A

CALL

TO

THE UNCONVERTED.

TO WHICH ARE ADDED,

SEVERAL VALUABLE ESSAYS.

BY RICHARD BAXTER.

WITH

AN INTRODUCTORY ESSAY,

BY THOMAS CHALMERS, D. D.

NEW-YORK:
LEAVITT & COMPANY, 191 BROADWAY.
1850.

INTRODUCTORY ESSAY.

Having already introduced to the notice of our readers one of Richard Baxter's most valuable Treatises,* in the Essay to which we adverted to the character and writings of this venerable author, we count it unnecessary at present to make any allusion to them, but shall confine our remarks to the subject of the three Treatises which compose the present volume, namely, "A Call to the Unconverted to turn and live;" "Now or Never;" and "Fifty Reasons why a sinner ought to turn to God this day without delay."

These Treatises are characterized by all that solemn earnestness, and urgency of appeal, for which the writings of this much-admired author are so peculiarly distinguished. He seems to look upon mankind solely with the eyes of the Spirit, and exclusively to recognise them in their spiritual relations, and in the great and essential elements of their immortal being. Their future destiny is the all-important concern which fills and engrosses his mind, and he regards nothing of any magnitude but what has a distinct bearing on their spiritual and eternal condition. His business, therefore, is always with the conscience; to which, in these Treatises, he makes the most forcible appeals, and which he plies with all those arguments which are fitted to awaken the sinner to a deep sense of the necessity and importance

* The Saints' Everlasting Rest, with an Essay by Mr. Erskine.

of immediate repentance. In his "Call to the Unconverted," he endeavours to move them by the most touching of all representations, the tenderness of a beseeching God waiting to be gracious, and not willing that any should perish; and while he employs every form of entreaty, which tenderness and compassion can suggest, to allure the sinner to "turn and live," he does not shrink from forcing on his convictions those considerations which are fitted to alarm his fears, the terrors of the Lord, and the wrath, not merely of an offended Lawgiver, but of a God of love, whose threatenings he disregards, whose grace he despises, and whose mercy he rejects. And aware of the deceitfulness of sin in hardening the heart, and in betraying the sinner into a neglect of his spiritual interests, he divests him of every refuge, and strips him of every plea for postponing his preparation for eternity. He forcibly exposes the delusion of convenient seasons, and the awful infatuation and hazard of delay; and knowing the magnitude of the stake at issue, he urges the sinner to immediate repentance, as if the fearful and almost absolute alternative were "Now or Never." And to secure the commencement of such an important work against all the dangers to which procrastination might expose it, he endeavours to arrest the sinner in his career of guilt and unconcern, and resolutely to fix his determination on "turning to God this day without delay."

There are two very prevalent delusions on this subject, which we should like to expose; the one regards the *nature*, and the other the *season* of repentance; both of which are pregnant with mischief to the minds of men. With regard to the first, much mischief has arisen from mistakes respecting the meaning of the term *repentance*. The word repentance occurs with two different meanings in the New Testament; and it is to be regretted, that two different words could not have been devised to express these. This is chargeable upon the poverty of our language; for it is to be observed, that in the original Greek the distinction in the meanings is pointed out by a distinction in the words. The employment of one term to denote two different things has the effect of confounding and misleading the understanding; and it is much to be wished, that every ambiguity of this kind were cleared away from that most interesting point in the process of a human soul, at which it turns from sin unto righteousness, and from the power of Satan unto God.

When, in common language, a man says, 'I repent of such an action,' he is understood to say, 'I am sorry for having done it.' The feeling is familiar to all of us. How often does the man of dissipation prove this sense of the word repentance, when he awakes in the morning, and, oppressed by the languor of his exhausted faculties, looks back with remorse on the follies and profligacies of the night that is past? How often does the man of unguarded conversation prove it, when he thinks of the friend whose feelings he has wounded by some hasty utterance which he cannot recall? How often is it proved by the man of business, when he reflects on the rash engagement which ties him down to a losing speculation? All these people would be perfectly understood when they say, 'We repent of these doings.' The word repentance so applied is about equivalent to the word regret. There are several passages in the New Testament where this is the undoubted sense of the word repentance. In Matt. xxvii. 3. the wretched Judas repented himself of his treachery; and surely, when we think of the awful denunciation uttered by our Saviour against the man who should betray him, that it were better for him if he had not been born, we will never confound the repentance which Judas experienced with that repentance which is unto salvation.

Now here lies the danger to practical Christianity. In the above-cited passage, to repent is just to regret, or to be sorry for; and this we conceive to be by far the most prevailing sense of the term in the English language. But there are other places where the same term is employed to denote that which is urged upon us as a duty—that which is preached for the remission of sins—that which is so indispensable to sinners, as to call forth the declaration from our Saviour, that unless we have it, we shall all likewise perish. Now, though repentance, in all these cases, is expressed by the same term in our translation as the repentance of mere regret, it is expressed by a different term in the original record of our faith. This surely might lead us to suspect a difference of meaning, and should caution us against taking up with that, as sufficient for the business of our salvation, which is short of saving and scriptural repentance. There may be an alternation of wilful sin, and of deep-felt sorrow, up to the very end of our history—there may be a presumptuous sin committed every day, and a sorrow regularly succeeding it. Sorrow may imbitter every act of sin—sorrow may darken every interval of sinful indulgence—and sorrow may give an unutterable anguish to the pains and the prospects of a deathbed. Couple all this with the circumstance that sorrow passes, in the common currency of our language, for repentance, and that repentance is made, by our Bible, to lie at the turning point from a state of condemnation to a state of acceptance with God; and it is difficult not to conceive that much danger may have arisen from this, leading to indistinct views of the nature of repentance, and to slender and superficial conceptions of the mighty change which is implied in it.

We are far from saying that the eye of Christians is not open to this danger—and that the vigiant care of Christian authors has not been employed n averting it. Where will we get a better definition of repentance unto life than in our Shorter Catechism? by which the sinner is represented not merely as grieving, but, along with his grief and hatred of sin, as turning from it unto God with full purpose of, and endeavour after new obedience But the mischief is, that the word repent has a common meaning, different from the theological; that wherever it is used, this common meaning is apt to intrude itself, and exert a kind of habitual imposition upon the understanding—that the influence of the single word carries it over the influence of the lengthened explanation—and thus it is that, for a steady progress in the obedience of the gospel, many persevere, to the end of their days, in a wretched course of sinning and of sorrowing, without fruit and without amendment.

To save the practically mischievous effect arising from the application of one term to two different things, one distinct and appropriate term has been suggested for the saving repentance of the New Testament. The term repentance itself has been restricted to the repentance of mere sorrow, and is made equivalent to regret; and for the other, able translators have adopted the word reformation. The one is expressive of sorrow for our past conduct; the other is expressive of our renouncing it. It denotes an actual turning from the habits of life that we are sorry for. Give us, say they, a change from bad deeds to good deeds, from bad habits to good habits, from a life of wickedness to a life of conformity to the requirements of heaven, and you give us reformation.

Now there is often nothing more unprofitable than a dispute about words; but if a word has got into common use, a common and generally understood meaning is attached to it; and if this meaning does not just come up to the thing which we want to express by it, the application of that word to that thing has the same misleading effects as in the case already alluded to. Now, we have much the same kind of exception to allege against the term reformation, that we have alleged against the term repentance. The term repentance is inadequate—and why? because, in the common use of it, it is equivalent to regret, and regret is short of the saving change that is spoken of in the New Testament. On the very same principle, we count the term reformation to be inadequate. We think that, in common language, a man would receive the appellation of a reformed man upon the mere change of his outward habits, without any reference to the change of mind and of principle which gave rise to it. Let the drunkard give up his excesses—let the backbiter give up his evil speakings—let the extortioner give up his unfair charges—and we would apply to one and all of them, upon the mere change of their external doings, the character of reformed men. Now, it is evident that the drunkard may give up his drunkenness, because checked by a serious impression of the injury he has been doing to his health and his circumstances. The backbiter may give up his evil speaking, on being made to perceive that the hateful practice has brought upon him the contempt and alienation of his neighbours. The extortioner may give up his unfair charges, upon taking it into calculation that his business is likely to suffer by the desertion of his customers. Now, it is evident, that though in each of these cases there has been what the world would call reformation, there has not been scriptural repentance. The deficiency of this term consists in its having been employed to denote a mere change in the deeds or in the habits of the outward man; and if employed as equivalent to repentance, it may delude us into the idea that the change by which we are made meet for a happy eternity is a far more slender and superficial thing than it really is. It is of little importance to be told that the translator means it only in the sense of a reformed conduct, proceeding from the influence of a new and a right principle within. The common meaning of the word will, as in the former instance, be ever and anon intruding itself, and get the better of all the formal cautions, and all the qualifying clauses of our Bible commentators.

But, will not the original word itself throw some light upon this important question? The repentance which is enjoined as a duty—the repentance which is unto salvation—the repentance which sinners undergo when they pass to a state of acceptance with God from a state of enmity against him—these are all one and the same thing, and are expressed by one and the same word in the original language of the New Testament. It is different from the word which expresses the repentance of sorrow; and if translated according to the parts of which it is composed, it signifies neither more nor less than *a change of mind*. This of itself is sufficient to prove the inadequacy of the term reformation—a term which is often applied to a man upon the mere change of his conduct, without ever adverting to the state of his mind, or to the kind of change in motive and in principle which it has undergone. It is true, that there can be no change in the conduct without some change in the inward principle. A reformed drunkard, before careless about health or fortune, may be so far changed as to become impressed with these considerations; but this change is evidently short of that which the Bible calls repentance toward God. It is a change that may, and has taken place in many a mind, when there was no effectual sense of the God who is above us, and of the eternity which is before us. It is a change, brought about by the prospect and the calculation of worldly advantages; and, in the enjoyment of these advantages, it hath its sole reward. But it is not done unto God, and God will not accept of it as done unto him. Reformation may signify nothing more than the mere surface-dressing of those decencies, and proprieties, and accomplishments, and civil and prudential duties, which, however fitted to secure a man's acceptance in society, may, one and all of them, consist with a heart alienated from God, and having every principle and affection of the inner man away from him. True, it is such a change as the man will reap benefit from, as his friends will rejoice in, as the world will call reformation; but it is not such a change as will make him meet for heaven, and is deficient in its import from what our Saviour speaks of when he says, "I tell you nay, except ye repent, ye shall all likewise perish."

There is no single word in the English language which occurs to us as fully equal to the faithful rendering of the term in the original. Renewedness of mind, however awkward a phrase this may be, is perhaps the most nearly expressive of it. Certain it is, that it harmonizes with those other passages of the Bible where the process is described by which saving repentance is brought about. We read of being transformed by the renewing of our minds, of the renewing of the Holy Ghost, of being renewed in the spirit of our minds. Scriptural repentance, therefore, is that deep and radical change whereby a soul turns from the idols of sin and of self unto God, and devotes every movement of the inner and the outer man, to the captivity of his obedience. This is the change which, whether it be expressed by one word or not in the English language, we would have you well to understand; and reformation or change in the outward conduct, instead of being saving and scriptural repentance, is what, in the language of John the Baptist, we would call a fruit meet for it. But if mischief is likely to arise, from the want of an adequate word in our language, to that repentance which is unto salvation, there is one effectual preservative against it—a firm and consistent exhibition of the whole counsel and revelation of God. A man who is well read in his New Testament, and reads it with docility, will dismiss all his meagre conceptions of repentance, when he comes to the following statements:—"Except a man be born again, he cannot see the kingdom of God." "Except ye be converted, and become as little children, ye shall not enter into the kingdom of heaven." "If any man have not the

Spirit of Christ, he is none of his." "The carnal mind is enmity against God; and if ye live after the flesh, ye shall die; but if ye, through the Spirit, do mortify the deeds of the body, ye shall live." "By the washing of regeneration ye are saved." "Be not then conformed to this world, but be ye transformed by the renewing of your minds." Such are the terms employed to describe the process by which the soul of man is renewed unto repentance; and, with your hearts familiarized to the mighty import of these terms, you will carry with you an effectual guarantee against those false and flimsy impressions, which are so current in the world, about the preparation of a sinner for eternity.

Another delusion which we shall endeavour to expose, is a very mischievous application of the parable of the labourers in the vineyard, contained in the twentieth chapter of the Gospel by Matthew. The interpretation of this parable, the mischief and delusion of which we shall endeavour to lay open, is, that it relates to the call of individuals, and to the different periods in the age of each individual at which this call is accepted by them. We almost know nothing more familiar to us, both in the works of authors, and in the conversation of private Christians, than when the repentance of an aged man is the topic, it is represented as a case of repentance at the eleventh hour of the day. We are far from disputing the possibility of such a repentance, nor should those who address the message of the gospel ever be restrained from the utterance of the free call of the gospel, in the hearing of the oldest and most inveterate sinner whom they may meet with. But what we contend for, is, that this is not the drift of the parable. The parable relates to the call of nations, and to the different periods in the age of the world at which this call was addressed to each of them, and not, as we have already observed, to the call of individuals, and to the different periods in the age of each individual at which this call is ac cepted by them.* It is not true that the labourers who began to work in the vineyard on the first hour of the day, denote these Christians who began to remember their Creator, and to render the obedience of the faith unto his Gospel with their first and earliest education. It is not true, that they who entered into this service on the third hour of the day, denote those Christians, who after a boyhood of thoughtless unconcern about the things of eternity, are arrested in the season of youth, by a visitation of seriousness, and betake themselves to the faith and the following of the Saviour who died for them. It is not true, that they who were hired

---

* To render our argument more intelligible, we shall briefly state what we conceive to be the true explanation of the parable. In the verses preceding the parable, Peter had stated the whole amount of the surrender that he and his fellow disciples had made by the act of following after Jesus; and it is evident, that they all looked forward to some great and temporal remuneration—some share in the glories of the Israelitish monarchy—some place of splendour or distinction under that new government, which they imagined was to be set up in the world; and they never conceived any thing else, than that in this altered state of things, the people of their own country were to be raised to high pre-eminence among the nations which had oppressed and degraded them. It was in the face of this expectation, that our Saviour uttered a sentence, which we meet oftener than once among his recorded sayings in the New Testament, " Many that are first shall be last, and the last shall be first." The Israelites, whom God distinguished at an early period of the world, by a revelation of himself, were first invited in the doing of his will (which is fitly enough represented by working in his vineyard) to the possession of his favour, and the enjoyment of his rewards. This offer to work in that peculiar vineyard, where God assigned to them a performance, and bestowed on them a recompense, was made to Abraham and to his descendants at a very early period in history; and a succession of prophets and righteous men were sent to renew the offer, and the communications from God to the world followed the stream of ages, down to the time of the utterance of this parable. And a few years, afterwards, the same offers, and the same

on the sixth and ninth hours, denote those Christians, who, after having spent the prime of their youthful vigour in alienation from God, and perhaps run out some mad career of guilt and profligacy, put on their Christianity along with the decencies of their sober and established manhood. Neither is it true, that the labourers of the eleventh hour, the men who had stood all day idle, represent those aged converts who have put off their repentance to the last—those men who have renounced the world when they could not help it—those men who have put on Christianity, but not till they had put on their wrinkles—those men who have run the varied stages of depravity, from the frivolous unconcern of

---

invitations, were addressed to another people; and at this late period, at this eleventh hour, the men of those countries which had never before been visited by any authoritative call from heaven, had this call lifted up in their hearing, and many Gentiles accepted that everlasting life, of which the Jews counted themselves unworthy. And as to the people of Israel, who valued themselves so much on their privileges—who had turned all the revelations, by which their ancestors had been honoured, into a matter of distinction and of vain security—who had ever been in the habit of eyeing the profane Gentiles with all that contempt which is laid upon outcasts, this parable received its fulfilment at the time when these Gentiles, by their acceptance of the Saviour, were exalted to an equal place among the chiefest favourites of God; and these Jews, by their refusal of him, had their name rooted out from among the nations—and those first and foremost in all the privileges of religion, are now become the last. Now this we conceive to be the real design of the parable. It was designed to reconcile the minds of the disciples to that part of the economy of God, which was most offensive to their hopes and to their prejudices. It asserted the sovereignty of the Supreme Being in the work of dispensing his calls and his favours among the people whom he had formed. It furnished a most decisive and silencing reproof to the Jews, who were filled with envy against the Gentiles; and who, even those of them that embraced the Christian profession, made an obstinate struggle against the admission of those Gentiles into the church on equal terms with themselves.

a boy, and the appalling enormities of misled and misguided youth, and the deep and determined worldliness of middle age, and the clinging avarice of him, who, while with slow and tottering footsteps he descends the hill of life, has a heart more obstinately set than ever on all its interests, and all its sordid accumulations, but who, when death taps at the door, awakes from his dream, and thinks it now time to shake away his idolatrous affections from the mammon of unrighteousness.

Such are the men who, after having taken their full swing of all that the world could offer, and of all that they could enjoy of it, defer the whole work of preparation for eternity to old age, and for the hire of the labourers of the eleventh hour, do all that they can in the way of sighs, and sorrows, and expiations of penitential acknowledgment. What! will we offer to liken such men to those who sought the Lord early, and who found him? Will we say that he who repents when old, is at all to be compared to him, who bore the whole heat and burden of a life devoted throughout all its stages to the glory and the remembrance of the Creator? Who, from a child, trembled at the word of the Lord, and aspired after a conformity to all his ways? Who, when a young man, fulfilled that most appropriate injunction of the apostle, "Be thou strong?" Who fought it with manly determination against all the enemies of principle by which he was surrounded, and spurned the enticements of vicious acquaintances away from him; and nobly stood it out, even though unsupported and alone, against the unhallowed contempt of a whole multitude of scorners; and with intrepid defiance to all the assaults of ridicule, maintained a firmness, which no wile could seduce from the posts of vigilance; and cleared his unfaltering way through all the allurements of a perverse and crooked generation. Who, even in the midst of a most withering atmosphere on every side of him, kept all his purposes unbroken, and all his delicacies untainted. Who, with the rigour of self-command, combined the softening lustre which a pure and amiable modesty sheds over the moral complexion of him who abhors that which is evil, and cleaves to that which is good, with all the energy of a holy determination. Can that be a true interpretation, which levels this youth of promise and of accomplishment, with his equal in years, who is now prosecuting every guilty indulgence, and crowns the audacity of his rebellion by the mad presumption, that ere he dies, he shall be able to propitiate that God, on the authority of all whose calls, and all whose remonstrances he is now trampling? Or follow each of them to the evening of their earthly pilgrimage—will you say that the penitent of the eleventh hour, is at all to be likened to him who has given the whole of his existence to the work and the labour of Christianity? to him who, after a morning of life adorned with all the gracefulness we have attempted to describe, sustains through the whole of his subsequent history such a high and ever-brightening example, that his path is like the shining light, which shineth more and more unto the perfect day; and every year he lives, the graces of an advancing sanctification form into a richer assemblage of all that is pure, and lovely, and honourable, and of good report; and when old age comes, it brings none of the turbulence or alarm of an unfinished preparation along with it—but he meets death with the quiet assurance of a man who is in readiness, and hails his message as a friendly intimation; and as he lived in the splendour of ever-increasing acquirements, so he dies in all the radiance of anticipated glory.

This interpretation of the parable cannot be sus tained; and we think, that, out of its own mouth, a condemnation may be stamped upon it. Mark this peculiarity. The labourers of the eleventh hour are not men who got the offer before, but men who for the first time received a call to work in the vineyard; and they may therefore well represent the people of a country, who, for the first time, received the overtures of the Gospel. The answer they gave to the question, Why stand you so long idle? was, that no man had hired them. We do not read of any of the labourers of the third, or sixth, or ninth hours, refusing the call at these times, and afterwards rendering a compliance with the evening call, and getting the penny for which they declined the offer of working several hours, but afterwards agreed, when the proposal was made, that they should work one hour only. They had a very good answer to give, in excuse for their idleness. They never had been called before. And the oldest men of a Pagan country have the very same answer to give, on the first arrival of Christian missionaries amongst them. But we have no part nor lot in this parable. We have it not in our power to offer any such apology. There is not one of us who can excuse the impenitency of the past, on the plea that no man has called us. This is a call that has been sounded in our ears, from our very infancy. Every time we have seen a bible in our shelves, we have had a call. Every time we have heard a minister in the pulpit, we have had a call. Every time we have heard the generous invitation, "Ho, every one that thirsteth, come ye unto the waters," we have had a solemn, and what ought to have been a most impressive, call. Every time that a parent has plied us with a good advice, or a neighbour come forward with a friendly persuasion, we have had a call. Every time that the Sabbath bell has rung for us to the house of God, we have had a call. These are all so many distinct and repeated calls. These are past events in our life, which rise in judgment against us, and remind us, with a justice of argument that there is no evading, that we have no right whatever to the privileges of the eleventh hour.

This, then, is the train to which we feel ourselves directed by this parable. The mischievous interpretation which has been put upon it, has wakened up our alarms, and set us to look at the delusion which it fosters, and, if possible, to drag out to the light of day, the fallacy which lies in it. We should like to reduce every man to the feeling of the alternative of repentance now or repentance never. We should like to flash it upon your convictions, that, by putting the call away from you now, you put your eternity away from you. We should like to expose the whole amount of that accursed infatuation which lies in delay. We should like to arouse every soul out of its lethargies, and giving no quarter to the plea of a little more sleep, and a little more slumber, we should like you to feel as if the whole of your future destiny hinged on the very first movement to which you turned yourselves.

The work of repentance must have a beginning; and we should like you to know, that, if not begun to-day, the chance will be less of its being begun to-morrow. And if the greater chance has failed, what hope can we build upon the smaller?—and a chance too that is always getting smaller. Each day, as it revolves over the sinner's head, finds him a harder, and a more obstinate, and a more helplessly enslaved sinner, than before. It was this consideration which gave Richard Baxter such earnestness and such urgency in his "Call." He knew that the barrier in the way of the sinner's return, was strengthened by every act of resistance to the call which urges it. That the refusal of this moment hardened the man against the next attack of a Gospel argument that is brought to bear upon him. That if he attempted you now, and he failed, when he came back upon you, he would find himself working on a more obstinate and uncomplying subject than ever. And therefore it is, that he ever feels as if the present were his only opportunity. That he is now upon his vantage ground, and he gives every energy of his soul to the great point of making the most of it. He will put up with none of your evasions. He will consent to none of your postponements. He will pay respect to none of your more convenient seasons. He tells you, that the matter with which he is charged, has all the urgency of a matter in hand. He speaks to you with as much earnestness as if he knew that you were going to step into eternity in half an hour. He delivers his message with as much solemnity as if he knew that this was your last meeting on earth, and that you were never to see each other till you stood together at the judgment-seat. He knew that some mighty change must take place in you, ere you be fit for entering into the presence of God; and that the time in which, on every plea of duty and of interest, you should bestir yourselves to secure this, is the present time. This is the distinct point he assigns to himself; and the whole drift of his argument, is to urge an instantaneous choice of the better part, by telling you how you multiply every day the obstacles to your future repentance, if you begin not the work of repentance now.

Before bringing our Essay to a close, we shall make some observations on the mistakes concerning repentance which we have endeavoured to expose, and adduce some arguments for urging on the consciences of our readers the necessity and importance of immediate repentance.

1. The work of repentance is a work which must be done ere we die; for, unless we repent, we shall all likewise perish. Now, the easier this work is in our conception, we will think it the less necessary to enter upon it immediately. We will look upon it as a work that may be done at any time, and let us, therefore, put it off a little longer, and a little longer. We will perhaps look forward to that retirement from the world and its temptations which we figure old age to bring along with it, and falling in with the too common idea, that the evening of life is the appropriate season of preparation for another world, we will think that the author is bearing

too closely and too urgently upon us, when, in the language of the Bible, he speaks of "*to-day*," while it is called to-day, and will let us off with no other repentance than repentance "*now*,"—seeing that now only is the accepted time, and now only the day of salvation, which he has a warrant to proclaim to us. This dilatory way of it is very much favoured by the mistaken and very defective view of repentance which we have attempted to expose. We have some how or other got into the delusion, that repentance is sorrow, and little else; and were we called to fix upon the scene where this sorrow is likely to be felt in the degree that is deepest and most overwhelming, we would point to the chamber of the dying man. It is awful to think that, generally speaking, this repentance of mere sorrow is the only repentance of a deathbed. Yes! we will meet with sensibility deep enough and painful enough there—with regret in all its bitterness—with terror mustering up its images of despair, and dwelling upon them in all the gloom of an affrighted imagination; and this is mistaken, not merely for the drapery of repentance, but for the very substance of it. We look forward, and we count upon this—that the sins of a life are to be expunged by the sighing and the sorrowing of the last days of it. We should give up this wretchedly superficial notion of repentance, and cease, from this moment, to be led astray by it. The mind may sorrow over its corruptions at the very time that it is under the power of them. To grieve because we are under the captivity of sin is one thing—to be released from that captivity is another. A man may weep most bitterly over the perversities of his moral constitution; but to change that constitution is a different affair. Now, this is the mighty work of repentance. He who has undergone it is no longer the servant of sin. He dies unto sin, he lives unto God. A sense of the authority of God is ever present with him, to wield the ascendancy of a great master-principle over all his movements—to call forth every purpose, and to carry it forward, through all the opposition of sin and of Satan, into accomplishment. This is the grand revolution in the state of the mind which repentance brings along with it. To grieve because this work is not done, is a very different thing from the doing of it. A deathbed is the very best scene for acting the first; but it is the very worst for acting the second. The repentance of Judas has often been acted there. We ought to think of the work in all its magnitude, and not to put it off to that awful period when the soul is crowded with other things, and has to maintain its weary struggle with the pains, and the distresses, and the shiverings, and the breathless agonies of a deathbed.

2. There are two views that may be taken of the way in which repentance is brought about, and whichever of them is adopted, delay carries along with it the saddest infatuation. It may be looked upon as a step taken by man as a voluntary agent, and we would ask you, upon your experience of the powers and the performances of humanity, if a deathbed is the time for taking such a step? Is this a time for a voluntary being exercising a vigorous control over his own movements? When racked with pain, and borne down by the pressure of a sore and overwhelming calamity? Surely the greater the work of repentance is, the more ease, the more time, the more freedom from suffering, is necessary for carrying it on; and, therefore, addressing you as voluntary beings, as beings who will and who do, we call upon you to seek God early that you may find him—to haste, and make no delay in keeping his commandments. The other view is, that repentance is not a self-originating work in man, but the work of the Holy Spirit in him as the subject of its influences. This view is not opposite to the former. It is true that man wills and does at every step in the business of his salvation; and it is as true that God works in him so to will and to do. Take this last view of it then. Look on repentance as the work of God's

Spirit in the soul of man, and we are furnished with a more impressive argument than ever, and set on higher vantage for urging you to stir yourselves, and set about it immediately. What is it that you propose? To keep by your present habits, and your present indulgences—and build yourselves up all the while in the confidence that the Spirit will interpose with his mighty power of conversion upon you, at the very point of time that you have fixed upon as convenient and agreeable? And how do you conciliate the Spirit's answer to your call then? Why, by doing all you can to grieve, and to quench, and to provoke him to abandon you now. Do you feel a motion towards repentance at this moment? If you keep it alive, and act upon it, good and well. But if you smother and suppress this motion, you resist the Spirit—you stifle his movements within you; it is what the impenitent do day after day, and year after year—and is this the way for securing the influences of the Spirit at the time that you would like them best? When you are done with the world, and are looking forward to eternity because you cannot help it? God says, "My Spirit will not always strive with the children of men." A good and a free Spirit he undoubtedly is, and, as a proof of it, he is now saying, "Let whosoever will, come and drink of the water of life freely." He says so now, but we do not promise that he will say so with effect upon your deathbeds, if you refuse him now. You look forward then for a powerful work of conversion being done upon you, and yet you employ yourselves all your life long in raising and multiplying obstacles against it. You count upon a miracle of grace before you die, and the way you take to make yourselves sure of it, is to grieve and offend him while you live, who alone can perform the miracle. O what cruel deceits will sin land us in! and how artfully it pleads for a "little more sleep, and a little more slumber; a little more folding of the hands to sleep." We should hold out no longer, nor make not such an abuse of the forbearance of

God: we will treasure up wrath against the day of wrath if we do so. The genuine effect of his goodness is to lead to repentance; let not its effect upon us be to harden and encourage ourselves in the ways of sin. We should cry now for the clean heart and the right spirit; and such is the exceeding freeness of the Spirit of God, that we will be listened to. If we put off the cry till then, the same God may laugh at our calamity, and mock when our fear cometh.

3. Our next argument for immediate repentance is, that we cannot bring forward, at any future period of your history, any considerations of a more prevailing or more powerfully moving influence than those we *may* bring forward at this moment. We can tell you now of the terrors of the Lord. We can tell you now of the solemn mandates which have issued from his throne—and the authority of which is upon one and all of you. We can tell you now, that though, in this dead and darkened world, sin appears but a very trivial affair—for every body sins, and it is shielded from execration by the universal countenance of an entire species lying in wickedness—yet it holds true of God, what is so emphatically said of him, that he cannot be mocked, nor will he endure it that you should riot in the impunity of your wilful resistance to him and to his warnings. We can tell you now, that he is a God of vengeance; and though, for a season, he is keeping back all the thunder of it from a world that he would like to reclaim unto himself, yet, if you put all his expostulations away from you, and will not be reclaimed, these thunders will be let loose upon you, and they will fall on your guilty heads, armed with tenfold energy, because you have not only defied his threats, but turned your back on his offers of reconciliation. These are the arguments by which we would try to open our way to your consciences, and to awaken up your fears, and to put the inspiring activity of hope into your bosoms, by laying before you those invitations which are address-

ed to the sinner, through the peace-speaking blood of Jesus, and, in the name of a beseeching God, to win your acceptance of them. At no future period can we address arguments more powerful and more affecting than these. If these arguments do not prevail upon you, we know of none others by which a victory over the stubborn and uncomplying will can be accomplished, or by which we can ever hope to beat in that sullen front of resistance wherewith you now so impregnably withstand us. We feel that, if any stout-hearted sinner shall rise from the perusal of these Treatises with an unawakened conscience, and give himself to an act of wilful disobedience, we feel as if, in reference to him, we had made our last discharge, and it fell powerless as water spilt on the ground, that cannot be gathered up again. We would not cease to ply him with our arguments, and tell him, to the hour of death, of the Lord God, merciful and gracious, who is not willing that any should perish, but that all should turn to him, and live. And if in future life we should meet him at the eleventh hour of his dark and deceitful day—a hoary sinner, sinking under the decrepitude of age, and bending on the side of the grave that is open to receive him—even then we would testify the exceeding freeness of the grace of God, and implore his acceptance of it. But how could it be away from our minds that he is not one of the evening labourers of the parable? We had met with him at former periods of his existence, and the offer we make him now we made him then, and he did what the labourers of the third, and sixth, and ninth hours of the parable did not do—he rejected our call to hire him into the vineyard; and this heartless recollection, if it did not take all our energy away from us, would leave us little else than the energy of despair. And therefore it is, that we speak to you now as if this was our last hold of you. We feel as if on your present purpose hung all the preparations of your future life, and all the rewards or all the horrors of your coming eternity. We will

not let you off with any other repentance than repentance now; and if this be refused now, we cannot, with our eyes open to the consideration we have now urged, that the instrument we make to bear upon you afterwards is not more powerful than we are wielding now, coupled with another consideration which we shall insist upon, that the subject on which the instrument worketh, even the heart of man, gathers, by every act of resistance, a more uncomplying obstinacy than before; we cannot, with these two thoughts in our mind, look forward to your future istory, without seeing spread over the whole path it the iron of a harder impenitency—the sullen gloom of a deeper and more determined alienation.

4. Another argument, therefore, for immediate repentance is, that the mind which resists a present call or a present reproof, undergoes a progressive hardening towards all those considerations which arm the call of repentance with all its energy. It is not enough to say, that the instrument by which repentance is brought about, is not more powerful to-morrow than it is to-day; it lends a most tremendous weight to the argument, to say further, that the subject on which this instrument is putting forth its efficiency, will oppose a firmer resistance to-morrow than it does to-day. It is this which gives a significancy so powerful to the call of "To-day while it is to-day, harden not your hearts;" and to the admonition of "Knowest thou not, O man, that the goodness of God leadeth thee to repentance; but after, thy hardness and impenitent heart treasurest up wrath against the day of wrath and revelation of the righteous judgments of God?" It is not said, either in the one or in the other of these passages, that, by the present refusal, you cut yourself off from a future invitation. The invitation may be sounded in your hearing to the last half hour of your earthly existence, engraved in all those characters of free and gratuitous kindness which mark the beneficent religion of the New Testament.

But the present refusal hardens you against the power and tenderness of the future invitation. This is the fact in human nature to which these passages seem to point, and it is the fact through which the argument for immediate repentance receives such powerful aid from the wisdom of experience. It is this which forms the most impressive proof of the necessity of plying the young with all the weight and all the tenderness of earnest admonition, that the now susceptible mind might not turn into a substance harder and more uncomplying than the rock which is broken in pieces by the powerful application of the hammer of the word of God.

The metal of the human soul, so to speak, is like some material substances. If the force you lay upon it do not break it, or dissolve it, it will beat it into hardness. If the moral argument by which it is plied now, do not so soften the mind as to carry and to overpower its purposes, then, on another day, the argument may be put forth in terms as impressive—but it falls on a harder mind, and, therefore, with a more slender efficiency. If the threat, that ye who persist in sin shall have to dwell with the devouring fire, and to lie down amid everlasting burnings, do not alarm you out of your iniquities from this very moment, then the same threat may be again cast out, and the same appalling circumstances of terror be thrown around it, but it is all discharged on a soul hardened by its inurement to the thunder of denunciations already uttered, and the urgency of menacing threatenings already poured forth without fruit and without efficacy. If the voice of a beseeching God do not win upon you now, and charm you out of your rebellion against him, by the persuasive energy of kindness, then let that voice be lifted in your hearing on some future day, and though armed with all the power of tenderness it ever had, how shall it find its entrance into a heart sheathed by the operation of habit, that universal law, in more impenetrable obstinacy? If, with the earliest dawn of your understanding, you have been offered the hire of the morning labourer and have refused it, then the parable does not say that you are the person who at the third, or sixth, or ninth, or eleventh hour, will get the offer repeated to you. It is true, that the offer is unto all and upon all who are within reach of the hearing of it. But there is all the difference in the world between the impression of a new offer, and of an offer that has already been often heard and as often rejected—an offer which comes upon you with all the familiarity of a well-known sound that you have already learned how to dispose of, and how to shut your every feeling against the power of its gracious invitations—an offer which, if discarded from your hearts at the present moment, may come back upon you, but which will have to maintain a more unequal con test than before, with an impenitency ever strengthening, and ever gathering new hardness from each successive act of resistance. And thus it is that the point for which we are contending is not to carry you at some future period of your lives, but to carry you at this moment. It is to work in you the instantaneous purpose of a firm and a vigorously sustained repentance; it is to put into you all the freshness of an immediate resolution, and to stir you up to all the readiness of an immediate accomplishment--it is to give direction to the very first footstep you are now to take, and lead you to take it as the commencement of that holy career, in which all old things are done away, and all things become new--it is to press it upon you, that the state of the alternative, at this moment, is "now or never"—it is to prove how fearful the odds are against you, if now you suffer the call of repentance to light upon your consciences, and still keep by your determined posture of careless, and thoughtless, and thankless unconcern about God. You have resisted to-day, and by that resistance you have acquired a firmer metal of resistance against the power of every future warning that may be brought to bear upon you. You have stood your ground against the urgency of the most earnest admonitions, and against the dreadfulness of the most terrifying menaces. On that ground you have fixed yourself more immovably than before; and though on some future day the same spiritual thunder be made to play around you, it will not shake you out of the obstinacy of your determined rebellion.

It is the universal law of habit, that the feelings are always getting more faintly and feebly impressed by every repetition of the cause which excited them, and that the mind is always getting stronger in its active resistance to the impulse of these feelings, by every new deed of resistance which it performs; and thus it is, that if you refuse us now, we have no other prospect before us than that your course is every day getting more desperate and more irrecoverable, your souls are getting more hardened, the Spirit is getting more provoked to abandon those who have so long persisted in their opposition to his movements. God, who says that his Spirit will not always strive with the children of men, is getting more offended. The tyranny of habit is getting every day a firmer ascendancy over you; Satan is getting you more helplessly involved among his wiles and his entanglements; the world, with all the inveteracy of those desires which are opposite to the will of the Father, is more and more lording it over your every affection. And what, we would ask, what is the scene in which you are now purposing to contest it, with all this mighty force of opposition you are now so busy in raising up against you? What is the field of combat to which you are now looking forward, as the place where you are to accomplish a victory over all those formidable enemies whom you are at present arming with such a weight of hostility, as, we say, within a single hairbreadth of certainty, you will find to be irresistible? O the bigness of such a misleading infatuation! The proposed scene in which this battle for eternity is to be fought, and this victory for the crown of glory to be won, is a deathbed. It is when the last messenger stands by the couch of the dying man, and shakes at him the terrors of his grisly countenance, that the poor child of infatuation thinks he is to struggle and prevail against all his enemies; against the unrelenting tyranny of habit—against the obstinacy of his own heart, which he is now doing so much to harden—against the Spirit of God who perhaps long ere now has pronounced the doom upon him, "He will take his own way, and walk in his own counsel; I shall cease from striving, and let him alone"—against Satan, to whom every day of his life he has given some fresh advantage over him, and who will not be willing to lose the victim on whom he has practised so many wiles, and plied with success so many delusions. And such are the enemies whom you, who wretchedly calculate on the repentance of the eleventh hour, are every day mustering up in greater force and formidableness against you; and how can we think of letting you go, with any other repentance than the repentance of the precious moment that is now passing over you, when we look forward to the horrors of that impressive scene, on which you propose to win the prize of immortality, and to contest it singlehanded and alone, with all the weight of opposition which you have accumulated against yourselves—a deathbed—a languid, breathless, tossing, and agitated deathbed; that scene of feebleness, when the poor man cannot help himself to a single mouthful—when he must have attendants to sit around him, and watch his every wish, and interpret his every signal, and turn him to every posture where he may find a moment's ease, and wipe away the cold sweat that is running over him—and ply him with cordials for thirst, and sickness, and insufferable languor. And this is the time, when occupied with such feelings, and beset with such agonies as these, you propose to crowd within the compass of a few wretched days, the work of winding up the concerns of a neglected eternity!

5. But it may be said, if repentance be what you represent it, a thing of such mighty import, and such impracticable performance, as a *change of mind*, in what rational way can it be made the subject of a precept or an injunction? you would not call upon the Ethiopian to change his skin—you would not call upon the leopard to change his spots; and yet you call upon us to change our minds. You say, "Repent;" and that too in the face of the undeniable doctrine, that man is without strength for the achievement of so mighty an enterprise. Can you tell us any plain and practicable thing that you would have us to perform, and that we may perform to help on this business? This is the very question with which the hearers of John the Baptist came back upon him, after he had told them in general terms to repent, and to bring forth fruits meet for repentance. He may not have resolved the difficulty, but he pointed the expectation of his countrymen to a greater than he for the solution of it. Now that Teacher has already come, and we live under the full and the finished splendour of his revelation. O that the greatness and difficulty of the work of repentance, had the effect of shutting you up into the faith of Christ! Repentance is not a paltry, superficial reformation. It reaches deep into the inner man, but not too deep for the searching influences of that Spirit which is at his giving, and which worketh mightily in the hearts of believers. You should go then under a sense of your difficulty to Him. Seek to be rooted in the Saviour, that you may be nourished out of his fulness, and strengthened by his might. The simple cry for a clean heart, and a right spirit, which is raised from the mouth of a believer, brings down an answer from on high, which explains all the difficulty and overcomes it. And if what we have said of the extent and magnitude of repentance, should have the effect to give a deeper feeling than before of the wants under which you labour; and shall dispose you to seek after a closer and more habitual union with Him

who alone can supply them, then will our call to repent have indeed fulfilled upon you the appointed end of a preparation for the Saviour. But recollect now is your time, and now is your opportunity, for entering on the road of preparation that leads to heaven. We charge you to enter this road at this moment, as you value your deliverance from hell, and your possession of that blissful place where you shall be for ever with the Lord—we charge you not to parry and to delay this matter, no not for a single hour—we call on you by all that is great in eternity—by all that is terrifying in its horrors—by all that is alluring in its rewards—by all that is binding in the authority of God—by all that is condemning in the severity of his violated law, and by all that can aggravate this condemnation in the insulting contempt of his rejected gospel;—we call on you by one and all of these considerations, not to hesitate but to flee—not to purpose a return for to-morrow, but to make an actual return *this very day*—to put a decisive end to every plan of wickedness on which you may have entered—to cease your hands from all that is forbidden—to turn them to all that is required—to betake yourselves to the appointed Mediator, and receive through him, by the prayer of faith, such constant supplies of the washing of regeneration and renewing of the Holy Ghost, that, from this moment, you may be carried forward from one degree of grace unto another, and from a life devoted to God here, to the elevation of a triumphant, and the joys of a blissful eternity hereafter.

T. C.

St. Andrew's, October, 1825

CONTENTS.

THE GREAT SUCCESS WHICH ATTENDED THF CALL WHEN FIRST PUBLISHED.

It may be proper to prefix an account of this book given by Mr. Baxter himself, which was found in his study, after his death, in his own words:

'I published a short treatise on conversion, entitled, A Call to the Unconverted. The occasion of this was my converse with Bishop Usher while I was at London; who, approving my method and directions for Peace of Conscience, was importunate with me to write directions suited to the various states of Christians, and also against particular sins. I reverenced the man, but disregarded these persuasions, supposing I could dc nothing but what is done better already: but when he was dead, his words went deeper to my mind, and I purposed to obey his counsel; yet, so as that to the first sort of men, the ungodly, I thought vehement persuasions meeter than directions only: and so for such I published this little book, which God hath blessed with unexpected success, beyond all the rest that I have written, except The Saint's Rest. In a little more than a year, there were about twenty thousand of them printed by my own consent, and about ten thousand since, beside many thousands by stolen impressions, which poor men stole for lucre's sake. Through God's mercy I have information of almost whole households converted by this small book which I set so light by: and, as if all this in England, Scotland, and Ireland, were not mercy enough to me, God, since I was silenced hath sent it over in his message to many beyond the seas; for when Mr. Elliot had printed all the Bible in the Indian language, he next translated this my *Call to the Unconverted*, as he wrote to us here. And yet God would make some farther use of it; for Mr. Stoop, the pastor of the French Church in London, being driven hence by the displeasure of his superiors, was pleased to translate it into French. I hope it will not be unprofitable there; nor in Germany, where it is printed in Dutch.'

It may be proper also to mention Dr. Bates's account of the author, and of this useful treatise. In his sermon at Mr. BAXTER's funeral, he thus says: 'His books of practical divinity have been effectual for more conversions of sinners to God than any printed in our time; and while the church remains on earth, will be of continual efficacy to recover lost souls. There is a vigorous pulse in them, that keeps the reader awake and attentive.' His Call to the Unconverted, how small in bulk, but how powerful in virtue! Truth speaks in it with that authority and efficacy, that it makes the reader to lay his hand upon his heart, and find that he has a soul and a conscience, though he lived before as if he had none. He told some friends, that six brothers were converted by reading that CALL; and that every week he received letters of some converted by his books. This he spake with most humble thankfulness, that God was pleased to use him as an instrument for the salvation of souls.

PREFACE.

To all unsanctified Persons that shall read this Book; especially of my hearers in the Borough and Parish of Kidderminster.

MEN AND BRETHREN,

THE eternal GOD, that made you for a life everlasting, and hath redeemed you by his only Son, when you had lost it and yourselves, being mindful of you in your sin and misery, hath indited the gospel, and sealed it by his Spirit, and commanded his ministers to preach it to the world, that pardon being freely offered you, and Heaven being set before you, he might call you off from your fleshly pleasures, and from following after this deceitful world, and acquaint you with the life that you were created and redeemed for, before you are dead and past remedy. He sendeth you not prophets or apostles, that receive their message by immediate revelation; but yet he calleth you by his ordinary ministers, who are commissioned by him to preach the same gospel which Christ and his apostles first delivered. The Lord seeth how you forget him and your latter end, and how light you make of everlasting things, as men that understand not what they have to do or suffer. He seeth how bold you are in sin, and how fearless of his threatenings, and how careless of your souls, and how the works of infidels are in your lives, while the belief of Christians is in your mouths. He seeth the dreadful day at hand, when your sorrows will begin, and you must lament all this with fruitless cries in torment and desperation: and then the remembrance of your folly will tear your hearts, if true conversion now prevent it not. In compassion to your sinful miserable souls, the Lord, that better knows your case than you can know it, hath made it our duty to speak to you in his name, (2 Cor. v. 19.) and to tell you plainly of your sin and misery, and what will be your end, and how sad a change you will shortly see, if yet you go on a little longer. Having bought you at so dear a rate as the blood of his Son Jesus Christ, and made you so free and general a promise of pardon, and grace, and everlasting glory; he commandeth us to tender all this to you, as the gift of God, and to entreat you to consider of the necessity and worth of what he offers. He sees and pities you, while you are drowned in worldly cares and pleasures, eagerly following childish toys, and wasting that short and precious time for a thing of nought, in which you should make ready for an everlasting life; and therefore he hath commanded us to call after you, and tell you how you lose your labour, and are about to lose your souls, and to tell you what greater and better things you might certainly have, if you would hearken to his call. Isa. lv. 1, 2, 3. We believe and obey the voice of God; and come to you on his message, who hath charged us to preach, and be instant with you in season and out of season, to lift up our voice like a trumpet, and show you your transgressions and your sins. Isa. lviii. 1.; 2 Tim. iv. 1, 2. But, alas! to the grief of our souls and your undoing, you stop your ears, you stiffen your necks, you harden your hearts; and send us back to God with groans, to tell him that we have done his message, but can do no good on you, nor scarcely get a sober hearing. Oh! that our eyes were as a fountain of tears, that we might lament our ignorant careless people, that have Christ before them, and pardon, and life, and heaven before them, and have not hearts to know or value them! that might have Christ, and grace, and glory, as well as others, if it were not for their wilful negligence and contempt! O that the Lord would fill our hearts with more compassion to these miserable souls, that we might cast ourselves even at their feet, and follow them to their houses, and speak to them with our bitter tears. For, long have we preached to many of them in vain. We study *plainness* to make them understand; and many of them will not understand us; we study serious piercing words, to make them *feel*, but they will not feel. If the *greatest* matters would work with them, we should awake them; if the *sweetest* things would work, we should entice them and win their hearts; if the most *dreadful* things would work, we should at least affright them from their wickedness; if *truth* and certainty would take with them, we should soon convince them; if the God that made them, and the Christ that bought them, might be heard, the case would soon be altered with them; if *scripture* might be heard, we should soon prevail; if *reason*, even the best and strongest reason, might be heard, we should not doubt but we should speedily convince them; if *experience* might be heard, even their own experience and the experience of all the world, the matter would be mended; yea, if the *conscience* within them might be heard, the case would be better with them than it is. But if nothing can be heard, what then shall we do for them? If the dreadful God of heaven be slighted, who then shall be regarded? if the inestimable love and blood of a Redeemer be made light of, what then shall be valued? If heaven have no desirable glory with them, and everlasting joys be nothing worth; if they can jest at hell, and dance about the bottomless pit, and play with the consuming fire, and that when God and man do warn them of it, what shall we do for such souls as these?

Once more, in the name of the God of heaven, I shall do the message to you which he hath commanded us, and leave it in these standing lines to convert you or condemn you: to change you, or rise up in judgment against you, and to be a witness to your faces, that once you had a *serious call* to turn. Hear all you that are drudges of the world, and the servants of flesh and Satan! that spend your days in looking after prosperity on earth, and drown your conscience in drinking, and gluttony, and idleness, and foolish sports, and know your sin, and yet will sin, as if you set God at defiance, and bid him do his worst and spare not! Hearken, all you that mind not God, and have no heart to holy things, and feel no savour in the word or worship of the Lord, or in the thoughts or mention of eternal life; that are careless of your immortal souls, and never bestow one hour in inquiring what case they are in, whether sanctified or unsanctified, and whether you are ready to appear before the Lord! Hearken all you that, by sinning in light, have sinned yourselves into infidelity, and do not believe the word of God. He that hath an ear to hear let him hear the gracious and yet dreadful call of God! His eye is all this while upon you. Your sins are registered, and you shall surely hear of them all again. God keepeth the book now; and he will write it all upon your consciences with his terrors; and then you also shall keep it yourselves! O sinners, that you but knew what you are doing, and whom you are all this while offending! The sun itself is darkness before the glory of that Majesty which you daily abuse and carelessly provoke. The sinning angels were not able to stand before him, but were cast down to be tormented with devils. And dare such silly worms as you so carelessly offend, and set yourselves against your Maker! O that you did but a little know what case that wretched soul is in, that hath engaged the living God against him! The word of his mouth, that made thee, can unmake thee; the frown of his face will cut thee off and cast thee out into utter darkness. How eager are the devils to be doing with thee that have tempted thee, and do but wait for the word from God to take and use thee as their own! and then in a moment thou wilt be in hell. If God be against thee, all things are against thee: this world is but thy prison, for all thou so lovest it; thou art but reserved in it to the day of wrath (Job xxi. 30.); the Judge is coming, thy soul is even going. Yet a little while, and thy friend shall say of thee, 'He is dead;' and thou shalt see the things that thou now dost despise, and feel that which now thou wilt not believe. Death will bring such an argument as thou canst not answer; an argument that shall effectually confute thy cavils against the word and ways of God, and all thy self-conceited dotages. And then how soon will thy mind be changed? Then be an unbeliever if thou canst; stand then to all thy former words, which thou wast wont to utter against a holy and a heavenly life. Make good that cause then before the Lord, which thou wast wont to plead against thy teachers; and against the people that feared God. Then stand to thy old opinions and contemptuous thoughts of the diligence of the saints: make ready now thy strongest reasons, and stand up then before the Judge, and plead like a man for thy fleshly, thy worldly, thy ungodly life. But know that thou wilt have one to plead with, that will not be outfaced by thee; nor so easily put off as we thy fellow-creatures. O poor soul! there is nothing but a slender veil of flesh between thee and that amazing sight, which will quickly silence thee, and turn thy tone, and make thee of another mind! As soon as death hath drawn this curtain, thou shalt see that which will quickly leave thee speechless. And how quickly will that day and hour come! When thou hast had but a few more merry hours, and but a few more pleasant draughts and morsels, and a little more of the honours and riches of the world, thy portion will be spent, and thy pleasures ended, and all is then gone that thou settest thy heart upon; of all that thou soldest thy Saviour and salvation for, there is nothing left but the heavy reckoning. As a thief, that sits merrily spending the money which he hath stolen, in an alehouse, when men are riding in post haste to apprehend him, so is it with you. While you are drowned in cares or fleshly pleasures, and making merry with your own shame, death is coming in post haste to seize upon you, and carry your souls to such a place and state as now you little know or think of. Suppose, when you are bold and busy in your sin, that a messenger were but coming post from London to apprehend you and take away your lives; though you saw him not, yet if you knew that he was coming, it would mar your mirth, and you would be thinking of the haste he makes, and hearkening when he knocked at your door. O that you could but see what haste Death makes, though he has not yet overtaken you! No post so swift. No messenger more sure. As sure as the sun will be with you in the morning, though it hath many thousand and hundred thousand miles to go in the night, so sure will Death be quickly with you: and then where is your sport and pleasure? Then will you jest and brave it out? Then will you jeer at them that warned you? Then is it better to be a believing saint or a sensual worldling? And then whose shall all these things be that you have gathered? Luke xii. 19, 20, 21. Do you not observe that days and weeks are quickly gone, and nights and mornings come apace, and speedily succeed each other? You sleep, but your damnation slumbereth not; you linger, but your judgment this long time lingereth not, to which you are reserved for punishment. 2 Pet. ii. 3, 4, 5, 8, 9. O that you were wise to understand this, and that you did consider your latter end! Deut. xxxii. 29. He that hath an ear to hear, let him hear the call of God in this day of his salvation.

O careless sinners! that you did but know the love that you unthankfully neglect, and the preciousness of the blood of Christ which you despise! O that you did but know the riches of the gospel! O that you did but know, a little know, the certainty, and the glory, and blessedness of that everlasting life, which now you will not set your hearts upon, nor be persuaded first and diligently to seek. Heb. xi. 6, and xii. 28; and Matt. vi 13. Did you but know the endless life with God which you now neglect, how quickly would you cast away your sin, how quickly would you change your mind and life, your course and company, and turn the streams of your affections, and lay your care another way How resolutely would you scorn to yield to such temptations as now deceive you and carry you away? How zealously would you bestir yourselves for that most blessed life? How earnest would you be with God in prayer? How diligent in hearing and learning, and inquiring? How serious in meditating on the laws of God? Ps. i. 2. How fearful of sinning in thought, word, and deed? and how careful to please God and grow in holiness? O what a changed people you would be! And why should not the certain word of God be believed by you, and prevail with you, which openeth to you these glorious and eternal things?

Yea, let me tell you that even here on earth, you little know the difference between the life which you refuse, and the life which you choose? The sanctified are conversing with God, when you dare scarce think of him, and when you are conversing with but earth and flesh. Their conversation is in heaven, when you are utter strangers to it, and your belly is your God, and you are minding earthly things. Phil. iii. 18, 19, 20. They are seeking after the face of God, when you seek for nothing higher than this world. They are busily laying up for an endless life, where they shall be equal with the angels, (Luke xx. 36.) when you are taken up with a shadow and a transitory thing of nought.

How low and base is your earthly, fleshly, sinful life, in comparison of the noble and spiritual life of true believers? Many a time have I looked on such men with grief and pity, to see them trudge about the world, and spend their lives, and care, and labour, for nothing but a little food and raiment, or a little fading pelf, or fleshly pleasures, or empty honours, as if they had no higher things to mind. What difference is there between the lives of these men and of the beasts that perish, that spend their time in working and eating, and living, but that they may live? They taste not of the inward heavenly pleasures upon which believers taste and live. I had rather have a little of their comfort, which the forethoughts of their heavenly inheritance afford them, though I had all their scorns and sufferings with it, than to have all your pleasures and treacherous prosperity. I would not have one of your secret pangs of conscience, and dark and dreadful thoughts of death and the life to come, for all that ever the world hath done for you, or all that you can reasonably hope that it should do. If I were in your unconverted carnal state, and knew but what I know, and believe but what I now believe, methinks my life would be a foretaste of hell. How oft should I be thinking of the terrors of the Lord, and of the dismal day that is hastening on! Sure death and hell would be still before me. I should think of them by day, and dream of them by night; I should lie down in fear, and rise in fear, and live in fear, lest death should come before I were converted. I should have small felicity in any thing that I possessed, and little pleasure in any company, and little joy in any thing in the world, as long as I knew myself to be under the curse and wrath of God. I should be still afraid of hearing that voice, Thou fool, this night shall thy soul be required of thee. Luke xii. 20. And that fearful sentence would be written upon my conscience, There is no peace, saith my God, to the wicked. Isaiah xlviii. 22. lvii. 21. O poor sinners! It is a more joyful life than this, that you might live, if you were but willing, but truly willing to hearken to Christ, and come home to God. You might then draw near to God with boldness, and call him your Father, and comfortably trust him with your souls and bodies. If you look upon the promises, you may say, They are all mine. If upon the curse, you may say, From this I am delivered. When you read the law, you may see what you are saved from. When you read the Gospel, you may see him that redeemed you, and see the course of his love, and holy life, and sufferings, and trace him in his temptations, tears, and blood, in the work of your salvation. You may see death conquered, and heaven opened, and your resurrection and glorification provided for in the resurrection and glorification of the Lord. If you look on the saints, you may say, They are my brethren and companions. If on the unsanctified, you may rejoice to think that you are saved from that state. If you look upon the heavens, the sun, and moon, and stars innumerable, you may think and say, My Father's face is infinitely more glorious; it is higher matters that He hath prepared for his saints; yonder is but the outward court of heaven. The blessedness that He hath promised me is so much higher that flesh and blood cannot behold it. If you think of the grave, you may remember that the glorified Spirit, a living Head, and a loving Father, have all so near a relation to your dust, that it cannot be forgotten or neglected, but will more certainly revive than the plants and flowers in the spring: because that the soul is still alive that is the root of the body; and Christ is alive, that is the root of both. Even death, which is the king of fears, may be remembered and entertained with joy, as being the day of your deliverance from the remnant of sin and sorrow, and the day which you believed, and hoped, and waited for, when you shall see the blessed things which you had heard of, and shall find by present joyful experience what it was to choose the better part, and to be a sincere believing saint. What say you, sir? Is not this a more delightful life, to be assured of salvation and ready to die, than to live as the ungodly, that have their hearts overcharged with surfeiting, and drunkenness, and the cares of this life, and so that day comes upon them unawares? Luke xxi. 34, 36. Might you not live a comfortable life, if once you were made the heirs of heaven, and sure to be saved when you leave the world? O look about you then, and think what you do, and cast not away such hopes as these for very nothing. The flesh and world can give you no such hopes or comforts.

And besides all the misery that you bring upon yourselves, you are the troublers of others as long as you are unconverted. You trouble magistrates to rule you by their laws; you trouble ministers by resisting the light and guidance which they offer you. Your sin and misery are the greatest grief and trouble to them in the world. You trouble the commonwealth, and draw the judgments of God upon you. It is you that most disturb the holy peace and order of the churches, and hinder our union and reformation, and are the shame and trouble of the churches where you intrude, and of the places where you are. Ah, Lord! how heavy and sad a case is this, that even in England, where the gospel doth abound above any other nation in the world, where teaching is so plain and common, and all the helps we can desire are at hand; when the sword has been hewing us, and judgment has run as a fire through the land; when deliverances have relieved us, and so many admirable mercies have engaged us to God, and to the Gospel, and a holy life; that, after all this, our cities, and towns, and countries, shall abound with multitudes of unsanctified men, and swarm with so much sensuality, as every where, to our grief, we see? One would have thought, that after all this light, and all this experience, and all these judgments and mercies of God, the people of this nation should have joined together, as one man, to turn to the Lord, and should have come to their godly teacher, and lamented all their former sins, and desired him to join with them, in public humiliation, to confess them openly, and beg pardon of them from the Lord, and should have craved his instruction for the time to come, and be glad to be ruled by the Spirit within, and the ministers of Christ without, according to the word of God. One would think that, after such reason and Scripture evidence as they hear, and after all these means and mercies, there should not be an ungodly person left among us, nor a worldling, nor a drunkard, nor a hater of reformation, nor an enemy to holiness, to be found in all our towns and countries. If we be not all agreed about some ceremonies or forms of government, one would think that, before this, we should have been agreed to live a holy and heavenly life, in obedience to God, his word, and ministers, and in love and peace with one another. But, alas! how far are our people from this course! Most of them, in most places, do set their hearts on earthly things, and seek not "first the kingdom of God and the righteousness thereof," but look on holiness as a needless thing: their families are prayerless, or else a few heartless lifeless words must serve instead of hearty fervent daily prayers (or perhaps only on the Lord's day, in the evening:) their children are not taught the knowledge of Christ, and the covenant of grace, nor brought up in the nurture of the Lord, though they firmly promised all this at their baptism.

They instruct not their servants in the matters of salvation; but so their work be done, they care not. There are more railing speeches in their families than gracious words that tend to edification. How few are the families that fear the Lord, and inquire at his word and ministers how they should live, and what they should do, and are willing to be taught and ruled, and that heartily look after everlasting life! And those few that God hath made so happy are commonly the by-word of their neighbours. When we see some live in drunkenness, and some in pride and worldliness, and most of them have little care of their salvation, though the cause be gross and past all controversy, yet will they hardly be convinced of their misery, and more hardly recovered and reformed; but, when we have done all that we are able to save them from their sins, we leave the most of them as we find them. And if, according to the law of God, we cast them out of the communion of the church, when they have obstinately rejected all our admonitions, they rage at us as if we were their enemies, and their hearts are filled with malice against us, and they will sooner set themselves against the Lord, and his laws, and church, and ministers, than against their deadly sins. This is the doleful case of England: we have magistrates that countenance the ways of godliness, and a happy opportunity for unity and reformation is before us, and faithful ministers long to see the right ordering of the church and of the ordinances of God: but the power of sin in our people doth frustrate almost all. Nowhere almost can a faithful minister set up the unquestionable discipline of Christ, or put back the most scandalous impenitent sinners from the communion of the church and participation of the sacraments, but the most of the people rail at them and revile them; as if these ignorant careless souls were wiser than their teachers, or than God himself. And thus, in the day of our visitation, when God calls upon us to reform his church, though magistrates seem willing, and faithful ministers seem willing, yet are the multitude of the people still unwilling, and have so blinded themselves, and hardened their hearts, that, even in these days of light and grace, they are the obstinate enemies of light and grace, and will not be brought by the calls of God to see their folly, and know what is for their good. O that the people of England knew at least in this their day, the things that belong unto their peace, before they are hid from their eyes! Luke xix. 42.

O foolish miserable souls! Gal. iii. 1. Who hath bewitched your minds into such madness, and your hearts unto such deadness, that you should be such mortal enemies to yourselves, and go on so obstinately towards damnation, that neither the word of God, nor the persuasions of men, can change your minds, or hold your hands, or stop you, till you are past remedy! Well, sinners! this life will not last always; this patience will not wait upon you still. Do not think that you shall abuse your Maker and Redeemer, and serve his enemies, and debase your souls, and trouble the world, and wrong the church, and reproach the godly, and grieve your teachers, and hinder reformation, and all this upon free cost. You know not yet what this must cost you, but you must shortly know, when the righteous God shall take you in hand, who will handle you in another manner than the sharpest magistrates or the plainest dealing pastors did, unless you prevent the everlasting torments, by a sound conversion and a speedy obeying of the call of God, "He that hath an ear to hear, let him hear," while mercy hath a voice to call."

One objection I find most common in the mouths of the ungodly, especially of late years; they say, 'We can do nothing without God, we cannot have grace, if God will not give it us; and, if he will, we shall quickly turn; if he have not predestinated us, and will not turn us, how can we turn ourselves, or be saved? It is not in him that wills nor in him that runs.' And thus they think they are excused.

I have answered this formerly, and in this book; but let me now say this much. 1. Though you cannot cure yourselves, you can hurt and poison yourselves. It is God that must sanctify your hearts; but who corrupted them? Will you wilfully take poison, because you cannot cure yourselves? Methinks you should the more forbear it. You should the more take heed of sinning, if you cannot mend what sin doth mar. 2. Though you cannot be converted without the special grace of God, yet you must know that God giveth his grace in the use of his holy means which he hath appointed to that end; and common grace may enable you to forbear your gross sinning (as to the outward act) and to use those means. Can you truly say, that you do as much as you are able to do? Are you not able to go by an alehouse door, or to forbear the company that hardeneth you in sin? Are you not able to hear the word, and think of what you heard when you come home, and to consider with yourselves of your own condition and of everlasting things? Are you not able to read good books from day to day, at least on the Lord's day, and to converse with those that fear the Lord? You cannot say that you have done what you are able. 3. And therefore you must know that you can forfeit the grace and help of God by your wilful sinning or negligence, though you cannot without grace, turn to God. If you will not do what you can, it is just with God to deny you that grace by which you might do more. 4. And, for God's decrees, you must know that they separate not the end and means, but tie them together. God never decreed to save any but the sanctified, nor to damn any but the unsanctified. God doth as truly decree whether your land this year shall be barren or fruitful, and just how long you shall live in the world, as he hath decreed whether you shall be saved or not; and yet you would think that man but a fool that would forbear ploughing and sowing, and say, 'If God hath decreed that my ground shall bear corn, it will bear, whether I plough and sow or not. If God have decreed that I shall live, I shall live, whether I eat or not; but, if he have not, it is not eating that will keep me alive.' Do you know how to answer such a man, or do you not? If you do, then you know how to answer yourselves; for, the case is alike: God's decree is as peremptory about your bodies as your souls: if you do not then try first these conclusions upon your bodies, before you venture to try them on your souls: see first whether God will keep you alive without food or raiment, and whether he will give you corn without tillage and labour, and whether he will bring you to your journey's end without your travel or carriage; and if you speed well in this, then try whether he will bring you to heaven without your diligent use of means, and sit down and say, We cannot sanctify ourselves.

Well, sirs, I have but three requests to you, and I have done.

First, That you will seriously read over this small treatise; and, if you have such as need it in your families, that you would read it over and over to them; and if those that fear God would go now and then to their ignorant neighbours, and read this or some other book to them of this subject, they might be a means of winning souls. If we cannot entreat so small a labour of men for their own salvation, as to read such short instructions as these, they set little by themselves and will most justly perish.

Secondly, When you have read over this book, I would entreat you to go alone and ponder a little what you have read, and bethink you, as in the sight of God, whether it be not true, and do not nearly touch your souls, and whether it be not time to look about you. And also entreat you, that you will upon your knees beseech the Lord that he will open your eyes to understand the truth, and turn your hearts to the love of God, and beg of him all that saving grace which you have so long neglected, and follow it on from day to day, till your hearts be changed. And withal, that you will go to your pastors, (that are set over you to take care of the health and safety of your souls, as physicians do for the health of your bodies,) and desire them to direct you what course to take, and acquaint them with your spiritual estate, that you may have the benefit of their advice and ministeral help.

Or, if you have not a faithful pastor at home, make use of some other in so great a need.

Thirdly, When, by reading, consideration, prayer, and ministerial advice, you are once acquainted with your sin and misery, with your duty and remedy, delay not, but presently forsake your sinful company and courses, and turn to God, and obey his call. As you love your souls, take heed that ye go not on against so loud a call of God, and against your own knowledge and conscience, lest it go worse with you in the day of judgment than with Sodom and Gomorrah. Inquire of God, as a man that is willing to know the truth, and not be a wilful cheater of his soul. Search the holy Scriptures daily, and see whether these things be so or not: try impartially whether it be safer to trust heaven or earth, and whether it be better to follow God or man, the Spirit or the flesh, and better to live in holiness or sin, and whether an unsanctified state be safe for you to abide in one day longer; and when you have found out which is best, resolve accordingly, and make your choice without any more ado. If you will be true to your own souls, and do not love everlasting torments, I beseech you, as from the Lord, that you will but take this reasonable advice. O what happy towns and countries, and what a happy nation might we have, if we could but persuade our neighbours to agree to such a necessary motion! What joyful men would all faithful ministers be, if they could but see their people truly heavenly and holy; this would be the unity, the peace, the safety, the glory, of our churches; the happiness of our neighbours, and the comfort of our souls. Then how comfortably should we preach pardon and peace to you, and deliver the sacraments, which are the seals of peace to you! And with what love and joy might we live among you! At your deathbed how boldly might we comfort and encourage your departing souls! And, at your burial, how comfortably might we leave you in the grave, in expectation to meet your souls in heaven, and to see your bodies raised to that glory!

But, if still the most of you will go on in a careless, ignorant, fleshly, worldly, or unholy life, and all our desires and labours cannot so far prevail as to keep you from the wilful damning of yourselves, we must then imitate our Lord, who delighteth himself in those few that are jewels, and in a little flock that shall receive the kingdom, when the most shall reap the misery which they sowed. In nature excellent things are few. The world hath not many suns, or moons; it is but a little of the earth that is gold or silver. Princes and nobles are but a small part of the sons of men: and it is no great number that are learned, judicious, or wise, here in this world. And, therefore, if the gate being strait and very narrow, there be but few that find salvation, yet God will have his glory and pleasure in those few. And, when Christ shall come with his mighty angels in flaming fire, taking vengeance on them that know not God and obey not the gospel of our Lord Jesus Christ, his coming will be glorified in his saints, and admired in all true believers. 2 Thess. i. 7, 8, 9, 10.

And for the rest, as God the father vouchsafed to create them, and God the Son disdained not to bear the penalty of their sins upon the cross, and did not judge such sufferings in vain, though he knew that by refusing the sanctification of the Holy Ghost they would finally destroy themselves, so we, that are his ministers, though these be not gathered, judge not our labour wholly lost. See Isa. xlix. 5.

Reader, I have done with thee, when thou hast perused this book; but sin hath not yet done with thee, even those that thou thoughtest had been forgotten long ago, and Satan hath not yet done with thee, though now he be out of sight, and God hath not yet done with thee, because thou wilt not be persuaded to have done with the deadly reigning sin. I have written thee this persuasive, as one that is going into another world, where the things are seen that I here speak of, and as one tnat knoweth thou must be shortly there thyself. As ever thou wilt meet me with comfort before the Lord that made us; as ever thou wilt escape the everlasting plagues prepared for the final neglecters of salvation, and for all that are not sanctified by the Holy Ghost; and love not the communion of the saints as members of the holy catholic church; and as ever thou hopest to see the face of Christ the Judge, and of the majesty of the Father, with peace and comfort, and to be received into glory when thou art turned naked out of this world; I beseech thee, I charge thee, to hear and obey the CALL of God, and resolvedly to turn, that thou mayst live. But, if thou wilt not, even when thou hast no true reason for it, but because thou wilt not, I summon thee to answer it before the Lord, and require thee there to bear me witness that I gave thee warning, and that thou wast not condemned for want of a call to turn and live, but because thou wouldst not believe it, and obey it; which also must be the testimony of

Thy serious Monitor,

RICHARD BAXTER

December 11, 1657.

A CALL

TO THE UNCONVERTED.

EZEKIEL XXXIII. 11.

Say unto them, As I live, saith the Lord God, I have no pleasure in the death of the wicked; but that the wicked turn from his way and live: turn ye, turn ye from your evil ways; for why will ye die, O house of Israel?

It hath been the astonishing wonder of many a man as well as me, to read in the holy Scriptures how few will be saved, and that the greatest part even of those that are called, will be everlastingly shut out of the kingdom of heaven, and be tormented with the devils in eternal fire. Infidels believe not this when they read it, and therefore they must feel it; those that do believe it, are forced to cry out with Paul, (Rom. xi. 13,) "O the depth of the riches both of the wisdom and knowledge of God! How unsearchable are his judgments, and his ways past finding out!" But nature itself doth teach us all to lay the blame of evil works upon the doers; and therefore when we see any heinous thing done, a principle of justice doth provoke us to inquire after him that did it, that the evil of the work may return the evil of shame upon the author. If we saw a man killed and cut in pieces by the way, we would presently ask, Oh! who did this cruel deed? If the town was wilfully set on fire, you would ask, what wicked wretch did this? So when we read that many souls will be miserable in hell for ever, we must needs think with ourselves, how comes this to pass? and whose fault is it? Who is it that is so cruel as to be the cause of such a thing as this? and we can meet with few that will own the guilt. It is indeed confessed by all, that Satan is the cause; but that doth not resolve the doubt, because he is not the principal cause. He doth not force men to sin, but tempts them to it, and leaves it to their own wills whether they will do it or not. He doth not carry men to an alehouse and force open their mouths and pour in the drink; nor doth he hold them that they cannot go to God's service; nor doth he force their hearts from holy thoughts. It lieth therefore between God himself and the sinner; one of them must needs be the principal cause of all this misery, whichever it is, for there is no other to lay it upon; and God disclaimeth it; he will not take it upon him; and the wicked disclaim it usually, and they will not take it upon them, and this is the controversy that is here managing in my text.

The Lord complaineth of the people; and the people think it is the fault of God. The same controversy is handled, chap. xviii. 25; they plainly say, "that the way of the Lord is not equal." So here they say, verse 19, "If our transgressions and our sins be upon us, and we pine away in them, how shall we then live?" As if they should say, if we must die, and be miserable, how can we help it? as if it were not their fault but God's. But God, in my text, doth clear himself of it, and telleth them how they may help it if they will, and persuadeth them to use the means, and if they will not be persuaded, he lets them know that it is the fault of themselves; and if this will not satisfy them, he will not forbear to punish them. It is he that will be the Judge, and he will judge them according to their ways; they are no judge of him or of themselves. as wanting authority, and wisdom, and impartiality, nor is it the cavilling and quarrelling with God that shall serve their turn, or save them from the execution of justice at which they murmur.

The words of this verse contain, 1. God's purgation or clearing himself from the blame of their destruction. This he doth not by disowning his law, that the wicked shall die, nor by disowning his judgments and execution according to that law, or giving them any hope that the law shall not be executed; but by professing that it is not their death that he takes pleasure in, but their returning rather, that they may live; and this he confirmeth to them by his oath. 2. An express exhortation to the wicked to return; wherein God doth not only command, but persuade and condescend also to reason the case with them. Why will they die? The direct end of this exhortation is, that they may turn and live. The secondary or reserved ends, upon supposition that this is not attained, are these two: First, To convince them by the means which he used, that it is not the fault of God if they be miserable. Secondly, To convince them from their manifest wilfulness in rejecting all his commands and persuasions, that it is the fault of themselves, and they die, even because they will die.

The substance of the text doth lie in these observations following:—

Doctrine 1. It is the unchangeable law of God, that wicked men must turn or die.

Doctrine 2. It is the promise of God, that the wicked shall live, if they will but turn.

Doctrine 3. God takes pleasure in men's conversion and salvation, but not in their death or damnation: he had rather they would return and live, thar go on and die.

Doctrine 4. This is a most certain truth, which because God would not have men to question, he hath confirmed it to them solemnly by his oath.

Doctrine 5. The Lord doth redouble his commands and persuasions to the wicked to turn.

Doctrine 6. The Lord condescendeth to reason the case with them; and asketh the wicked why they will die?

Doctrine 7. If after all this the wicked will not turn, it is not the fault of God that they perish but of themselves; their own wilfulness is the cause of their own damnation; they therefore die because they will die.

Having laid the text open in these propositions, I shall next speak somewhat of each of them in order, though very briefly.

Doctrine 1. It is the unchangeable law of God, that wicked men must turn, or die.

If you will believe God, believe this: there is but one of these two ways for every wicked man, either conversion or damnation. I know the wicked will hardly be persuaded either of the truth or equity of this. No wonder if the guilty quarrel with the law. Few men are apt to believe that which they would not have to be true, and fewer would have that to be true which they apprehend to be against them. But it is not quarrelling with the law, or with the judge, that will save the malefactor. Believing and regarding the law might have prevented his death; but denying and accusing it will but hasten it. If it were not so, a hundred would bring their reason against the law, for one that would bring his reason to the law, and men would rather choose to give their reasons why they should not be punished, than to hear the commands and reasons of their governors which require them to obey. The law was not made for you to judge, but that you might be ruled and judged by it.

But if there be any so blind as to venture to question either the truth or the justice of this law of God,

I shall briefly give you that evidence of both, which, methinks, should satisfy a reasonable man.

And first, if you doubt whether this be the word of God, or not, besides a hundred other texts, you may be satisfied by these few :—Matt. xviii. 3. "Verily I say unto you, except ye be converted and become as little children, ye cannot enter into the kingdom of God." John iii. 3. "Verily, verily, I say unto you, except a man be born again, he cannot see the kingdom of God." 2 Cor. v. 17. "If any man be in Christ, he is a new creature; old things are passed away ; behold, all things are become new." Col. iii. 9, 10. "Ye have put off the old man with his deeds, and have put on the new man, which is renewed in knowledge after the image of him that created him." Heb. xii. 14. "Without holiness none shall see God." Rom. viii. 8, 9. "So then they that are in the flesh cannot please God. Now if any man have not the Spirit of Christ, he is none of his." Gal. vi. 15. "For in Christ Jesus neither circumcision availeth any thing, nor uncircumcision, but a new creature." 1 Pet. i. 3. "According to his abundant grace he hath begotten us to a lively hope." Ver. 23. "Being born again, not of corruptible seed, but of incorruptible, by the word of God, which liveth and abideth for ever." 1 Pet. ii. 1, 2. "Wherefore laying aside all malice, and all guile, and hypocrisies, and envies, and evil speaking, as new born babes desire the sincere milk of the word, that ye may grow thereby." Psalm ix. 17. "The wicked shall be turned into hell, and all the nations that forget God." Psalm xi. 4. "And the Lord loveth the righteous, but the wicked his soul hateth."

As I need not stay to open these texts which are so plain, so I think I need not add any more of that multitude which speak the like. If thou be a man that dost believe the word of God, here is already enough to satisfy thee, that the wicked must be converted or condemned. You are already brought so far, that you must either confess that this is true, or say plainly, you will not believe the word of God. And if once you be come to that pass, there is but small hopes of you: look to yourselves as well as you can, for it is like you will not be long out of hell. You would be ready to fly in the face of him that should give you the lie; and yet dare you give the lie to God? But if you tell God plainly you will not believe him, blame him not if he never warn you more, or if he forsake you, and give you up as hopeless; for to what purpose should he warn you, if you will not believe him? Should he send an angel from heaven to you, it seems you would not believe? For an angel can speak but the word of God; and if an angel should bring you any other gospel, you are not to receive it, but to hold him accursed. Gal. i. 8. And surely there is no angel to be believed before the Son of God, who came from the Father to bring us this doctrine. If he be not to be believed, then all the angels in heaven are not to be believed. And if you stand on these terms with God, I shall leave you till he deal with you in a more convincing way. God hath a voice that will make you hear. Though he entreat you to hear the voice of his gospel, he will make you hear the voice of his condemning sentence, without entreaty. We cannot make you believe against your wills; but God will make you feel against your wills.

But let us hear what reason you have why you will not believe this word of God, which tells us that the wicked must be converted, or condemned. I know your reason; it is because that you judge it unlikely that God should be so unmerciful: you think it cruelty to damn men everlastingly for so small a thing as a sinful life. And this leads us to the second thing, which is to justify the equity of God in his laws and judgments.

And first, I think you will not deny but that it is most suitable to an immortal soul, to be ruled by laws that promise an immortal reward, and threaten an endless punishment. Otherwise the law should not be suited to the nature of the subject, who will not be fully ruled by any lower means than the hopes or fears of everlasting things: as it is in cases of temporal punishment, if a law were now made that the most heinous crimes shall be punished with a hundred years' captivity, this might be of some efficacy, as being equal to our lives. But, if there had been no other penalties before the flood, when men lived eight or nine hundred years, it would not have been sufficient, because men would know that they might have so many hundred years impunity afterwards. So it is in our present case.

2. I suppose that you will confess, that the promise of an endless and inconceivable glory is not so unsuitable to the wisdom of God, or the case of man: and why then should you not think so of the threatening of an endless and unspeakable misery!

3. When you find it in the word of God that so it is, and so it will be, do ye think yourselves fit to contradict this word? Will you call your Maker to the bar, and examine his word upon the accusation of falsehood? Will you sit upon him, and judge him by the law of your conceits? Are you wiser, and better, and more righteous than he? Must the God of heaven come to school to you to learn wisdom? Must Infinite Wisdom learn of folly, and Infinite Goodness be corrected by a swinish sinner, that cannot keep himself an hour clean? Must the Almighty stand at the bar of a worm? O horrid arrogancy of senseless dust! shall ever mole, or clod, or dunghill, accuse the sun of darkness, and undertake to illuminate the world? Where were you when the Almighty made the laws, that he did not call you to his counsel? Surely he made them before you were born, without desiring your advice; and you came into the world too late to reverse them, if you could have done so great a work. You should have stepped out of your nothingness and have contradicted Christ when he was on earth, or Moses before him, or have saved Adam and his sinful progeny from the threatened death, that so there might have

been no need of Christ. And what if God withdraw his patience and sustaining power, and let you drop into hell while you are quarrelling with his word, will you then believe that there is a hell?

4. If sin be such an evil that it requireth the death of Christ for its expiation, no wonder if it deserve our everlasting misery.

5. And if the sin of the devils deserved an endless torment, why not also the sin of man?

6. And methinks you should perceive that it is not possible for the best of men, much less for the wicked, to be competent judges of the desert of sin. Alas! we are both blind and partial. You can never know fully the desert of sin, till you fully know the evil of sin; and you can never fully know the evil of sin, till you fully know, 1. The excellency of the soul which it deformeth. 2. And the excellency of holiness which it obliterates. 3. The reason and excellency of the law which it violates. 4. The excellency of the glory which it despises. 5. The excellency and office of reason which it treadeth down. 6. No, nor till you know the infinite excellency, almightiness and holiness of that God against whom it is committed. When you fully know all these, you shall fully know the desert of sin besides. You know that the offender is too partial to judge the law, or the proceeding of his judge. We judge by feeling which blinds our reason. We see, in common worldly things, that most men think the cause is right which is their own, and that all is wrong that is done against them; and let the most wise or just impartial friends persuade them to the contrary, and it is all in vain. There are few children but think the father is unmerciful, or dealeth hardly with them if he whip them. There is scarce the vilest wretch but thinketh the church doth wrong him if they excommunicate him: or scarce a thief or murderer that is hanged, but would accuse the law and judge of cruelty, if that would serve their turn.

7. Can you think that an unholy soul is fit for

heaven? Alas, they cannot love God here, nor do him any service which he can accept. They are contrary to God; they loathe that which he most loveth, and love that which he abhorreth. They are incapable of that imperfect communion with him which his saints here partake of. How then can they live in that perfect love of him, and full delights and communion with him, which is the blessedness of heaven? Ye do not accuse yourselves of unmercifulness, if you make not your enemy your bosom counsellor; or if you take not your swine to bed and board with you: no, nor if you take away his life though he never sinned; and yet you will blame the absolute Lord, the most wise and gracious Sovereign of the world, if he condemn the unconverted to perpetual misery.

USE.—I beseech you now, all that love your souls, that, instead of quarrelling with God and with his word, you will presently stoop to it, and use it for your good. All you that are yet unconverted in this assembly, take this as the undoubted truth of God:—You must, ere long, be converted or condemned; there is no other way but to turn or die. When God, that cannot lie, hath told you this; when you hear it from the Maker and Judge of the world, it is time for him that hath ears to hear. By this time you may see what you have to trust to. You are but dead and damned men, except you will be converted. Should I tell you otherwise, I should deceive you with a lie. Should I hide this from you, I should undo you, and be guilty of your blood, as the verses before my text assure me. Verse 8. "When I say to the wicked man, O wicked man, thou shalt surely die; if thou dost not speak to warn the wicked from his way, that wicked man shall die in his iniquity; but his blood will I require at thine hand." You see then, though this be a rough and unwelcome doctrine, it is such as we must preach, and you must hear. It is easier to hear of hell than feel it. If your necessities did not require it, we would not gall your tender ears with truths that seem so harsh and grievous. Hell would not be so full, if people were but willing to know their case, and to hear and think of it. The reason why so few escape it is, because they strive not to enter in at the strait gate of conversion, and go the narrow way of holiness, while they have time: and they strive not, because they are not awakened to a lively feeling of the danger they are in; and they are not awakened because they are loth to hear or think of it: and that is partly through foolish tenderness and carnal self love, and partly because they do not well believe the word that threateneth it. If you will not thoroughly believe this truth, methinks the weight of it should force you to remember it, and it should follow you, and give you no rest till you are converted. If you had but once heard this word by the voice of an angel, "Thou must be converted," or "condemned: turn, or die:" would it not stick in your minds, and haunt you night and day? so that in your sinning you would remember it, as if the voice were still in your ears, "Turn, or die!" O happy were your souls if it might thus work with you and never be forgotten, or let you alone till it have driven home your hearts to God. But if you will cast it out by forgetfulness or unbelief, how can it work to your conversion and salvation? But take this with you to your sorrow, though you may put this out of your minds, you cannot put it out of the Bible, but there it will stand as a sealed truth, which you shall experimentally know for ever, that there is no other way but turn, or die.

O what is the matter then that the hearts of sinners are not pierced with such a weighty truth? A man would think now, that every unconverted soul that hears these words should be pricked to the heart, and think with themselves, 'This is my own case,' and never be quiet till they found themselves converted. Believe it, sirs, this drowsy careless temper will not last long. Conversion and condemnation are both of them awakening things, and one of them will make you feel ere long. I can foretell it as truly as if I saw it with my eyes, that either grace or hell will shortly bring these matters to the quick, and make you say, 'What have I done? what a foolish wicked course have I taken?' The scornful and the stupid state of sinners will last but a little while; as soon as they either turn or die, the presumptuous dream will be at an end, and then their wits and feeling will return.

But I foresee there are two things that are likely to harden the unconverted, and make me lose all my labour, except they can be taken out of the way; and that is the misunderstanding on those two words, the *wicked* and *turn*. Some will think to themselves, 'It is true, the wicked must turn or die; but what is that to me, I am not wicked; though I am a sinner, all men are.' Others will think, 'It is true that we must turn from our evil ways, but I am turned long ago; I hope this is not now to do.' And thus while wicked men think they are not wicked, but are already converted, we lose all our labour in persuading them to turn. I shall therefore, before I go any further, tell you here who are meant by the wicked; and who they are that must turn or die; and also what is meant by turning, and who they are that are truly converted. And this I have purposely reserved for this place, preferring the method that fits my end.

And here you may observe, that in the sense of the text, a wicked man and a converted man are contraries. No man is a wicked man that is converted; and no man is a converted man that is wicked; so that to be a wicked man and to be an unconverted man, is all one; and therefore in opening one, we shall open both.

Before I can tell you what either wickedness or conversion is, I must go to the bottom, and fetch up the matter from the beginning.

It pleased the great Creator of the world to make three sorts of living creatures. Angels he made pure sprits without flesh, and therefore he made them only for heaven, and not to dwell on earth. Brutes were made flesh, without immortal souls, and therefore they were made only for earth, and not for heaven. Man is of a middle nature, between both, as partaking of both flesh and spirit, and therefore he was made both for heaven and earth. But as his flesh is made to be but a servant to his spirit, so is he made for earth but as his passage or way to heaven, and not that this should be his home or happiness. The blessed state that man was made for, was to behold the glorious majesty of the Lord, and to praise him among his Holy Angels, and to love him, and to be filled with his love for ever. And as this was the end that man was made for, so God did give him means that were fitted to the attaining of it. These means were principally two: First the right inclination and disposition of the mind of man. Secondly, The right ordering of his life and practice. For the first, God suited the disposition of man unto his end, giving him such knowledge of God as was fit for his present state, and a heart disposed and inclined to God in holy love. But yet he did not fix or confirm him in this condition, but, having made him a free agent, he left him in the hands of his own free will. For the second, God did that which belonged to him; that is, he gave him a perfect law, required him to continue in the love of God, and perfectly to obey him. By the wilful breach of this law, man did not only forfeit his hopes of everlasting life, but also turned his heart from God, and fixed it on these lower fleshly things, and hereby blotted out the spiritual image of God from his soul; so that man did both fall short of the glory of God, which was his end, and put himself out of the way by which he should have attained it, and this both as to the frame of his heart, and of his life. The holy inclination and love of his soul to God, he lost, and instead of it he contracted an inclination and love to the pleasing of his flesh, or carnal self, by earthly things; growing strange to God and acquainted with the creature. And the course of this life was suited to the bent and inclination of his heart; he lived to his carnal self, and not to God; he sought the creature, for the pleasing of his flesh, instead of seeking to please the Lord. With this nature or corrupt inclination, we are all now born into the world; "for who can bring a clean thing out of an unclean?" Job xiv. 4. As a lion hath a fierce and cruel nature before he doth devour; and an adder hath a venomous nature before she sting, so in our infancy we have those sinful natures or inclinations, before we think, or speak, or do amiss. And hence springeth all the sin of our lives; and not only so, but when God hath of his mercy, provided us a remedy, even the Lord Jesus Christ, to be the Saviour of our souls, and bring us back to God again, we naturally love our present state, and are loth to be brought out of it, and therefore are set against the means of our recovery: and though custom hath taught us to thank Christ for his good-will, yet carnal self persuades us to refuse his remedies, and to desire to be excused, when we are commanded to take the medicines which he offers, and are called to forsake all and follow him to God and glory.

I pray you read over this leaf again, and mark it; for in these few words you have a true description of our natural state, and consequently of wicked man; for every man that is in the state of corrupted nature is a wicked man, and in a state of death.

By this also you are prepared to understand what it is to be converted: to which end you must further know, that the mercy of God, not willing that man should perish in his sin, provided a remedy, by causing his Son to take our nature, and being, in one person, God and man, to become a mediator between God and man, and by dying for our sins on the cross, to ransom us from the curse of God and the power of the devil. And having thus redeemed us, the Father hath delivered us into his hands as his own. Hereupon the Father and the Mediator do make a new law and covenant for man, not like the first, which gave life to none but the perfectly obedient, and condemned man for every sin; but Christ hath made a law of grace, or a promise of pardon and everlasting life to all that, by true repentance, and by faith in Christ, are converted unto God; like an act of oblivion, which is made by a prince to a company of rebels, on condition they will lay down arms and come in, and be loyal subjects for the time to come.

But, because the Lord knoweth that the heart of man is grown so wicked, that, for all this, men will not accept of the remedy if they be left to themselves, therefore the Holy Ghost hath undertaken it as his office to inspire the Apostles, and seal up the Scriptures by miracles and wonders, and to illuminate and convert the souls of the elect.

So by this much you see, that as there are three persons in the Trinity, the Father, the Son, and he Holy Ghost, so each of these persons have their several works, which are eminently ascribed to them.

The Father's works were, to create us, to rule us, as his rational creatures, by the law of nature, and judge us thereby; and in mercy to provide us a Redeemer when we were lost; and to send his Son, and accept his ransom.

The works of the Son for us were these: to ransom and redeem us by his suffering and righteousness; to give out the promise or law of grace, and rule and judge the world as their Redeemer, on terms of grace: and to make intercession for us, that the benefits of his death may be communicated; and to send the Holy Ghost, which the Father also doth by the Son.

The works of the Holy Ghost, for us, are these· to indite the holy Scriptures, by inspiring and guiding the Apostles, and sealing the word, by his miraculous gifts and works, and the illuminating and exciting the ordinary ministers of the gospel, and so enabling them and helping them to publish that word; and by the same word illuminating and converting the souls of men. So that as you could not have been reasonable creatures, if the Father had not created you, nor have had any access to God, if the Son had not redeemed you, so neither can you have a part in Christ, or be saved, except the Holy Ghost do sanctify you.

So that by this time you may see the several causes of this work. The Father sendeth the Son: the Son redeems us and maketh the promise of grace: the Holy Ghost inditeth and sealeth this gospel: the Apostles are the secretaries of the Spirit to write it: the preachers of the gospel to proclaim it, and persuade men to open it: and the Holy Ghost doth make their preaching effectual, by opening the hearts of men to entertain it. And all this to repair the image of God upon the soul, and to set the heart upon God again, and take it off the creature and carnal self to which it is revolted, and so to turn the current of the life into a heavenly course, which before was earthly; and all this by entertaining of Christ by faith, who is the Physician of the soul.

By what I have said, you may see what it is to be wicked, and what it is to be converted; which, I think, will yet be plainer to you, if I describe them as consisting of their several parts. And for the first, a wicked man may be known by these three things:—

First, He is one who placeth his chief affections on earth, and loveth the creature more than God, and his fleshly prosperity above the heavenly felicity. He savoureth the things of the flesh, but neither discerneth nor savoureth the things of the Spirit; though he will say, that heaven is better than earth, yet he doth not really so esteem it to himself. If he might be sure of earth, he would let go heaven, and had rather stay here than be removed thither. A life of perfect holiness in the sight of God, and in his love and praises for ever in heaven, doth not find such liking with his heart, as a life of health, and wealth, and honour here upon earth. And though he falsely profess that he loves God above all, yet indeed he never felt the power of divine love within him, but his mind is more set on the world or fleshly pleasures than on God. In a word, whoever loves earth above heaven, and fleshly prosperity more than God, is a wicked unconverted man.

On the other hand, a converted man is illuminated to discern the loveliness of God, and so far believeth the glory that is to be had with God, that his heart is taken up with it and set more upon it than any thing in this world. He had rather see the face of God, and live in his everlasting love and praises, than have all the wealth or pleasures of the world. He seeth that all things else are vanity, and nothing but God can fill the soul; and therefore let the world go which way it will, he layeth up his treasures and hopes in heaven, and for that he is resolved to let go all. As the fire doth mount upward, and the needle that is touched with the loadstone still turns to the north, so the converted soul is inclined unto God. Nothing else can satisfy him: nor can he find any content and rest but in his love. In a word, all that are converted do esteem and love God better than all the world, and the heavenly felicity is dearer to them than their fleshly prosperity. The proof of what I have said you may find in these places of Scripture: Phil. iii. 18, 21. Matt. vi. 19, 20, 21. Col. iii. 1—4. Rom. viii. 5—9, 18, 23. Psalm lxxiii. 25, 26.

Secondly, A wicked man is one that makes it the principal business of his life to prosper in the world, and attain his fleshly ends. And though he may read, and hear, and do much in the outward duties of religion, and forbear disgraceful sins, yet this is all but by the by, and he never makes it the principal business of his life to please God, and attain everlasting glory, and puts off God with the leavings of the world, and gives him no more service than the flesh can spare, for he will not part with all for heaven.

On the contrary, a converted man is one that makes it the principal care and business of his life to please God, and to be saved, and takes all the blessings of this life but as accommodations in his journey towards another life, and useth the creature in subordination to God; he loves a holy life, and longs to be more holy; he hath no sin but what he hateth, and longeth, and prayeth, and striveth to be rid of. The drift and bent of his life is for God, and if he sin, it is contrary to the very bent of his heart and life; and therefore he riseth again and lamenteth it, and dares not wilfully live in any known sin. There is nothing in this world so dear to him but he can give it up to God, and forsake it for him and the hopes of glory. All this you may see in Col. iii. 1—5. Matt. vi. 20, 33. Luke xviii. 22, 23, 29. Luke xiv. 18, 24, 26, 27. Rom. viii. 13. Gal. v. 24. Luke xii. 21, &c.

Thirdly, The soul of a wicked man did never truly discern and relish the mystery of redemption, nor thankfully entertain an offered Saviour, nor is he taken up with the love of the Redeemer, nor willing to be ruled by him as the Physician of his soul, that he may be saved from the guilt and power of his sins, and recovered to God; but his heart is insensible of this unspeakable benefit, and is quite against the healing means by which he should be recovered. Though he may be willing to be outwardly religious, yet he never resigns up his soul to Christ, and to the motions and conduct of his word and Spirit.

On the contrary, the converted soul having felt himself undone by sin, and perceiving that he hath lost his peace with God and hopes of heaven, and is in danger of everlasting misery, doth thankfully entertain the tidings of redemption, and believing in the Lord Jesus as his only Saviour, resigns himself up to him for wisdom, righteousness, sanctification, and redemption. He takes Christ as the life of his soul, and lives by him, and uses him as a salve for every sore, admiring the wisdom and love of God in this wonderful work of man's redemption. In a word, Christ doth even dwell in his heart by faith, and the life that he now liveth, is by the faith of the Son of God, that loved him, and gave himself for him; yea, it is not so much he that liveth, as Christ in him. For these, see Job i. 11, 12. and iii. 19, 20. Rom. viii. 9. Phil. iii. 7—10. Gal. ii. 20. Job xv. 2, 3, 4. 1 Cor. i. 20. ii. 2.

You see now in plain terms from the Word of God, who are the wicked and who are the converted. Ignorant people think, that if a man be no swearer, nor curser, nor railer, nor drunkard, nor fornicator, nor extortioner, nor wrong any body in his dealings, and if he come to church and say his prayers, he cannot be a wicked man. Or if a man that hath been guilty of drunkenness, swearing or gaming, or the like vices, do but forbear them for the time to come, they think that this is a converted man. Others think if a man that hath been an enemy, and scorner at godliness, do but approve it, and be hated for it by the wicked, as the godly are, that this must needs be a converted man. And some are so foolish as to think that they are converted, by taking up some new opinion, and falling into some dividing party. And some think, if they have but been affrighted by the fears of hell, and had convictions of conscience; and thereupon have purposed and promised amendment, and take up a life of civil behaviour, and outward religion, that this must needs be true conversion. And these are the poor deluded souls that are like to lose the benefit of all our persuasions; and when they hear that the wicked must turn or die, they think that this is not spoken to them, for they are not wicked, but are turned already. And therefore it is that Christ told some of the rulers of the Jews who were greater and more civil than the common people, that "publicans and harlots go into the kingdom of Christ before them." Matt. xxi. 31. Not that a harlot or gross sinner can be saved without conversion; but because it was easier to make these gross sinners perceive their sin and misery, and the necessity of a change, than the more civil sort, who delude themselves by thinking that they are converted already, when they are not.

O sirs, conversion is another kind of work than most are aware of. It is not a small matter to bring an earthly mind to heaven, and to show man the amiable excellences of God, till he be taken up in such love to him that can never be quenched; to break the heart for sin, and make him fly for refuge to Christ, and thankfully embrace him as the life of his soul; to have the very drift and bent of the heart and life changed; so that a man renounceth that which he took for his felicity, and placeth his felicity where he never did before; and lives not to the same end, and drives not on the same design in the world, as he formerly did. In a word, he that is in Christ is a "new creature: old things are passed away: behold, all things are become new." 2 Cor. v. 17. He hath a new understanding, a new will and resolution, new sorrows, and desires, and love, and delight; new thoughts, new speeches, new company, (if possible,) and a new conversation. Sin, that before was a jesting matter with him, is now so odious and terrible to him, that he flies from it as from death. The world, that was so lovely in his eyes, doth now appear but as vanity and vexation: God, that was before neglected, is now the only happiness of his soul: before he was forgotten, and every lust preferred before him, but now he is set next the heart, and all things must give place to him; the heart is taken up in the attendance and observance of him, is grieved when he hides his face, and never thinks itself well without him. Christ himself, that was wont to be slightly thought of, is now his only hope and refuge, and he lives upon him as on his daily bread; he cannot pray without him, nor rejoice without him, nor think, nor speak, nor live without him. Heaven itself, that before was looked upon but as a tolerable reserve, which he hoped might serve his turn better than hell, when he could not stay any longer in the world, is now taken for his home, the place of his only hope and rest, where he shall see, and love, and praise that God that hath his heart already. Hell, that did seem before but as a bugbear to frighten men from sin, doth now appear to be a real misery, that is not to be ventured on, nor jested with. The works of holiness, of which before he was weary, and thought to be more than needful, are now both his recreation, and his business, and the trade that he lives upon. The Bible, which was before to him but almost as a common book, is now as the law of God; as a letter written to him, and subscribed with the name of the Eternal Majesty; it is the rule of his thoughts, and words, and deeds; the commands are binding, the threats are dreadful, and the promises of it speak life to his soul. The godly, that seemed to him but like other men, are now the most excellent and happy on earth. And the wicked that were his playfellows, are now his grief; and he that could laugh at their sins, is readier now to weep for their sin and misery:—Psalm xvi. 3. xv. 4. Phil. iii. 18. "but to the saints that are in the earth, and to the excellent, in whom is all my delight." "In whose eyes a vile person is contemned; but he honoureth them that fear the Lord: he that sweareth to his own hurt, and changeth not." "For many walk, of whom I have told you often, and now tell you even weeping, that they are the enemies of the cross of Christ." In short, he hath a new end in his thoughts, and a new way in his endeavours, and therefore his heart and life are new. Before, his carnal self was his end, and his pleasure and worldly profits and credit were his way; and now God and everlasting glory are his end, and Christ, and the Spirit, and word, and ordinances. Holiness to God, and righteousness and mercy to men, these are his way. Before, self was the chief ruler, to which the matters of God and conscience must stoop and give place; and now God, in Christ, by the Spirit, word and ministry, is the chief ruler, to whom both self and all the matters of self, must give place. So that this is not a change in one, or two, or twenty points, but in the whole soul, and in the very end and bent of the conversation. A man may step out of one path into another, and yet have his face the same way, and be still going towards the same place; but it is another matter to turn quite back, and take his journey quite the contrary way, to a contrary place. So it is here; a man may turn from drunkenness to thriftiness, and forsake his good fellowship, and other gross disgraceful sins, and set upon some duties of religion, and yet be still going to the same end as before, intending his carnal self above all, and giving it still the government of his soul; but when he is converted, this self is denied, and taken down, and God is set up, and his face is turned the contrary way: and he that before was addicted to himself, and lived to himself, is now, by sanctification, devoted to God, and liveth unto God. Before, he asked himself what he should do with his time, his parts, and his estate, and for himself he used them; but now he asketh God what he shall do with them, and useth them for him. Before he would please God so far as might accord with the pleasure of his flesh and carnal self, but not to any great displeasure of them; but now he will please God, let flesh and self be never so much displeased. This is the great change that God will make upon all that shall be saved.

You can say, that the Holy Ghost is our sanctifier; but do you know what sanctification is? Why, this is what I have now opened to you; and every man and woman in the world must have this, or be condemned to everlasting misery. They must turn or die.

Do you believe all this, sirs, or do you not?

Surely you dare not say, you do not; for it is past a doubt or denial. These are not controversies, where one learned pious man is of one mind, and another of another; where one party saith this, and the other saith that. Every sect among us that deserve to be called Christians, are all agreed in this that I have said; and if you will not believe the God of truth, and that in a case where every set and party do believe him, you are utterly inexcusable.

But if you do believe this, how comes it to pass that you live so quietly in an unconverted state? Do you know that you are converted? and can you find this wonderful change upon your souls? Have you been thus born again, and made new? Are not these strange matters to many of you, and such as you never felt within yourselves? If you cannot tell the day or week of your change, or the very sermon that converted you, yet do you find that the work is done, and such a change indeed there is, and that you have such hearts as are before described? Alas! the most do follow their worldly business, and little trouble their minds with such thoughts. And if they be restrained from scandalous sins, and can say, "I am no whoremonger, nor thief, nor curser, nor swearer, nor tippler, nor extortioner; I go to church, and say my prayers;" they think that this is true conversion, and they shall be saved as well as any. Alas! this is foolish cheating of yourselves. This is too much contempt of an endless glory, and too gross neglect of your immortal souls. Can you make so light of heaven and hell? Your corpse will shortly lie in the dust, and angels or devils will presently seize upon your souls; and every man or woman of you all will shortly be among other company, and in another case than now you are. You will dwell in these houses but a little longer; you will work in your shops and fields but a little longer; you will sit in these seats and dwell on this earth but a little longer; you will see with these eyes, and hear with these ears, and speak with these tongues, but a little longer, till the resurrection-day; and can you make shift to forget this? O what a place will you shortly be in of joy or torment! O what a sight will you shortly see in heaven or hell! O what thoughts will shortly fill your hearts with unspeakable delight or horror! What work will you be employed in! to praise the Lord with saints and angels, or to cry out in fire unquenchable with devils; and should all this be forgotten? And all this will be endless, and sealed up by an unchangeable decree. Eternity, eternity will be the measure of your joys or sorrows: and can this be forgotten? And all this is true, sirs, most certainly true. When you have gone up and down a little longer, and slept and awaked a few times more, you will be dead and gone, and find all true that now I tell you: and yet can you now so much forget it? You shall then remember that you heard this sermon, and that, this day or this place, you were reminded of these things, and perceive them matters a thousand times greater than either you or I could here conceive; and yet shall they be now so much forgotten?

Beloved friends, if the Lord had not awakened me to believe and to lay to heart these things myself, I should have remained in a dark and selfish state, and have perished for ever; but if he have truly made me sensible of them, it will constrain me to compassionate you as well as myself. If your eyes were so far opened as to see hell, and you saw your neighbours, that were unconverted, dragged thither with hideous cries; though they were such as you accounted honest people on earth, and feared no such danger themselves, such a sight would make you go home and think of it, and think again, and make you warn all about you, as that lost worldling (Luke xvi. 28.) would have had his brethren warned, lest they come to that place of torment. Why, faith is a kind of sight; it is the eye of the soul, the evidence of things not seen. If I believe God, it is next to seeing; and therefore I beseech you excuse me, if I be half as earnest with you about these matters, as if I had seen them. If I must die to-morrow, and it were in my power to come again from another world, and tell you what I had seen, would you not be willing to hear me? and would you not believe, and regard what I should tell you? If I might preach one sermon to you after I am dead, and have seen what is done in the world to come, would you not have me plainly speak the truth, and would you not crowd to hear me, and would you not lay it to heart? But this must not be; God hath his appointed way of teaching you by Scriptures and ministers, and he will not humour unbelievers so far as to send men from the dead to them, and alter his established way; if any man quarrel with the sun, God will not humour him so far as to set up a clearer light. Friends, I beseech you regard me now, as you would do if I should come from the dead to you; for I can give you as full assurance of the truth of what I say to you, as if I had been there and seen it with my eyes: for it is possible for one from the dead to deceive you; but Jesus Christ can never deceive you; the Word of God delivered in Scripture, and sealed by miracles, and holy workings of the Spirit, can never deceive you. Believe this or believe nothing. Believe and obey this, or you are undone. Now, as ever you believe the word of God, and as ever you care for the salvation of your souls, let me beg of you this reasonable request, and I beseech you deny me not: That you would, without any more delay, when you are gone from hence, remember what you have heard, and enter into an earnest search of your hearts, and say to yourselves—It is so indeed; must I turn or die? Must I be converted or condemned? It is time for me then to look about me before it be too late. O why did not I look after this till now? Why did I venturously put off or neglect so great a business? Was I awake, or in my wits? O blessed God, what a mercy is it that thou didst not cut off my life all this while, before I had any certain hope of eternal life! Well, God forbid that I should neglect this work any longer. What state is my soul in? Am I converted, or am I not? Was ever such a change or work done upon my soul? Have I been illuminated by the word and Spirit of the Lord, to see the odiousness of sin, the need of a Saviour, the love of Christ, and the excellences of God and glory? Is my heart broken or humbled within me, for my former life? Have I thankfully entertained my Saviour and Lord, that offered himself with pardon and life for my soul? Do I hate my former sinful life, and the remnant of every sin that is in me? Do I fly from them as my deadly enemies? Do I give up myself to a life of holiness and obedience to God? Do I love it, and delight in it? Can I truly say that I am dead to the world, and carnal self, and that I live for God and the glory which he hath promised? Hath heaven more of my estimation and resolution than earth? And is God the dearest and highest in my soul? Once, I am sure, I lived principally to the world and flesh, and God had nothing but some heartless services, which the world could spare, and which were the leavings of the flesh. Is my heart now turned another way? Have I a new design and a new end, and a new train of holy affections? Have I set my hopes and heart in heaven? And is it not the scope, and design, and bent of my heart, to get well to heaven, and see the glorious face of God, and live in his love and praise? And when I sin, is it against the habitual bent and design of my heart? And do I conquer all gross sins, and am I weary and willing to be rid of my infirmities? This is the state of converted souls. And thus it must be with me, or I must perish. Is it thus with me indeed, or is it not? It is time to get this doubt resolved before the dreadful Judge resolve it. I am not such a stranger to my own heart and life, but I may somewhat perceive whether I am thus converted or not: if I be not, it will do me no good to flatter my soul with false conceits and hopes. I am resolved no more to deceive myself, but endeavour to know truly whether I be converted or not: that if I be, I may rejoice in it, and glorify my gracious Lord, and comfortably go on till I reach the crown: and if I am not, I may set myself to beg and seek after the grace that should convert me, and may turn without any more delay. For, if I find in time that I am out of the way, by the help of Christ I may turn and be recovered; but if I stay till either my heart be forsaken of God in blindness or hardness, or till I be catched away by death, it is then too late. There is no place for repentance and conversion then; I know it must be now or never.

Sirs, this is my request to you, that you will but take your hearts to task, and thus examine them till you see if it may be, whether you are converted or not? And if you cannot find it out by your own endeavours, go to your ministers, if they be faithful and experienced men, and desire their assistance. The matter is great; let not bashfulness, nor carelessness hinder you. They are set over you, to advise you, for the saving of your soul, as physicians advise you for the curing of your bodies. It undoes many thousands that they think they are in the way to salvation, when they are not; and think that they are converted when it is no such thing. And then when we call to them daily to turn they go away as they came, and think that this concerns not them; for they are turned already, and hope they shall do well enough in the way that they are in, at least if they pick the fairest path, and avoid some of the foulest steps, when, alas! all this while they live but to the world and flesh, and are strangers to God and eternal life; and are quite out of the way to heaven. And all this because we cannot persuade them to a few serious thoughts of their condition, and to spend a few hours in the examining of their states. Are there not many self-deceivers who hear me this day that never bestowed one hour, or quarter of an hour, in all their lives, to examine their souls, and try whether they are truly converted or not? O merciful God, that will care for such wretches that care no more for themselves, and that will do so much to save them from hell, and help them to heaven, who will do so little for it themselves! If all that are in the way to hell, and in the state of damnation, did but know it, they durst not continue in it. The greatest hope that the devil hath of bringing you to damnation without a rescue, is by keeping you blindfold, and ignorant of your state, and making you believe that you may do well enough in the way that you are in. If you knew that you were out of the way to heaven, and were lost for ever if you should die as you are; durst you sleep another night in the state that you are in? Durst you live another day in it? Could you heartily laugh, or be merry in such a state? What! And not know but you may be snatched away to hell in an hour? Sure it would constrain you to forsake your former company and courses, and to betake yourselves to the ways of holiness, and the communion of saints. Sure it would drive you to cry to God for a new heart, and to seek help of those that are fit to counsel you. There are none of you that cares not for being damned. Well, then I beseech you presently make inquiry into your hearts, and give them no rest till you find out your condition, that if it be good, you may rejoice in it, and go on; and if it be bad, you may presently look about you for recovery, as men that believe they must turn or die. What say you, sirs, will you resolve and promise to be at thus much labour for your own souls? Will you fall upon this self-examination when you come home? Is my request unreasonable? Your consciences know it is not. Resolve on it then, before you stir; knowing how much it concerneth your souls. I beseech you, for the sake of that God that doth command you, at whose bar you will all shortly appear, that you do not deny me this reasonable request. For the sake of those souls that must turn or die, I beseech you deny me not; but make it your business to understand your own conditions, and build upon sure ground, and know whether you are converted or not; and venture not your souls on negligent security.

But perhaps you will say, 'What if we should find ourselves yet unconverted, what shall we do then?' This question leads me to my second Doctrine; which will do much to the answering of it, to which I now proceed.

DOCTRINE 2. It is the promise of God, that the wicked shall live, if they will but turn, unfeignedly and thoroughly turn.

The Lord here professeth that this is what he takes pleasure in, that the wicked turn and live. Heaven is made as sure to the converted, as hell is to the unconverted. Turn and live, is as certain a truth as Turn or die. God was not bound to provide us a Saviour, nor open to us a door of hope, nor call us to repent and turn, when once we had cast ourselves away by sin. But he hath freely done it to magnify his mercy. Sinners, there are none of you shall have cause to go home, and say I preach desperation to you. Do we use to shut the door of mercy against you? O that you would not shut it up against yourselves! Do we use to tell you that God will have no mercy on you, though you turn and be sanctified? When did you ever hear a preacher say such a word? You that cavil at the preachers of the gospel, for desiring to keep you out of hell, and say, that they preach desperation; tell me if you can, when did you ever hear any sober man say, that there is no hope for you, though you repent, and be converted? No, it is the direct contrary that we daily proclaim from the Lord; and whoever is born again, and by faith and repentance doth become a new creature, shall certainly be saved and so far are we from persuading you to despair of this, that we persuade you not to make any doubt of it. It is life, not death, that is the first part of our message to you; our commission is to offer salvation, certain salvation; a speedy, glorious, everlasting salvation, to every one of you; to the poorest beggar as well as the greatest lord; to the worst of you, even to drunkards, swearers, worldlings, thieves, yea, to the despisers and reproachers of the holy way of salvation. We are commanded by the Lord our Master, to offer you a pardon for all that is past, if you will but now at last return and live; we are commanded to beseech and entreat you to accept the offer, and return; to tell you what preparation is made by Christ; what mercy stays for you; what patience waiteth for you; what thoughts of kindness God hath towards you; and how happy, how certainly and unspeakably happy you may be if you will. We have indeed also a message of wrath and death, yea, of a twofold wrath and death; but neither of them is our principal message. We must tell you of the wrath that is on you already, and the death that you are born under, for the breach of the law of works; but this is but to show you the need of mercy, and to provoke you to esteem the grace of the Redeemer. And we tell you nothing but the truth, which you must know; for who will seek for physic that knows not that he is sick? Our telling you of your misery, is not that which makes you miserable, but driveth you out to seek for mercy. It is you that have brought this death upon yourselves. We tell you also of another death, even remediless, and much greater torment, that will fall on those that will not be converted. But as this is true, and must be told you, so it is but the last and saddest part of our message. We are first to offer you mercy, if you will turn; and it is only those that will not turn, nor hear the voice of mercy, to whom we must foretell damnation. Will you but cast away your transgressions, delay no longer, but come away at the call of Christ, and be converted, and become new creatures, and we have not a word of damning wrath or death to speak against you. I do here, in the name of the Lord of Life, proclaim to you all that hear me this day, to the worst of you, to the greatest, to the oldest sinner, that you may have mercy and salvation, if you will but turn. There is mercy in God, there is sufficiency in the satisfaction of Christ, the promise is free, and full, and universal; you may have life, if you will but turn. But then, as you love your souls, remember what turning it is that the Scripture speaks of. It is not to mend the old house, but to pull down all, and build anew on Christ, the Rock, and sure foundation. It is not to mend somewhat in a carnal course of life, but to mortify the flesh, and live after the Spirit. It is not to serve the flesh and the world, in a more reformed way, without any scandalous disgraceful sins, and with a certain kind of religiousness; but it is to change your master, and your works, and end; and to set your face the contrary way, and do all for the life that you never saw, and dedicate yourselves and all you have to God. This is the change that must be made, if you will live.

Yourselves are witnesses now, that it is salvation, and not damnation, that is the great doctrine I preach to you, and the first part of my message to you. Accept of this, and we shall go no further with you; for we would not so much as affright, or trouble you with the name of damnation, without necessity.

But if you will not be saved, there is no remedy, but damnation must take place; for there is no middle place between the two; you must have either life or death.

And we are not only to offer you life, but to show you the grounds on which we do it, and call you to believe that God doth mean, indeed, as he speaks; that the promise is true, and extended conditionally to you, as well as others; and that heaven is no fancy, but a true felicity.

If you ask, Where is your commission for this offer? Among a hundred texts of scripture, I will show it to you in these few:

First, You see it here in my text, and the following verses, and in the 18th of Ezekiel, as plain as can be spoken; and in 2 Cor. v. 17—21, you have the very sum of our commission; "If any man be in Christ, he is a new creature: old things are passed away; behold, all things are become new. And all things are of God, who hath reconciled us to himself by Jesus Christ, and hath given to us the ministry of reconciliation; to wit, that God was in Christ reconciling the world unto himself, not imputing their trespasses to them, and hath committed unto us the word of reconciliation. Now then we are ambassadors for Christ, as though God did beseech you by us: we pray you in Christ's stead, be ye reconciled unto God. For he hath made him to be sin for us, who knew no sin; that we might be made the righteousness of God in him." So Mark xvi. 15, 16. "Go ye into all the world, and preach the gospel to every creature. He that believeth, (that is with such a converting faith as is expressed) and is baptized, shall be saved; and he that believeth not, shall be damned." And Luke xxiv. 46, 47. "Thus it behoved Christ to suffer, and to rise from the dead the third day: and that repentance (which is conversion) and remission of sins should be preached in his name among all nations." And, Acts v. 30, 31. "The God of our fathers raised up Jesus, whom ye slew, and hanged on a tree: him hath God exalted with his right hand, to be a Prince and a Saviour, to give repentance to Israel, and forgiveness of sins." And Acts xiii. 38, 39. "Be it known unto you, therefore, men and brethren, that through this man is preached unto you the forgiveness of sins; and by him all that believe are justified from all things, from which ye could not be justified by the law of Moses." And lest you think this offer is restrained to the Jews, see Gal. vi. 15. "For in Christ Jesus, nei ther circumcision availeth any thing, nor uncircumcision, but a new creature." And Luke xiv. 17. "Come, for all things are now ready."

You see by this time that we are commanded to offer life to you all, and to tell you from God, That if you will turn, you may live.

Here you may safely trust your souls; for the love of God is the fountain of this offer, (John iii. 16,) and the blood of the Son of God hath purchased it; the faithfulness and truth of God is engaged to make the promise good; miracles oft sealed the truth of it; preachers are sent through the world to proclaim it; the sacraments are instituted and used for the solemn delivery of the mercy offered to them that will accept it; and the Spirit doth open the heart to entertain it, and is itself the earnest of the full possession. So that the truth of it is past controversy, that the worst of you all, and every one of you, if you will but be converted, may be saved.

Indeed, if you will needs believe that you shall be saved without conversion, then you believe a falsehood; and if I should preach that to you, I should preach a lie. This were not to believe God, but the devil and your own deceitful hearts. God hath his promise of life, and the devil hath his promise of life. God's promise is, Return and live. The devil's promise is, You shall live whether you turn or not. The words of God are, as I have showed you, "Except ye be converted and become as little children, ye cannot enter into the kingdom of heaven." Matt. xviii. 3. "Except a man be born again, he cannot enter into the kingdom of God." John iii. 3, 5. "Without holiness none shall see God." Heb. xii. 14. The devil's word, "You may be saved without being born again and converted; you may do well enough without being holy, God doth but frighten you; he is more merciful than to do as he saith, he will be better to you than his word." And, alas, the greatest part of the world believe this word of the devil, before the word of God; just as our sin and misery came into the world. God said to our first parents, "If ye eat ye shall die;" and the devil contradicted him, and said, "Ye shall not die:" and the woman believed the devil before God. So now the Lord saith, Turn or die: and the devil saith, You shall not die, if you do but cry for God's mercy at last, and give over the acts of sin when you can practise it no longer. And this is the word that the world believes. O heinous wickedness, to believe the devil before God.

And yet that is not the worst; but blasphemously they call this a believing and trusting in God, when they put him in the shape of Satan, who was a liar from the beginning; and when they believe that the word of God is a lie, they call this a trusting God and say they believe in him, and trust in him for salvation. Where did ever God say, that the unregenerate, unconverted, unsanctified, shall be saved? Show me such a word in scripture. I challenge you if you can. Why this is the devil's word, and to believe it is to believe the devil, and the sin that is commonly called presumption; and do you call this a believing and trusting in God? There is enough in the word of God to comfort and strengthen the heart of the sanctified; but not a word to strengthen the hands of wickedness, nor to give men the least hope of being saved, though they be never sanctified.

But if you will turn, and come into the way of mercy, the mercy of the Lord is ready to entertain you. Then trust God for salvation, boldly and confidently; for he is engaged by his word to save you. He will be a father to none but his children; and he will save none but those that forsake the world, the devil, and the flesh, and come into his family to be members of his Son, and have communion with his saints. But if they will not come in, it is the fault of themselves: his doors are open; he keeps none back; he never sent such a message as this to any of you, 'It is now too late; I will not receive thee, though thou be converted.' He might have done so and done you no wrong; but he did not; he doth not to this day. He is still ready to receive you, if you were but ready unfeignedly, and with all your hearts to turn. And the fulness of this truth will yet more appear in the two following doctrines, which I shall therefore next proceed to, before I make any further application of this.

DOCTRINE 3. God taketh pleasure in men's conversion and salvation, but not in their death or damnation. He had rather they would turn and live, than go on and die.

I shall first teach you how to understand this, and then clear up the truth of it to you.

And for the first you must observe these following things: 1. A simple willingness or complacency is the first act of the will following the single apprehension of the understanding, before it proceedeth to compare things together; but the choosing act of the will is a following act, and supposeth the comparing practical act of the understanding; and these two acts may often be carried to contrary objects, without any fault at all in the person.

2. An unfeigned willingness may have divers degrees; some things I am so far willing of as that I will do all that lieth in my power to accomplish it, and some things I am truly willing another should do, when yet I will not do all that I am ever able to procure it, having many reasons to dissuade me therefrom, though yet I will do all that belongs to me to do.

3. The will of a ruler, as such, is manifested in making and executing laws: but the will of man in his simple natural capacity, or as absolute lord of his own, is manifested in desiring or resolving of events.

4. A ruler's will, as lawgiver, is first and principally that his laws be obeyed, and not at all that the penalty be executed on any, but only on supposition that they will not obey his laws; but a ruler's will,

as judge, supposeth the law already either kept or broken, and therefore he resolveth our reward or punishment accordingly.

Having given you those necessary distinctions, I shall next apply them to the case in hand, in these following propositions:—

1. It is in the glass of the word and creatures, that in this life we must know God; and so according to the nature of man we ascribe to him understanding and will, removing all the imperfections that we can, because we are capable of no higher positive conceptions of him.

2. And on the same grounds we do, with the scripture, distinguish between the acts of God's will, as diversified from the respects or the objects, though as to God's essence they are all one.

3. And the bolder, because that when we speak of Christ, we have the more ground for it from his human nature.

4. And thus we say, that the simple complacency, will, or love of God, is to all that is naturally or morally good, according to the nature and degree of its goodness, and so he hath pleasure in the conversion and salvation of all, which yet will never come to pass.

5. And God, as Ruler and Lawgiver of the world, had so far a practical will for their salvation, as to make them a free deed of gift of Christ and life, and an act of oblivion for all their sins, so be if they will not unthankfully reject it; and to command his messengers to offer this gift to all the world, and persuade them to accept it. And so he doth all that, as Lawgiver or Promiser, belongs to him to do for their salvation.

6. But yet he resolveth, as Lawgiver, that they that will not turn shall die; and as Judge, when their day of grace is past he will execute that degree.

7. So that he thus unfeignedly willeth the conversion of those that never will be converted, but not as absolute Lord with the fullest efficacious resolu-

tion, nor as a thing which he resolveth shall undoubtedly come to pass, or would engage all his power to accomplish. It is in the power of a prince to set a guard upon a murderer, to see that he shall not murder, and be hanged; but if, upon good reason, he forbear this, and do but send to his subjects to warn and entreat them not to be murderers, I hope he may well say that he would not have them murder and be hanged; he takes no pleasure in it, but rather that they forbear and live, and if he do more for some upon some special reason, he is not bound to do so by all. The king may well say to all murderers and felons in the land, 'I have no pleasure in your death, but rather that you would obey my laws and live; but if you will not, I am resolved, for all this, that you shall die.' The judge may truly say to a thief, or the murderer, 'Alas, I have no delight in thy death; I had rather thou hadst kept the law and saved thy life; but seeing thou hast not, I must condemn thee, or else I should be unjust.' So, though God have no pleasure in your damnation, and therefore calls upon you to return and live, yet he hath pleasure in the demonstration of his own justice, and the executing his laws; and therefore he is, for all this, fully resolved, that if you will not be converted, you shall be condemned. If God was so much against the death of the wicked, as that he were resolved to do all that he can to hinder it, then no man shall be condemned; whereas Christ telleth you, that few will be saved. But so far God is against your damnation, as that he will teach you, and warn you, and set before you life and death, and offer you your choice, and command his ministers to entreat you not to destroy yourselves, but accept his mercy, and so to leave you without excuse. But if this will not do, and if still you be unconverted, he professeth to you, he is resolved on your damnation, and hath commanded us to say to you in his name, verse 8, "O wicked man thou shalt surely die!" And Christ hath little less than sworn it, over and over, with a "verily, verily, except ye be converted and born again, ye cannot enter into the kingdom of heaven." Matt. xviii. 3. John iii. 3. Mark that he saith "you cannot." It is in vain to hope for it, and in vain to dream that God is willing for it; for it is a thing that cannot be.

In a word, you see then the meaning of the text, that God, the great Lawgiver of the world, doth take no pleasure in the death of the wicked, but rather that they turn and live; though yet he be resolved that none shall live but those that turn; and as a judge even delighteth in justice, and manifesting his hatred of sin, though not in their misery, which they have brought upon themselves, in itself considered.

And for the proofs of the point, I shall be very brief in them, because I suppose you easily believe it already.

1. The very gracious nature of God proclaimed: "And the Lord passed by before him, and proclaimed, The Lord, the Lord God, merciful and gracious, long-suffering, and abundant in goodness and truth, keeping mercy for thousands, forgiving iniquity, and transgression, and sin, and that will by no means clear the guilty;" (Exod. xxiv. 6. and xxvi. 6.) and frequently elsewhere, may assure you of this, That he hath no pleasure in your death.

2. If God had more pleasure in thy death, than in thy conversion and life, he would not have so frequently commanded thee in his word, to turn; he would not have made thee such promises of life, if thou wilt but turn; he would not have persuaded thee to it by so many reasons. The tenor of his gospel proveth the point.

3. And his commission that he hath given to the ministers of the gospel, doth fully prove it. If God had taken more pleasure in thy damnation, than in thy conversion and salvation, he would never have charged us to offer you mercy, and to teach you the way of life, both publicly and privately: and to en-

treat and beseech you to turn and live; to acquaint you with your sins, and foretell you of your danger; and to do all that possibly we can for your conversion, and to continue patiently so doing, though you should hate or abuse us for our pains. Would God have done this, and appointed his ordinances for your good, if he had taken pleasure in your death?

4. It is proved also by the course of his providence. If God had rather you were damned than converted and saved, he would not second his word with his works, and entice you by his daily kindness to himself, and give you all the mercies of this life, which are his means "to lead you to repentance," (Rom. ii. 4.) and bring you so often under his rod to lead you to your senses; he would not set so many examples before your eyes, no, nor wait on you so patiently as he does from day to day, and year to year. These are not signs of one that taketh pleasure in your death. If this had been his delight, how easily could he have had thee long ago in hell? How oft, before this, could he have catched thee away in the midst of thy sins with a curse, or oath, or lie in thy mouth, in thy ignorance, and pride, and sensuality? When thou wert last in thy drunkenness, or last deriding the ways of God, how easily could he have stopped thy breath, and tamed thee with plagues, and made thee sober in another world! Alas! how small a matter is it for the Almighty to rule the tongue of the profanest railer, and tie the hands of the most malicious persecutor, or calm the fury of the bitterest of his enemies, and make them know that they are but worms? If he should but frown upon thee thou wouldst drop into thy grave. If he gave commission to one of his angels to go and destroy ten thousand sinners, how quickly would it be done! how easily can he lay thee upon the bed of languishing, and make thee lie roaring there in pain, and make thee eat the words of reproach which thou hast spoken against his servants, his word, his worship, and his holy ways, and make thee send to beg

their prayers whom thou didst despise in thy presumption? How easily can he lay that flesh under pains, and groans, and make it too weak to hold thy soul, and make it more loathsome than the dung of the earth? That flesh which now must have what it loves, and must not be displeased, though God be displeased; and must be humoured in meat, and drink, and clothes, whatever God say to the contrary, how quickly would the frowns of God consume it? When thou wast passionately defending thy sin, and quarrelling with them that would have drawn thee from it, and showing thy spleen against the reprover, and pleading for the works of darkness; how easily could God have snatched thee away in a moment, and set thee before his dreadful Majesty, where thou shouldst see ten thousand times ten thousand glorious angels waiting on his throne, and have called thee there to plead thy cause, and asked thee 'What hast thou now to say against thy Creator, his truth, his servants, or his holy ways? Now plead thy cause, and make the best of it thou canst. Now what canst thou say in excuse of thy sins? Now give account of thy worldliness and fleshly life, of thy time, of all the mercies thou hast had.' O how thy stubborn heart would have melted, and thy proud looks be taken down, and thy countenance be appalled, and thy stout words turned into speechless silence, or dreadful cries, if God had but set thee thus at his bar, and pleaded his own cause with thee, which thou hast here so maliciously pleaded against! How easily can he at any time say to thy guilty soul, Come away, and live in that flesh no more till the resurrection, and it cannot resist! A word of his mouth would take off the poise of thy present life, and then all thy parts and powers would stand still; and if he say unto thee, Live no longer, or, live in hell, thou couldst not disobey.

But God hath yet done none of this, but hath patiently forborne thee, and mercifully upheld thee, and given thee that breath, which thou didst breathe out against him, and given those mercies which thou didst sacrifice to thy flesh, and afforded thee that provision which thou spentest to sanctify thy greedy throat: he gave thee every minute of that time which thou didst waste in idleness, or drunkenness, or worldliness; and doth not all his patience and mercy show that he desired not thy damnation? Can the candle burn without the oil? Can your houses stand without the earth to bear them? No more can you live an hour without the support of God. And why did he so long support thy life, but to see when thou wouldst bethink thee of the folly of thy ways, and return and live? Will any man purposely put arms into his enemy's hands to resist him, or hold a candle to a murderer that is killing his children, or to an idle servant that plays or sleeps the while? Surely it is to see whether thou wilt at last return and live, that God hath so long waited on thee.

5. It is further proved by the suffering of his Son, that God taketh no pleasure in the death of the wicked. Would he have ransomed them from death at so dear a rate? Would he have astonished angels and men by his condescension? Would God have dwelt in flesh, and have come in the form of a servant, and have assumed humanity into one person with the Godhead; and would Christ have lived a life of suffering, and died a cursed death for sinners, if he had rather taken pleasure in their death? Suppose you saw him but so busy in preaching and healing of them, as you find him in Mark iii. 21. or so long in fasting, as in Matt. iv. or all night in prayer, as in Luke vi. 12. or praying with the drops of blood trickling from him instead of sweat, as Luke xxii. 44. or suffering a cursed death upon the cross, and pouring out his soul as a sacrifice for our sins—would you have thought these the signs of one that delighted in the death of the wicked?

And think not to extenuate it by saying, that it was only for his elect: for it was thy sin, and the sin of all the world, that lay upon our Redeemer; and his sacrifice and satisfaction is sufficient for all, and the fruits of it are offered to one as well as another. But it is true, that it was never the intent of his mind to pardon and save any that would not, by faith and repentance, be converted. If you had seen and heard him weeping and bemoaning the state of disobedience in impenitent people:—Luke xix. 41, 42. "And when he was come near, he beheld the city, and wept over it, saying, if thou hadst known, even thou, at least in this thy day, the things which belong unto thy peace! but now they are hid from thine eyes." Or complaining of their stubbornness, as Matt. xxiii. 37. "O Jerusalem, Jerusalem, how often would I have gathered thy children together, even as a hen gathereth her chickens under her wings, and ye would not!" Or if you had seen and heard him on the cross, praying for his persecutors—Father, forgive them, for they know not what they do—would you have suspected that he had delighted in the death of the wicked, even of those that perish by their wilful unbelief? When God hath so loved, (not only loved, but so loved,) as to give his only begotten Son, that whosoever believeth in him (by an effectual faith) should not perish, but have everlasting life, I think he hath hereby proved, against the malice of men and devils, that he takes no pleasure in the death of the wicked, but had rather that they would "turn and live."

6. Lastly, If all this will not yet satisfy you, take his own word, that knoweth best his own mind, or at least believe his oath: but this leads me to the fourth doctrine.

DOCTRINE 4. The Lord hath confirmed to us by his oath, that he hath no pleasure in the death of the wicked, but rather that he turn and live; that he may leave man no pretence to question the truth of it.

If you dare question his word, I hope you dare not question his oath. As Christ hath solemnly protested that the unregenerate and unconverted cannot enter into the kingdom of heaven; (Matt. xviii. 3. John iii. 3;) so God hath sworn that his pleasure is not in their death, but in their conversion and life. And as the Apostle saith, (Heb. iv. 13—18,) Because he can swear by no greater, he sware by himself. 'For men verily swear by the greater: and an oath for confirmation is to them an end of strife. Wherein God, willing more abundantly to show unto the heirs of promise the immutability of his counsel, confirmed it by an oath; that by two immutable things in which it was impossible for God to lie, we might have strong consolation, who have fled for refuge to lay hold on the hope set before us: which hope we have as an anchor of the soul both sure and steadfast.' If there be any man that cannot reconcile this truth with the doctrine of predestination, or the actual damnation of the wicked, that is his own ignorance; he hath no pretence left to question or deny therefore the truth of the point in hand; for this is confirmed by the oath of God, and therefore must not be distorted, to reduce it to other points: but doubtful points must rather be reduced to it, and certain truths must be believed to agree with it, though our shallow minds hardly discern the agreement.

USE.—I do now entreat thee, if thou be an unconverted sinner that hearest these words, that thou wouldst ponder a little upon the forementioned doctrines, and bethink thyself awhile, who it is that takes pleasure in thy sin and damnation. Certainly, it is not God: he hath sworn for his part that he takes no pleasure in it. And I know it is not the pleasing of him that you intend. You dare not say that you drink, and swear, and neglect holy duties, and quench the motions of the Spirit to please God. That were as if you should reproach the prince, and break his laws, and seek his death, and say, you did all this to please him.

Who is it then that takes pleasure in your sin and death? Not any that bear the image of God, for they must be like minded to him. God knows, it is small pleasure to your faithful teachers to see you serve your deadly enemy, and madly venture your eternal state, and wilfully run into the flames of hell It is small pleasure to them to see upon your souls (in the sad effects) such blindness, and hard-heartedness, and carelessness, and presumption; such wilfulness in evil, and such unteachableness and stiffness against the ways of life and peace; they know these are marks of death, and of the wrath of God, and they know, from the word of God, what is like to be the end of them, and therefore it is no more pleasure to them, than to a tender physician to see the plague-marks broke out upon his patient. Alas, to foresee your everlasting torments, and know not how to prevent them! To see how near you are to hell, and we cannot make you believe it and consider it. To see how easily, how certainly you might escape, if we knew but how to make you willing. How fair you are for everlasting salvation, if you would turn and do your best, and make it the care and business of your lives! but you will not do it; if our lives lay on it, we cannot persuade you to it. We study day and night what to say to you, that may convince and persuade you, and yet it is undone: we lay before you the word of God, and show you the very chapter and verse where it is written, that you cannot be saved except you be converted; and yet we leave the most of you as we find you. We hope you will believe the word of God, though you believe not us, and regard it when we show you the plain scripture for it; but we hope in vain, and labour in vain as to any saving change upon your hearts! And do you think that this is a pleasant thing to us? Many a time, in secret prayer, we are fain to complain to God with sad hearts, 'Alas, Lord, we have spoken to them in thy name, but they little regard us; we have told them what thou bidst us tell them concerning the danger of an unconverted state, but they do not believe us: we have told them that thou hast protested that there is no peace to the wicked.' Isa. xlviii. 2, and lvii. 21. 'But the worst of them all will scarcely believe that they are wicked; we have showed them thy word, where thou hast said, that if they live after the flesh they shall die.' Rom. viii. 13. 'But they say, they will believe in thee, when they will not believe thee, and that they will trust in thee, when they give no credit to thy word; and when they hope that the threatenings of thy word are false, they will yet call this a hoping in God; and though we show them where thou hast said, that when a wicked man dieth, all his hopes perish, yet cannot we persuade them from their deceitful hopes.' Prov. xi. 7. 'We tell them what a base, unprofitable thing sin is; but they love it, and therefore will not leave it. We tell them how dear they buy this pleasure, and what they must pay for it in everlasting torment; and they bless themselves, and will not believe it, but will do as the most do; and because God is merciful, they will not believe him, but will venture their souls, come on it what will. We tell them how ready the Lord is to receive them, and this doth but make them delay their repentance and be bolder in their sin. Some of them say they purpose to repent, but they are still the same; and some say they do repent already, while yet they are not converted from their sins. We exhort them, we entreat them, we offer them our help, but we cannot prevail with them; but they that were drunkards, are drunkards still; and they that were voluptuous flesh-pleasing wretches, are such still; and they that were worldlings, are worldlings still; and they that were ignorant, and proud, and self-conceited, are so still. Few of them will see and confess their sin, and fewer will forsake it, but comfort themselves that all men are sinners, as if there were no difference between a converted sinner and an unconverted. Some of them will not come near us, when we are willing to instruct them, but think they know enough already, and need not our instruction ; and some of them will give us the hearing, and do what they list; and most of them are like dead men that cannot feel; so that when we tell them of the matters of everlasting consequence, we cannot get a word of it to their hearts. If we do not obey them, and humour them in baptizing the children of the most obstinately wicked, and giving them the Lord's Supper, and doing all that they would have us, though never so much against the word of God, they will hate us, and rail at us; but if we beseech them to confess, and forsake their sins, and save their souls, they will not do it. We tell them, if they will but turn, we will deny them none of the ordinances of God, neither baptism to their children, nor the Lord's Supper to themselves, but they will not hear us; they would have us disobey God and damn our own souls, to please them; and yet they will not turn and save their own souls to please God. They are wiser in their own eyes than all their teachers ; they rage and are confident in their own way, and if we were never so fain, we cannot change them. Lord, this is the case of our miserable neighbours, and we cannot help it; we see them ready to drop into hell, and we cannot help it ; we know if they would unfeignedly turn, they might be saved, but we cannot persuade them; if we would beg it of them on our knees, we cannot persuade them to it; if we would beg it of them with tears, we cannot persuade them ; and what more can we do ?

These are the secret complaints and moans that many a poor minister is fain to make. And do you think that he hath any pleasure in this ? Is it a pleasure to him to see you go on in sin, and cannot stop you ? to see you so miserable, and cannot so much as make you sensible of it ? to see you merry, when you are not sure to be an hour out of hell ? to think what you must for ever suffer, because you will not turn? and to think what an everlasting life of glory you wilfully despise and cast away? What sadder thing can you bring to their hearts, and how can you devise to grieve them more?

Who is it then that you please by your sin and death? It is none of your understanding godly friends. Alas, it is the grief of their souls to see your misery, and they lament you many a time when you give them little thanks for it, and when you have not hearts to lament yourselves.

Who is it then that takes pleasure in your sin? It is none but three great enemies of God, whom you renounced in your baptism, and now are turned falsely to serve.

1. The devil indeed takes pleasure in your sin and death: for this is the very end of all his temptations; for this he watches night and day; you cannot devise to please him better than to go on in sin. How glad is he when he sees thee going into the alehouse, or other sin, and when he heareth thee curse, or swear, or rail? How glad is he when he heareth thee revile the minister that would draw thee from thy sin, and help to save thee? These are his delight.

2. The wicked are also delighted in it; for it is agreeable to their nature.

3. But I know, for all this, that it is not the pleasing of the devil, that you intend, even when you please him; but it is your own flesh, the greatest and most dangerous enemy, that you intend to please. It is the flesh that would be pampered, that would be pleased in meat, and drink, and clothing; that would be pleased in your company, and pleased in applause and credit with the world, and pleased in sports, and lusts, and idleness; this is the gulf that devoureth all. This is the very god that you serve, for the scripture saith of such, that their bellies are their gods. Phil. iii. 19. But I beseech you stay a little and consider the business.

1. *Question.* Should your flesh be pleased before

your Maker? Will you displease the Lord, and displease your teacher, and your godly friends, and all to please your brutish appetites, or sensual desires? Is not God worthy to be the ruler of your flesh? If he shall not rule it, he will not save it; you cannot in reason expect that he should.

2. *Question.* Your flesh is pleased with your sin; but is your conscience pleased? Doth not it grudge within you, and tell you sometimes that all is not well, and that your case is not so safe as you make it to be; and should not your souls and consciences be pleased before your corruptible flesh?

3. *Question.* But is not your flesh preparing for its own displeasure also? It loves the bait, but doth it love the hook? It loves the strong drink and sweet morsels; it loves its ease, and sports and merriment; it loves to be rich, and well spoken of by men, and to be somebody in the world; but doth it love the curse of God? Doth it love to stand trembling before his bar, and to be judged to everlasting fire? Doth it love to be tormented with the devils for ever? Take all together; for there is no separating sin and hell, but only by faith and true conversion; if you will keep one, you must have the other. If death and hell be pleasant to thee, no wonder then if you go on in sin: but if they be not (as I am sure they are not,) then what if sin were never so pleasant, is it worth the loss of life eternal? Is a little drink, or meat, or ease; is the good word of sinners, is the riches of this world to be valued above the joys of heaven? Or are they worth the sufferings of eternal fire? Sirs, these questions should be considered before you go any further, by every man that hath reason to consider, and that believes he hath a soul to save or lose.

Well, the Lord here sweareth that he hath no pleasure in your death, but rather that you would turn and live; if yet you will go on and die rather than turn, remember it was not to please God that you did it: it was to please the world, and to please yourselves. And if men will damn themselves to please themselves, and run into endless torments for delight, and have not the wit, the hearts, the grace, to hearken to God or man that would reclaim them, what remedy but they must take what they get by it, and repent it in another manner, when it is too late? Before I proceed any further in the application, I shall come to the next doctrine, which gives me a fuller ground for it.

DOCTRINE 5. So earnest is God for the conversion of sinners, that he doubleth his commands and exhortations, with vehemency—Turn ye, turn ye, why will you die?

This doctrine is the application of the former, as by a use of exhortation, and accordingly I shall handle it. Is there ever an unconverted sinner that heareth these vehement words of God? Is there ever a man or woman in this assembly that is yet a stranger to the renewing sanctifying work of the Holy Ghost? It is a happy assembly, if it be not so with the most. Hearken then to the voice of your Maker, and turn to him by Christ without delay. Would you know the will of God? Why this is his will, that you presently turn. Shall the living God send so earnest a message to his creatures, and should they not obey? 2. Hearken then, all you that live after the flesh: the Lord that gave thee thy breath and being, hath sent a message to thee from heaven; and this is his message, *Turn ye, turn ye, why will ye die?*—He that hath ears to hear, let him hear. Shall the voice of the eternal Majesty be neglected? If he do but terribly thunder, thou art afraid. O but this voice doth more nearly concern thee. If he did but tell thee thou shalt die to-morrow, thou wouldest not make light of it. O but this word concerneth thy life or death everlasting. It is both a command and an exhortation. As if he had said to thee, "I charge thee upon the allegiance that thou owest to me thy Creator and Redeemer, that thou renounce the flesh, the world, and the devil, and turn to me that thou mayest live. I condescend to entreat thee, as thou either lovest or fearest him that made thee; as thou lovest thine own life, even thine everlasting life, turn and live: as ever thou wouldst escape eternal misery, turn, turn, for why wilt thou die?' And is there a heart in man, in a reasonable creature, that can once refuse such a message, such a command, such an exhortation as this? O what a thing, then, is the heart of man!

Hearken, then, all that love yourselves, and all that regard your own salvation; here is the most joyful message that was ever sent to the ears of man, "*Turn ye, turn ye, why will ye die?*" You are not yet shut up under desperation. Here is mercy offered you; turn, and you shall have it. O sirs! with what glad and joyful hearts should you receive these tidings! I know this is not the first time that you have heard it; but how have you regarded it, or how do you regard it now? Hear, all you ignorant, careless sinners, the word of the Lord. Hear, all you worldlings, you sensual flesh-pleasers; you gluttons, and drunkards, and whoremongers, and swearers; you railers and backbiters, slanderers and liars —*Turn ye, turn ye, why will ye die?*

Hear, all you cold and outside professors, and all that are strangers to the life of Christ, and never knew the power of his cross and resurrection, and never felt your hearts warmed with his love, and live not on him as the strength of your souls—"Turn ye, turn ye, why will ye die?"

Hear, all that are void of the love of God, whose hearts are not toward him, nor taken up with the hopes of glory, but set more by your earthly prosperity and delights than by the joys of heaven; all you that are religious but a little by the by, and give God no more than your flesh can spare; that have not denied your carnal selves, and forsaken all that you have for Christ, in the estimation and grounded resolution of your souls, but have some one thing in the world so dear to you, that you cannot spare it for Christ, if he required it, but will rather venture on his displeasure than forsake it—" Turn ye, turn ye, why will ye die?"

If you never heard it, or observed it before, remember that you were told from the word of God this day, that if you will but turn, you may live; and if you will not turn, you shall surely die.

What now will you do, sirs? What is your resolution? Will you turn, or will you not? Halt not any longer between two opinions. If the Lord be God, follow him: if your flesh be God, then serve it still. If heaven be better than earth and fleshly pleasures, come away, then, and seek a better country, and lay up your treasure where rust and moths do not corrupt, and thieves cannot break through and steal; and be awakened at last, with all your might to seek the kingdom that cannot be moved, Heb. xii. 28. and to employ your lives on a higher design, and turn the stream of your cares, and abours, another way than formerly you have done. But if earth be better than heaven, or will do more for you, or last you longer, then keep it, and make your best of it, and follow it still. Sirs, are you resolved what to do? If you be not, I will set a few more moving considerations before you, to see if reason will make you resolve.

Consider, first, what preparations mercy hath made for your salvation; and what pity it is, that any man should be damned after all this. The time was, when the flaming sword was in the way, and the curse of God's law would have kept thee back, if thou hadst been never so willing to turn to God. The time was, when thyself, and all the friends that thou hast in the world, could never have produced thee the pardon of thy sins past, though thou hadst never so much lamented and reformed them. But Christ hath removed this impediment, by the ransom of his blood. The time was, that

God was wholly unreconciled, as being not satisfied for the violation of his law; but now he is so far satisfied and reconciled, as that he hath made thee a free act of oblivion, and a free deed of gift of Christ and life, and offereth it to thee, and entreateth thee to accept it; and it may be thine, if thou wilt. For, "he was in Christ reconciling the world to himself, and hath committed to us the word of reconciliation." 2 Cor. v. 18, 19. Sinners, we too are commanded to deliver this message to you all, as from the Lord; "Come, for all things are ready." Luke xiv. 17. Are all things ready, and are you unready? God is ready to entertain you, and pardon all that you have done against him, if you will but come. As long as you have sinned, as wilfully as you have sinned, he is ready to cast all behind his back, if you will but come. Though you have been prodigals, and run away from God, and have staid so long, he is ready even to meet you, and embrace you in his arms, and rejoice in your conversion, f you will but turn. Even the worldlings and drunkards will find God ready to bid them welcome, if they will but come. Doth not this turn thy heart within thee? O sinner! if thou hast a heart of flesh, and not of stone in thee, methinks this should melt it. Shall the dreadful infinite Majesty of heaven even wait for thy returning, and be ready to receive thee, who hast abused him, and forgotten him so long? Shall he delight in thy conversion, that might at any time glorify his justice in thy damnation? and yet doth it not melt thy heart within thee, and art thou not yet ready to come in? Hast thou not as much reason to be ready to come, as God hath to invite thee and bid thee welcome?

But that is not all: Christ hath done his part on the cross, and made such way for thee to the Father, that, on his account, thou mayst be welcome, if thou wilt come. And yet art thou not ready?

A pardon is already expressly granted, and offered thee in the Gospel. And yet art thou not ready?

The ministers of the Gospel are ready to assist thee, to instruct thee, and pronounce the absolving words of peace to thy soul; they are ready to pray for thee, and to seal up thy pardon by the administration of the holy sacrament. And yet art thou not ready?

All that fear God about thee, are ready to rejoice in thy conversion, and to receive thee into the communion of saints, and to give thee the right hand of fellowship, yea, though thou hadst been one that had been cast out of their society: they dare not but forgive where God forgiveth, when it is manifest to them, by thy confession and amendment; they dare not so much as reproach thee with thy former sins, because they know that God will not upbraid thee with them. If thou hadst been never so scandalous, if thou wouldst but heartily be converted and come in, they would not refuse thee, let the world say what they would against it. And are all these ready to receive thee, and yet art thou not ready to come in?

Yea, heaven itself is ready: the Lord will receive thee into the glory of his saints. Vile as thou hast been, if thou wilt be but cleansed, thou mayest have a place before his throne; his angels will be ready to guard thy soul to the place of joy, if thou do but unfeignedly come in. And is God ready, the sacrifice of Christ ready, the promise ready, and pardon ready? are ministers ready, and the people of God ready, and heaven itself ready? and angels ready? and all these but waiting for thy conversion; and yet art thou not ready? What! not ready to live, when thou hast been dead so long? not ready to come to thy right understanding, as the prodigal is said to "come to himself," Luke xv. 17. when thou hast been beside thyself so long? Not ready to be saved, when thou art even ready to be condemned? Art thou not ready to lay hold on Christ, that would deliver thee, when thou art even ready to sink into damnation? Art thou not ready to be drawn from hell, when thou art even ready to be cast remediless into it? Alas, man! dost thou know what thou doest? If thou die unconverted, there is no doubt to be made of thy damnation; and thou art not sure to live an hour. And yet art thou not ready to turn and to come in? O miserable wretch! Hast thou not served the flesh and the devil long enough? Yet hast thou not enough of sin? Is it so good to thee, or so profitable for thee? Dost thou know what it is, that thou wouldst yet have more of it? Hast thou had so many calls, and so many mercies, and so many warnings, and so many examples? Hast thou seen so many laid in the grave, and yet art thou not ready to let go thy sins, and come to Christ? What! after so many convictions and pangs of conscience, after so many purposes and promises, art thou not yet ready to turn and live? O that thy eyes, thy heart, were opened to know how fair an offer is now made to thee! and what a joyful message it is that we are sent on, to bid thee come, for all things are ready!

II. Consider also, what calls thou hast to turn and live. How many, how loud, how earnest, how dreadful: and yet what encouraging, joyful calls! For the principal inviter is God himself. He that commandeth heaven and earth, commands thee to turn, and that presently, without delay. He commands the sun to run its course, and to rise upon thee every morning; and though it be so glorious an orb, and many times bigger than all the earth, yet it obeyeth him, and faileth not one minute of its appointed time. He commandeth all the planets, and the orbs of heaven, and they obey. He commandeth the sea to ebb and flow, and the whole creation to keep its course, and all obey him: the angels of heaven obey his will, when he sends them to minister to such worms as we on earth, Heb. i. 14; and yet if he command but a sinner to turn, he will not obey him. He only thinks himself wiser than God, and he cavils and pleads the cause of sin, and will not obey. If the Lord Almighty say the word, the heavens and all therein obey him: but if he call but a drunkard out of an ale house, he will not obey: or if he call a worldly fleshly sinner to deny himself, and mortify the flesh, and set his heart upon a better inheritance, he will not obey.

If thou hadst any love in thee, thou wouldst know the voice, and say, O this is my Father's call! how can I find in my heart to disobey? For the sheep of Christ "know and hear his voice, and they follow him, and he giveth them eternal life." John x. 4. If thou hadst any spiritual life and sense in thee, at least thou wouldst say, This call is the dreadful voice of God, and who dare disobey? For saith the prophet, (Amos iii. 8.) "The lion hath roared, who will not fear?" God is not a man, that thou shouldst dally and trifle with him. Remember what he said to Paul at his conversion, "*It is hard for thee to kick against the pricks.*" Acts ix. 5. Wilt thou yet go on and despise his word, and resist his Spirit, and stop thine ear against his call? who is it that will have the worst of this? Dost thou know whom thou disobeyedst, and contendest with, and what thou art doing? It were a far wiser, and easier task for thee to contend with the thorns, and spurn them with thy bare feet, and beat them with thy bare hands, or put thine head into the burning fire. "Be not deceived, God will not be mocked." Gal. vi. 7. Whoever else be mocked, God will not: you had better play with the fire in your thatch, than with the fire of his burning wrath. "For our God is a consuming fire." Heb. xii. 29. O how unmeet a match art thou for God! "It is a fearful thing to fall into his hands." Heb. x. 31. And therefore it is a fearful thing to contend with him, or resist him. As you love your own souls, take heed what you do: what will you say if he begin in wrath to plead with you? What will you do if he take you once in hand? will you then strive against his judgment, as now ye do against his grace? Isa. xxvii. 4, 5. "*Fury is not in me,*" saith the Lord: (that is) I delight not to destroy you: I do it, as it were unwillingly; but yet "*who will set the briers and thorns against me in battle? I would go through them; I would burn them together. Or let him take hold of my strength, that he may make peace with me.*" It is an unequal combat for the briers and stubble to make war with the fire.

And thus you see, who it is that calleth you, that would move you to hear his call, and turn: so consider also by what instruments, and how often, and how earnestly he doth it.

1. Every leaf of the blessed book of God hath, as it were, a voice, and calls out to thee, Turn, and live; turn, or thou wilt die. How canst thou open it, and read a leaf, or hear a chapter, and not perceive God bids thee turn?

2. It is the voice of every sermon that thou hearest: for what else is the scope and drift of all, but to call and persuade, and entreat thee for to turn.

3. It is the voice of many a motion of the Spirit that secretly speaks over these words again, and urgeth thee to turn.

4. It is likely, sometime it is the voice of thy own conscience. Art thou not sometimes convinced that all is not well with thee? And doth not thy conscience tell thee that thou must be a new man, and take a new course, and often call upon thee to return?

5. It is the voice of the gracious examples of the godly. When thou seest them live a heavenly life, and fly from the sin which is thy delight, this really calls on thee to turn.

6. It is the voice of all the works of God: for they also are God's books that teach thee this lesson, by shewing thee his greatness, and wisdom, and goodness, and calling thee to observe them, and admire the Creator. Psalm xix. 1, 2. "The heavens declare the glory of God, and the firmament showeth his handy work: day unto day uttereth speech, night unto night showeth knowledge." Every time the sun riseth unto thee, it really calleth thee to

turn, as if it should say, "What do I travel and compass the world for, but to declare to men the glory of their Maker, and to light them to do his work? And do I still find thee doing the work of sin, and sleeping out thy life in negligence? Awake thou that sleepest, and arise from the dead, and Christ shall give thee light." Ephes. v. 14. "The night is far spent, the day is at hand; it is now high time to awake out of sleep. Let us therefore cast off the works of darkness, and let us put on the armour of light. Let us walk honestly as in the day, not in rioting and drunkenness, not in chambering and wantonness, not in strife and envying, but put ye on the Lord Jesus Christ, and make not provision for the flesh, to fulfil the lusts thereof." Rom. xiii. 11—14. This text was the means of Austin's conversion.

7. It is the voice of every mercy thou dost possess; if thou couldst but hear and understand them, they all cry out unto thee, Turn. Why doth the earth bear thee, but to seek and serve the Lord? Why doth it afford thee its fruits, but to serve him? Why doth the air afford thee breath, but to serve him? Why do all the creatures serve thee with their labours and their lives, but that thou mightst serve the Lord of them and thee? Why doth he give thee time, and health, and strength, but only to serve him? Why hast thou meat, and drink, and clothes, but for his service? Hast thou any thing which thou hast not received? and if thou didst receive them, it is reason thou shouldst bethink thee from whom, and to what end and use thou didst receive them. Didst thou never cry to him for help in thy distress, and didst thou not then understand that it was thy part to turn and serve him, if he would deliver thee? He hath done his part, and spared thee yet longer, and tried thee another, and another year; and yet dost thou not turn? You know the parable of the unfruitful fig-tree, Luke xiii. 7—9. When the Lord had said, "Cut it down, why cumbereth it the ground?" he was entreated

to try it one year longer, and then if it proved not fruitful, to cut it down. Christ himself there makes the application twice over, ver. 3 and 5. "Except ye repent, ye shall all likewise perish." How many years hath God looked for the fruits of love and holiness from thee, and hath found none, and yet he hath spared thee? How many a time, by thy wilful ignorance, and carelessness, and disobedience, hast thou provoked justice to say, "Cut him down, why cumbereth he the ground?" And yet mercy hath prevailed, and patience hath forborne the fatal blow, to this day. If thou hadst the understanding of a man within thee, thou wouldst know that all this calleth thee to turn. "Dost thou think thou shalt still escape the judgment of God? or despisest thou the riches of his goodness, and forbearance, and long suffering? not knowing that the goodness of God leadeth thee to repentance. But, after thy hardness and impenitent heart, treasurest up unto thyself wrath against the day of wrath, and revelation of the righteous judgment of God; who will render to every man according to his deeds." Rom. ii. 3—6.

8. Moreover, it is the voice of every affliction to call thee to make haste and turn. Sickness and pain cry, Turn: and poverty, and loss of friends, and every twig of the chastening rod, cry, Turn; and yet wilt thou not hearken to the call? These have come near thee, and made thee feel; they have made thee groan, and can they not make thee turn?

9. The very frame of thy nature and being itself, bespeaketh thy return. Why hast thou reason, but to rule thy flesh, and serve thy Lord? Why hast thou an understanding soul, but to learn and know his will and do it? Why hast thou a heart within thee, that can love, and fear, and desire, but that thou shouldst fear him, and love him, and desire after him?

10. Yea, thine own engagements by promise to the Lord, call upon thee to turn and serve him.

Thou hast bound thyself to him by a baptismal covenant, and renounced the world, the flesh, and the devil. This thou hast confirmed by the profession of Christianity, and renewed it at Sacraments, and in times of affliction; and wilt thou promise and vow, and never perform and turn to God?

Lay all these together now, and see what should be the issue. The holy Scriptures call upon thee to turn; the ministers of Christ call upon thee to turn; the Spirit cries, Turn; thy conscience cries, Turn; the godly, by persuasions and examples cry, Turn; the whole world, and all the creatures therein that are presented to thy consideration cry, Turn; the patient forbearance of God cries, Turn; all the mercies which thou receivest cry, Turn; the rod of God's chastisement cries Turn; thy reason and the frame of thy nature bespeaks thy turning; and so do all thy promises to God; and yet art thou not resolved to turn?

III. Moreover, poor hard-hearted sinner, didst thou ever consider upon what terms thou standest all this while with Him that calleth on thee to turn? Thou art his own, and owest him thyself, and all thou hast; and may he not command his own? Thou art his absolute servant, and shouldst serve no other master. Thou standest at his mercy, and thy life is in his hand, and he is resolved to save thee upon no other terms; thou hast many malicious spiritual enemies, that would be glad if God would but forsake thee, and let them alone with thee, and leave thee to their will; how quickly would they deal with thee in another manner! and thou canst not be delivered from them but by turning unto God. Thou art fallen under his wrath by thy sin already; and thou knowest not how long his patience will yet wait. Perhaps this is the last year, perhaps the last day. His sword is even at thy heart, while the word is in thine ear; and if thou turn not, thou art a dead and undone man. Were thy eyes but open to see where thou standest, even upon the brink of hell, and to see how many thousands are there already that did not turn, thou wouldst see that it is time to look about thee.

Well, sirs, look inwards now and tell me how your hearts are affected with those offers of the Lord. You hear what is his mind: he delighteth not in your death; he calls to you, Turn, turn: it is a fearful sign if all this move thee not, or if it do but half move thee; and much more if it make thee more careless in thy misery, because thou hearest of the mercifulness of God. The working of the medicine will partly tell us whether there be any hope of the cure. O what glad tidings would it be to those that are now in hell, if they had but such a message from God! What a joyful word would it be to hear this, Turn and live! Yea, what a welcome word would it be to thyself, when thou hast felt that wrath of God but an hour! Or, if after a thousand or ten thousand years' torment, thou couldst but hear such a word from God, Turn and live; and yet wilt thou neglect it, and suffer us to return without our errand?

Behold, sinners, we are sent here as the messengers of the Lord, to set before you life and death. What say you? which of them will you choose? Christ standeth, as it were, by thee, with heaven in the one hand, and hell in the other, and offereth thee thy choice. Which wilt thou choose? The voice of the Lord maketh the rocks to tremble. Psalm xxix. And is it nothing to hear him threaten thee, if thou wilt not turn? Dost thou not understand and feel this voice, "Turn ye, turn ye, why will ye die?" Why? It is the voice of love, of infinite love, of thy best and kindest friend, as thou mightst easily perceive by the motion; and yet canst thou neglect it? It is the voice of pity and compassion. The Lord seeth whither thou art going better than thou dost, which makes him call after thee, Turn, turn. He seeth what will become of thee, if thou turn not. He thinketh with himself, Ah! this poor sinner will cast himself into endless torments, if he do not turn. I must in justice deal with him according to my righteous law.' And therefore he calleth after thee, Turn, turn. O sinner! If thou didst but know the thousandth part as well as God doth, the danger that is near you, and the misery that you are running into, we should have no more need to call after you to turn.

Moreover, this voice that calleth to thee, is the same that hath prevailed with thousands already, and called all to heaven that are now there; and they would not now for a thousand worlds that they had made light of it, and not turned to God. Now what are they possessing that turned at God's call? Now they perceive that it was indeed the voice of love, that meant them no more harm than their salvation; and if thou wilt obey the same call, thou shalt come to the same happiness. There are millions that must for ever lament that they turned not; but there is never a soul in heaven that is sorry that they were converted.

Well, sirs, are you yet resolved, or are you not? Do I need to say any more to you? What will you do? Will you turn or not? Speak, man, in thy heart to God, though you speak not out to me; speak, lest he take thy silence for denial; speak quickly, lest he never make thee the like offer more; speak resolvedly, and not waveringly, for he will have no indifferents to be his followers. Say in thine heart now, without any more delay, even before thou stir hence, 'By the grace of God I am resolved presently to turn. And because I know my own insufficiency, I am resolved to wait on God for his grace, and to follow him in his ways, and forsake my former courses and companions, and give up myself to the guidance of the Lord.'

Sirs, you are not shut up in the darkness of heathenism, nor in the desperation of the damned. Life is before you, and you may have it on reasonable terms, if you will; yea, on free cost, if you will accept it. The way of God lieth plain before you; the church is open to you. You may have Christ, and pardon, and holiness, if you will. What say you? Will you or will you not? If you say nay, or say nothing, and still go on, God is witness, and this congregation is witness, and your own consciences are witnesses, how fair an offer you had this day. Remember, you might have had Christ, and would not. Remember, when you have lost it, that you might have had eternal life, as well as others, and would not; and all because you would not turn!

But let us come to the next doctrine, and hear your reasons.

DOCTRINE 6. The Lord condescendeth to reason the case with unconverted sinners, and to ask them why they will die.

A strange disputation it is, both as to the controversy, and as to the disputants.

I. The controversy, or question propounded to dispute of is, Why wicked men will destroy themselves? or, Why they will rather die than turn; whether they have any sufficient reason for so doing?

II. The disputants are God and man: the most holy God, and wicked unconverted sinners.

Is it not a strange thing, which God doth here seem to suppose, that any man should be willing to die and be damned? yea, that this should be the case of the wicked? that is, of the greatest part of the world. But you will say, 'This cannot be; for nature desireth the preservation and felicity of itself; and the wicked are more selfish than others, and not less; and therefore how can any man be willing to be damned?'

To which I answer:—1. It is a certain truth that no man can be willing of any evil, as evil, but only as it hath some appearance of good; much less can any man be willing to be eternally tormented. Misery, as such, is desired by none. 2. But yet for all that, it is most true which God here teacheth us, that the cause why the wicked die is, because they will die. And this is true in several respects.

1. Because they will go the way that leads to hell, although they are told by God and man whither it goes and whither it ends; and though God hath so often professed in his word, that if they hold on in that way they shall be condemned; and that they shall not be saved unless they turn, Isa. xlviii. 22. lvii. 21. lix. 8, "There is no peace, saith the Lord, to the wicked." "The way of peace they know not; there is no judgment in their goings; they have made them crooked paths. Whosoever goeth therein, shall not know peace." They have the word and the oath of the living God for it, that if they will not turn, they shall not enter into his rest: and yet, wicked they are, and wicked they will be, let God and man say what they will: fleshly they are, and fleshly they will be, worldlings they are, and worldlings they will be, though God hath told them that the love of the world is enmity to God, and that if any man love the world (in that measure) the ove of the Father is not in him. James iv. 4.; I John ii. 15.; so that consequently these men are willing to be damned, though not directly; they are willing to walk in the way to hell, and love the certain cause of their torment; though they do not will hell itself, and do not love the pain which they must endure.

Is not this the truth of your case sirs? You would not burn in hell, but you will kindle the fire by your sins, and cast yourselves into it; you would not be tormented with devils for ever, but you will do that which will certainly procure it in spite of all that can be said against it. It is just as if you would say, 'I will drink this ratsbane, or other poison, but yet I will not die. I will cast myself headlong from the top of a steeple, but yet I will not kill myself. I will thrust this knife into my heart, but yet I will not take away my life. I will put this fire into the thatch of my house, but yet I will not burn it.' Just so it is with wicked men; they will be wicked, and they will live after the flesh and the world, and yet they would not be damned. But do you not know that the means lead to the end? and that God hath, by his righteous law, concluded that ye must repent or perish? He that will take poison, may as well say plainly, I will kill myself, for it will prove no better in the end; though perhaps he loved it for the sweetness of the sugar that was mixed with it; and would not be persuaded that it was poison, but that he might take it and do well enough; but it is not his conceits and confidence that will save his life. So if you will be drunkards, or fornicators, or worldlings, or live after the flesh, you may as well say plainly, We will be damned; for so you shall be unless you turn. Would you not rebuke the folly of a thief or murderer, that would say I will steal and kill, but I will not be hanged, when he knows that if he does the one, the judge in justice will see that the other be done? If he say I will steal and murder, he may as well say plainly, I will be hanged; and if you will go on in a carnal life, you may as well say plainly, We will go to hell.

2. Moreover, the wicked will not use those means without which there is no hope of their salvation. He that will not eat, may as well say plainly, he will not live, unless he can tell how to live without meat. He that will not go his journey, may as well say plainly he will not come to the end. He that falls into the water, and will not come out, nor suffer another to help him out, may as well say plainly, he will be drowned. So if you be carnal and ungodly, and will not be converted, nor use the means by which you should be converted, but think it more ado than needs, you may as well say plainly you will be damned; for if you have found out a way to be saved without conversion, you have done that which was never done before.

3. Yea, this is not all; but the wicked are unwilling even to partake of salvation itself; though they

may desire somewhat which they call by the name of heaven, yet heaven itself, considered in the true nature of the felicity, they desire not; yea, their hearts are quite against it. Heaven is a state of perfect holiness, and of continual love and praise to God, and the wicked have no heart to this. The imperfect love and praise and holiness which is here to be attained, they have no mind of; much less of that which is so much greater. The joys of heaven are of so pure and spiritual a nature, that the heart of the wicked cannot truly desire them.

So that by this time you may see on what ground it is that God supposeth that the wicked are willing of their own destruction. They will not turn, though they must turn or die: they will rather venture on certain misery, than be converted; and then to quiet themselves in their sins, they will make themselves believe that they shall nevertheless escape.

II. And as this controversy is matter of wonder, that ever men should be such enemies to themselves as wilfully to cast away their souls, so are the disputants too. That God should stoop so low as thus to plead the case with man; and that man should be so strangely blind and obstinate as to need all this in so plain a case; yea, and to resist all this, when their own salvation lieth upon the issue.

No wonder that they will not hear us that are men when they will not hear the Lord himself. As God saith, Ezek. iii. 7, when he sent the prophet to the Israelites. "The house of Israel will not hearken unto thee; for they will not hearken unto me; for all the house of Israel are impudent and hard-hearted." No wonder if they can plead against a minister, or a godly neighbour, when they will plead against the Lord himself, even against the plainest passages of his word, and think that they have reason on their side. When they weary the Lord with their words, they say, "Wherein have we wearied him?" Mal. ii. 17. The priests that despised his name durst ask, "Wherein have we despised thy name?" And "when they polluted his altar, and made the table of the Lord contemptible," they durst say, "Wherein have we polluted thee?" Mal. i. 6, 7. But "Wo unto him (saith the Lord) that striveth with his Maker! Let the potsherds strive with the potsherds of the earth: shall the clay say to him that fashioneth it, What makest thou?"

Quest.—But why is it that God will reason the case with man?

Answ.—1. Because that man being a reasonable creature, is accordingly to be dealt with, and by reason to be persuaded and overcome; God hath therefore endowed them with reason that they might use it for him. One would think a reasonable creature should not go against the clearest, the greatest reason in the world, when it is set before him.

2. At least, men shall see that God did require nothing of them that was unreasonable; but both in what he commandeth them, and what he forbids them, he hath all the right reason in the world on his side; and they have good reason to obey him,—but none to disobey. And thus even the damned shall be forced to justify God, and confess that it was only reasonable that they should have turned to him; and they shall be forced to condemn themselves, and confess that they had little reason to cast away themselves by the neglecting of his grace in the day of their visitation.

Use.—Look up your best and strongest reasons, sinners, if you will make good your way. You see now with whom you have to deal. What sayest thou, unconverted sensual sinner? Darest thou venture upon a dispute with God? Art thou able to confute him? Art thou ready to enter the lists? God asketh thee, Why wilt thou die? Art thou furnished with a sufficient answer? Wilt thou undertake to prove that God is mistaken, and that thou art in the right? O what an undertaking is that! Why, either he or you are mistaken, when he is for your conversion, and you are against it; he calls upon you to turn, and you will not; he bids you do it presently, even to-day, while it is called to-day, and you delay, and think it time enough hereafter. He saith it must be a total change, and you must be holy and new creatures, and born again: and you think that less may serve the turn, and that it is enough to patch up the old man, without becoming new. Who is in the right now? God or you? God calleth you to turn, and to live a holy life, and you will not;—by your disobedient lives, it appears you will not. If you will, why do you not? Why have you not done it all this while? And why do you not fall upon it yet? Your wills have the command of your lives. We may certainly conclude that you are unwilling to turn, when you do not turn. And why will you not?

Can you give any reason for it, that is worthy to be called a reason?

I that am but a worm, your fellow creature, of a shallow capacity, dare challenge the wisest of you all to reason the case with me, while I plead my Maker's cause; and I need not be discouraged when I know I plead but the cause that God pleadeth, and contend for him that will have the best at last. Had I but these two general grounds against you, I am sure that you have no good reason on your side.

I am sure it can be no good reason which is against the God of truth and reason. It cannot be light that is contrary to the sun. There is no knowledge in any creature but what it had from God; and therefore none can be wiser than God. It were fatal presumption for the highest angel to compare with his Creator! What is it then for a lump of earth, an ignorant sot, that knoweth not himself nor his own soul, that knoweth but little of the things which he seeth, yea, that is more ignorant than many of his neighbours, to set himself against the wisdom of the Lord! It is one of the fullest discoveries of the horrible wickedness of carnal men, and the stark-madness of such as sin, that so silly a mole dare contradict his Maker, and call in question the word of God: yea, that those people in our parishes, that are so ignorant that they cannot give us a reasonable answer concerning the very principles of religion, are yet so wise in their own conceit, that they dare question the plainest truths of God, yea, contradict them and cavil against them, when they can scarcely speak sense, and will believe them no further than agreeth with their foolish wisdom!

And as I know that God must needs be in the right, so I know the cause is so palpable and gross which he pleadeth against, that no man can have reason for it. Is it possible that a man can have any reason to break his Maker's laws, and reason to dishonour the Lord of glory, and reason to abuse the Lord that bought him? Is it possible that a man can have any good reason to damn his own immortal soul? Mark the Lord's question, Turn ye, turn ye, why will ye die? Is eternal death a thing to be desired? Are you in love with hell? What reason have you wilfully to perish? If you think you have some reason to sin, should you not remember that death is the wages of sin, Rom. vi. 23. and think whether you have any reason to undo yourselves, body and soul for ever? You should not only ask whether you love the adder, but whether you love the sting? It is such a thing for a man to cast away his everlasting happiness, and to sin against God, that no good reason can be given for it; but the more any one pleads for it, the more mad he showeth himself to be. Had you a lordship, or a kingdom offered you for every sin that you commit, it were not reason but madness to accept it. Could you by every sin obtain the highest thing on earth that flesh desireth, it were of no considerable value to persuade you in reason to commit it. If it were to please your greatest or dearest friends, or to obey the greatest prince on earth, or to save your lives, or to escape the great est earthly misery; all these are of no consideration to draw a man in reason to the committing of one sin. If it were a right hand or a right eye that would hinder your salvation, it is the most gainful way to cast it away, rather than to go to hell to save it; for there is no saving a part when you lose the whole. So exceedingly great are the matters of eternity, that nothing in this world deserveth once to be named in comparison with them; nor can any earthly thing, though it were life, or crowns, or kingdoms, be a reasonable excuse for the neglect of matters of such high and everlasting consequence. A man can have no reason to cross his ultimate end. Heaven is such a thing, that if you lose it, nothing can supply the want or make up the loss; and hell is such a thing, that if you suffer it, nothing can remove your misery, or give you ease and comfort; and therefore nothing can be a valuable consideration to excuse you for neglecting your own salvation; for, saith our Saviour "What shall it profit a man if he shall gain the whole world, and lose his own soul?" Mark, viii. 36.

O sirs, that you did but know what matters they are that we are now speaking to you of! you would have other kind of thoughts of these things. If the devil could come to them, the saints in heaven, that live in the sight and love of God, and should offer them sensual pleasures, or merry company, or sports to entice them away from God and glory, I pray you tell me, how do you think they would entertain the motion? Nay, or if he should offer them to be kings on the earth, do you think this would entice them down from heaven? O with what hatred and holy scorn would they reject the motion! And why should not you do so, that have heaven opened to your faith, if you had but faith to see it? There is never a soul in hell, but knows, by this time, that it was a mad exchange to let go heaven for fleshly pleasure; and that it is not a little mirth or pleasure, or worldly riches, or honour, or the good will or word of men, that will quench hell fire, or make him a gainer that loseth his soul. O if you had heard what I believe, if you had seen what I believe, and that on the credit of the word of God, you would say there can be no reason to warrant a man to destroy his soul; you durst not sleep quietly another night, before you had resolved to turn and live.

If you see a man put his hand into the fire till it burn off, you will marvel at it; but this is a thing that a man may have a reason for, as Bishop Cranmer had, when he burnt off his hand for subscribing to Popery. If you see a man cut off a leg, or an arm, it is a sad sight; but this is a thing, that a man may have a good reason for, as many a man hath it done to save his life. If you see a man give his body to be tormented with scourges and racks, or to be burned to ashes, and refuse deliverance when it is offered, this is a hard case to flesh and blood; but this a man may have good reason for, as you may see in Heb. xi. 33—36. and as many a hundred martyrs have done. But for a man to forsake the Lord that made him, and to run into the fire of hell, when he is told of it, and entreated to turn that he may be saved,—this is a thing that can have no reason in the world to justify or excuse it. For heaven will pay for the loss of any thing that we can lose to obtain it, or for any labour which we bestow for it; but nothing can pay for the loss of heaven.

I beseech you now let this word come nearer to your heart. As you are convinced that you have no reason to destroy yourselves, so tell me what reason have you to refuse to turn and live to God? What reason has the veriest worldling, or drunkard, or ignorant careless sinner of you all, why he should not be as holy as any you know, and be as careful for his soul as any other? Will not hell be as intolerable to you as to others? Should not your own souls be as dear to you as theirs to them? Hath not God as much authority over you? Why then will you not become a sanctified people, as well as they?

O sirs, when God bringeth the matter down to

the very principles of nature, and shows that you have no more reason to be ungodly than you have to damn your own souls,—if yet you will not understand and turn, it seems a desperate case that you are in.

And now, either you have good reason for what you do, or you have not: if not, will you go against reason itself? Will you do that which you have no reason for? But if you think you have, produce it, and make the best of your matter. Reason the case a little with me, your fellow-creature, which is far easier than to reason the case with God; tell me, man, here before the Lord, as if thou wert to die this hour, why shouldst thou not resolve to turn this day; before thou stir from the place thou standest in, what reason hast thou to deny or to delay? Hast thou any reason that satisfieth thine own conscience for it, or any that thou darest own and plead at the bar of God? If thou hast, let us hear them, bring them forth, and make them good. But, alas! what poor stuff, what nonsense, instead of reasons, do we daily hear from ungodly men! But for their necessity I should be ashamed to name them.

Object. 1. One saith, if none shall be saved but such converted and sanctified ones as you talk of, then heaven would be but empty; then God help a great many.

Answ. Why, it seems you think that God doth not know, or else that he is not to be believed! Measure not all by yourselves: God hath thousands and millions of his sanctified ones; but yet they are few in comparison of the world, as Christ himself hath told us, Matt. vii. 13, 14. Luke xi. 32. It better beseems you to make that use of this truth which Christ teacheth you: 'Strive to enter in at the strait gate; for strait is the gate, and narrow is the way, that leadeth unto life, and few there be that find it; but wide is the gate and broad is the way which leadeth to destruction, and many there be that go in thereat,' Luke xiii. 22—24. Fear not, little flock (saith Christ to his sanctified ones) for it is your Father's good pleasure to give you the kingdom. Luke xii. 32.

Object. 2. I am sure, if such as I go to hell, we shall have store of company.

Answ. And will that be any ease or comfort to you? Or do you think you may not have company enough in heaven? Will you be undone for company, or will you not believe that God will execute his threatenings, because there be so many that are guilty? These are all unreasonable conceits.

Object. 3. But all men are sinners, even the best of you all.

Answ. But all are not unconverted sinners. The godly live not in gross sins; and their very infirmities are their grief and burden, which they daily long, and pray, and strive to be rid of. Sin hath not dominion over them.

Object. 4. I do not see that professors are any better than other men; they will overreach and oppress, and are as covetous as any.

Answ. Whatever hypocrites are, it is not so with those that are sanctified. God hath thousands, and tens of thousands that are otherwise, though the malicious world doth accuse them of what they can never prove, and of that which never entered into their hearts; and commonly they charge them with heart-sins, which none can see but God, because they can charge them with no such wickedness in their lives, as they are guilty of themselves.

Object. 5. But I am no whoremonger, nor drunkard, nor oppressor; and therefore why should you call upon me to be converted?

Answ. As if you were not born after the flesh, and had not lived after the flesh, as well as others! Is it not as great a sin as any of these, for a man to have an earthly mind, and to love the world above God, and to have an unbelieving, unhumbled heart? Nay, let me tell you more, that many persons that avoid disgraceful sins, are as fast glued to the world, and as much slaves to the flesh, and as strange to

God, and averse to heaven in their more civil course as others are in their more shameful, notorious sins.

Object. 6. But I mean nobody any harm, nor do any harm; and why then should God condemn me?

Answ. Is it no harm to neglect the Lord that made thee, and the work for which thou camest into the world, and to prefer the creature before the Creator, and to neglect grace that is daily offered thee? It is the depth of thy sinfulness to be so insensible of it: the dead feel not that they are dead. If once thou wert made alive, thou wouldst see more amiss in thyself, and marvel at thyself for making so light of it.

Object. 7. I think you would make men mad, un der pretence of converting them: it is enough to rack the brains of simple people to muse so much on matters so high for them.

Answ. 1. Can you be more mad than you are already? or, at least, can there be a more dangerous madness than to neglect your everlasting welfare, and wilfully undo yourselves?

2. A man is never well in his wits till he be converted: he never knows God, nor knows sin, nor knows Christ, nor knows the world, nor himself, nor what his business is on earth, so as to set himself about it, till he be converted. The Scripture saith, that the wicked are unreasonable men, 2 Thess. iii. 2, and that the wisdom of the world is foolishness with God, 1 Cor. i. 20. and Luke xv. 17. It is said of the prodigal, that when he came to himself, he resolved to return. It is a wise world when men will disobey God, and run to hell, for fear of being out of their wits.

3. What is there in the work that Christ calls you to, that should drive a man out of his wits? Is it the loving God, and calling upon him, and comfortably thinking of the glory to come, and the forsaking of our sins, and loving one another, and delighting ourselves in the service of God? Are these such things as should make men mad?

4. And whereas you say that these matters are too high for us; you accuse God himself, for making this our work, and giving us his word, and commanding all that will be blessed to meditate on it day and night.—Are the matters which we are made for, and which we live for, too high for us to meddle with? This is plainly to unman us, and to make beasts of us, as if we were like them that must meddle with no higher matters than what belongs to flesh and earth. If heaven be too high for you to think on and provide for, it will be too high for you ever to possess.

5. If God should sometimes suffer any weak-headed persons to be distracted by thinking of eternal things, this is because they misunderstand them, and run without a guide: and of the two I had rather be in the case of such a one, than of the mad unconverted world, that take their distraction to be their wisdom.

Object. 8. I do not think that God cares so much what men think, or speak, or do, as to make so great a matter of it.

Answ. It seems then you take the word of God to be false: then what will you believe? But your own reason might teach you better, if you believe not the scriptures; for you see God sets not so light by us but that he vouchsafed to make us, and still preserveth us, and daily upholdeth us, and provideth for us; and will any wise man make a curious frame for nothing? Will you make or buy a clock or watch, and daily look at it, and not care whether it go true or false? Surely, if you believe not a particular eye of Providence observing your hearts and lives, you cannot believe or expect any particular Providence to observe your wants and troubles, or to relieve you; and if God had so little care for you as you imagine, you would never have lived till now; a hundred diseases would have striven which should first destroy you; yea, the devils would have haunted you, and fetched you away alive, as the great fishes devour the less, and as ravenous beasts and birds devour others. You cannot think that God made man for no end or use; and if he made him for any, it was surely for himself; and can you think he cares not whether his end be accomplished, and whether we do the work that we are made for?

Yea, by this atheistical objection, you make God to have made and upheld all the world in vain: for what are all other lower creatures for, but for man? What! doth the earth but bear us, and nourish us, and the beasts do serve us with their labours and lives, and so of the rest? And hath God made so glorious a habitation, and set man to dwell in it, and made all his servants; and now doth he look for nothing at his hands, nor care how he thinks, or speaks, or lives? This is most unreasonable.

Object. 9. It was a better world when men did not make so much ado in religion.

Answ. 1. It hath ever been the custom to praise the times past; that world that you speak of was wont to say it was a better world in their forefathers' days; and so did they of their forefathers. This is but an old custom, because we all feel the evil of our own times, but we see not that which was before us.

2. Perhaps you speak as you think. Worldlings think the world is at the best when it is agreeable to their minds, and when they have most mirth and worldly pleasure; and I doubt not but the devil, as well as you, would say, that then it was a better world; for then he had more service and less disturbance. But the world is at the best when God is most loved, regarded, and obeyed; and how else will you know when the world is good or bad, but by this?

Object. 10. There are so many ways and religions, that we know not which to be of, and therefore we will be even as we are.

Answ. Because there are many, will you be of that way that you may be sure is wrong? None are further out of the way than worldly, fleshly, unconverted sinners; for they do not only err in this or that opinion, as many sects do, but in the very scope and drift of their lives. If you were going a journey that your life lay on, would you stop or turn again, because you met with some cross-ways, or because you saw some travellers go the horse-way, and some the foot-way, and some perhaps break over the hedge, yea, and some miss the way? Or would you not rather be the more careful to inquire the way? If you have some servants that know not how to do your work right, and some that are unfaithful, would you take it well of any of the rest that would therefore be idle and do you no service, because they see the rest so bad?

Object. 11. I do not see that it goes any better with those that are so godly, than with other men; they are as poor, and in as much trouble as others.

Answ. And perhaps in much more, when God sees it meet. They take not earthly prosperity for their wages; they have laid up their treasure and hopes in another world; or else they are not Christians indeed; the less they have, the more is behind, and they are content to wait till then.

Object. 12. When you have said all that you can, I am resolved to hope well, and trust in God, and do as well as I can, and not make so much ado.

Answ. 1. Is that doing as well as you can, when you will not turn to God, but your heart is against his holy and diligent service? It is as well as you will, indeed, but that is your misery.

2. My desire is, that you should hope and trust in God. But for what is it that you will hope? Is it to be saved, if you turn and be sanctified? For this you have God's promise, and therefore hope for it and spare not. But if you hope to be saved without conversion and a holy life, this is not to hope in God, but in Satan, or yourselves; for God hath given you no such promise, but told you the contrary; but it is

Satan and self-love that made you such promises, and raised you to such hopes.

Well, if these, and such as these, be all you have to say against conversion and a holy life, your all is nothing, and worse than nothing; and if these, and such as these, seem reasons sufficient to persuade you to forsake God, and cast yourselves into hell, the Lord deliver you from such reasons, and from such blind understandings, and from such senseless hardened hearts. Dare you stand to aver one of these reasons at the bar of God? Do you think it will then serve your turn to say, 'Lord, I did not turn, because I had so much to do in the world, or because I did not like the lives of some professors, or because I saw men of so many minds!' O how easily will the light of that day confound and shame such reasonings as these! Had you the world to look after? Let the world which you served now pay you your wages, and save you if it can. Had you not a better world to look after first, and were ye not commanded to seek first God's kingdom and righteousness, and promised that other things should be added to you? Matt. vi. 33. And were ye not told, that godliness was profitable to all things, having the promise of this life, and of that which is to come? 1 Tim. iv. 8. Did the sins of professors hinder you? You should rather have been the more heedful, and learned, by their falls, to beware, and have been the more careful, and not to be more careless. It was the Scripture, and not their lives, that was your rule. Did the many opinions of the world hinder you? Why, the Scripture, that was your rule, did teach you but one way, and that was the right way. If you had followed that, even in so much as was plain and easy, you should never have miscarried. Will not such answers as these confound and silence you? If these will not, God hath those that will. When he asked the man, "Friend, how camest thou in hither, not having on a wedding-garment?" Matt. xxii. 12. that is, what dost thou in my Church among professed Christians, without a holy heart and life,—what answer did he make? Why the text saith, "he was speechless;" he had nothing to say. The clearness of the case, and the majesty of God, will then easily stop the mouths of the most confident of you, though you will not be put down by any thing we can say to you now, but will make good your cause, be it ever so bad. I know already that never a reason that now you can give me will do you any good at last, when your case must be opened before the Lord and all the world.

Nay, I scarce think that your own consciences are well satisfied with your reasons; for if they are, it seems then you have not so much as a purpose to repent. But if you do purpose to repent, it seems you do not put much confidence in your reasons which you bring against it.

What say you, unconverted sinners? Have you any good reasons to give why you should not turn, and presently turn with all your hearts? Or will you go to hell in despite of reason itself? Bethink you what you do in time, for it will shortly be too late to bethink you. Can you find any fault with God, or his work, or his wages? Is he a bad master? Is the devil, whom ye serve, a better? or is the flesh a better? Is there any harm in a holy life? Is a life of worldliness and ungodliness better? Do you think in your consciences that it would do you any harm to be converted and live a holy life? What harm can it do you? Is it harm to you to have the Spirit of Christ within you, and to have a cleansed purified heart? If it be bad to be holy, why doth God say, "Be ye holy, for I am holy?" 1 Pet. i. 15, 16. Lev. xx. 7. Is it evil to be like God? Is it not said that God made man in his own image? Why, this holiness is his image; this Adam lost, and this Christ by his word and Spirit would restore to you, as he doth to all that he will save. Why were you baptized into the Holy Ghost, and why do you baptize your children into the Holy Ghost, as your Sanctifier, if you will not be sanctified by him, but think it a hurt to you to be sanctified? Tell me truly, as before the Lord, though you are loth to live a holy life, had you not rather die in the case of those that do so, than of others? If you were to die this day, had you not rather die in the case of a converted man than of an unconverted? of a holy and heavenly man that of a carnal earthly man? and would you not say as Balaam, Numb. xxiii. 10. "Let me die the death of the righteous, and let my last end be like his!" And why will you not now be of the mind that you will be of then? First or last you must come to this, either to be converted, or to wish you had been, when it is too late.

But what is it that you are afraid of losing, if you turn? Is it your friends? You will but change them; God will be your friend, and Christ and the Spirit will be your friend, and every christian will be your friend. You will get one friend that will stand you in more stead than all the friends in the world could have done. The friends you lose would have but enticed you to hell, but could not have delivered you: but the friend you get will save you from hell, and bring you to his own eternal rest.

Is it your pleasures that you are afraid of losing? You think you shall never have a merry day again if once you be converted. Alas! that you should think it a greater pleasure to live in foolish sports and merriments, and please your flesh, than to live in the believing thoughts of glory, and in the love of God, and in righteousness, and peace, and joy in the Holy Ghost, in which the state of grace consisteth. Rom. xiv. 17. If it would be a greater pleasure for you to think of your lands and inheritance, if you were lord of all the country, than it is for a child to play at pins; why should it not be a greater joy to you to think of the kingdom of heaven being yours, than of all the riches or pleasures of the world? As it is but foolish childishness that makes children so delight in toys, that they would not leave them for all your lands, so it is but foolish worldliness, and fleshliness, and wickedness, that makes you so much delight in your houses and lands, and meat and drink, and ease and honour, as that you would not part with them for the heavenly delights. But what will you do for pleasure when these are gone? Do you not think of that? When your pleasures end in horror, and go out like a taper, the pleasures of the saints are then at the best. I have had myself but a little taste of the heavenly pleasures in the forethoughts of the blessed approaching day, and in the present persuasions of the love of God in Christ; but I have taken too deep a draught of earthly pleasures: so that you may see, if I be partial, it is on your side; and yet I must profess from that little experience, that there is no comparison. There is more joy to be had in a day, if the sun of life shine clear upon us, in the state of holiness, than in a whole life of sinful pleasures. "I had rather be a door-keeper in the house of God, than to dwell in the tents of wickedness." Ps. lxxxiv. 10. "A day in his courts is better than a thousand" any where else. Ps. lxxxiv. 10. The mirth of the wicked is like the laughter of a madman, that knows not his own misery; and therefore Solomon says of such laughter, "it is mad; and of mirth, what doth it?" Eccles. ii. 2. vii. 2—6. "It is better to go to the house of mourning, than to go to the house of feasting; for that is the end of all men, and the living will lay it to his heart. Sorrow is better than laughter; for by the sadness of the countenance the heart is made better. The heart of the wise is in the house of mourning; but the heart of fools is in the house of mirth. It is better to bear the rebuke of the wise, than to hear the song of fools; for as the crackling of thorns under a pot, so is the laughter of the fool." All the pleasure of fleshly things is but like the scratching of a man that hath the itch; it is his disease that makes him desire it, and a wise man had rather be without his pleasure than be troubled with his itch. Your loudest laughter is but like that of a man that is tickled; he laughs when he has no cause of joy. Judge, as you are men, whether this be a wise man's part. It is but your carnal unsanctified nature that makes a holy life seem grievous to you, and a course of sensuality seem more delightful. If you will but turn, the Holy Ghost will give you another nature and inclination, and then it will be more pleasant to you to be rid of your sin, than now it is to keep it; and you will then say, that you knew not what a comfortable life was till now, and that it was never well with you till God and holiness were your delight.

Quest. But how cometh it to pass that men should be so unreasonable in the matters of salvation? They have wit enough in other matters: what makes them so loth to be converted, that there should need so many words in so plain a case, and all will not do, but the most will live and die unconverted?

Answ. To name them only in a few words, the causes are these:

1. Men are naturally in love with the earth and flesh; they are born sinners, and their nature hath an enmity to God and goodness, as the nature of a serpent hath to a man: and when all that we can say goes against an habitual inclination of their natures, no marvel if it prevail little.

2. They are in darkness, and know not the very things they hear. Like a man that was born blind, and hears a high commendation of the light; but what will hearing do, unless he sees it? They know not what God is, nor what is the power of the cross of Christ, nor what the spirit of holiness is, nor what it is to live in love by faith: they know not the certainty, and suitableness, and excellency of the heavenly inheritance. They know not what conversion and a holy mind and conversation is, even when

they hear of it. They are in a mist of ignorance. They are lost and bewildered in sin; like a man that has lost himself in the night, and knows not where he is, nor how to come to himself again, till the day-light recover him.

3. They are wilfully confident that they need no conversion, but some partial amendment; and that they are in the way to heaven already; and are converted when they are not. And if you meet a man that is quite out of his way, you may long enough call on him to turn back again, if he will not believe you that he is out of the way.

4. They are become slaves to their flesh, and drowned in the world to make provision for it. Their lusts, and passions, and appetites have distracted them, and got such a hand over them, that they cannot tell how to deny them, or how to mind any thing else; so that the drunkard saith, I love a cup of good drink, and I cannot forbear it: the glutton saith, I love good cheer, and I cannot forbear; the fornicator saith, I love to have my lust fulfilled, and I cannot forbear; and the gamester loves to have his sports, and he cannot forbear. So that they are become even captivated slaves to their flesh, and their very wilfulness is become an impotency; and what they would not do, they say they cannot. And the worldling is so taken up with earthly things, that he hath neither heart, nor mind, nor time, for heavenly; but, as in Pharaoh's dream, Gen. xli. 4. the lean kine did eat up the fat ones; so this lean and barren earth doth eat up all the thoughts of heaven.

5. Some are so carried away by the stream of evil company, that they are possessed with hard thoughts of a godly life, by hearing them speak against it; or at least they think they may venture to do as they see most do, and so they hold on in their sinful ways; and when one is cut off, and cast into hell, and another snatched away from among them to the same condemnation,—it doth not much daunt them, because they see not whither they are gone. Poor

wretches, they hold on in their ungodliness for all this; for they little know that their companions are now lamenting it in torments. In Luke xvi. the rich man in hell would fain have had one to warn his five brethren, lest they should come to that place of torment. It is likely he knew their minds and lives, and knew that they were hasting thither, and little dreamt that he was there, yea, and would little have believed one that should have told them so. I remember a passage that a gentleman, yet living, told me he saw upon a bridge over the Severn.* A man was driving a flock of fat lambs, and something meeting them, and hindering their passage, one of the lambs leapt upon the wall of the bridge, and his legs slipping from under him, he fell into the stream; the rest seeing him, did, one after one, leap over the bridge into the stream, and were all or almost all drowned. Those that were behind did little know what was become of them that were gone before; but thought they might venture to follow their companions; but as soon as ever they were over the wall, and falling headlong, the case was altered. Even so it is with unconverted carnal men. One dieth by them, and drops into hell, and another follows the same way; and yet they will go after them, because they think not whither they are gone. O, but when death hath once opened their eyes, and they see what is on the other side of the wall, even in another world, then what would they give to be where they were!

6. Moreover, they have a subtle malicious enemy, that is unseen of them, and plays his game in the dark; and it is his principal business to hinder their conversion; and therefore to keep them where they are, by persuading them not to believe the Scriptures, or not to trouble their minds with these matters; or by persuading them to think ill of a godly life, or to think that more is enjoined than need be,

* Mr. R. Rowly, of Shrewsbury, upon Acham-Bridge.

and that they may be saved without conversion, and without all this stir; and that God is so merciful, that he will not damn any such as they; or at least, that they may stay a little longer, and take their pleasure, and follow the world a little longer yet, and then let it go, and repent hereafter. And by such juggling, deluding cheats as these, the devil keeps the most in his captivity, and leadeth them to his misery.

These, and such like impediments as these, do keep so many thousands unconverted, when God hath done so much, and Christ hath suffered so much, and ministers have said so much for their conversion: when their reasons are silenced and they are not able to answer the Lord that calls after them, "Turn ye, turn ye, why will ye die?" yet all comes to nothing with the greatest part of them; and they leave us no more to do after all, but to sit down and lament their wilful misery.

I have now showed you the reasonableness of God's commands, and the unreasonableness of wicked men's disobedience. If nothing will serve their turn, but men will yet refuse to turn, we are next to consider, who is in fault if they be damned. And this brings me to the last doctrine; which is,

DOCTRINE 7. That if after all this men will not turn, it is not the fault of God that they are condemned, but their own, even their own wilfulness. They die because they will, that is, because they will not turn.

If you will go to hell, what remedy? God here acquits himself of your blood; it shall not lie on him if you be lost. A negligent minister may draw it upon him; and those that encourage you or hinder you not in sin, may draw it upon them; but be sure of it, it shall not lie upon God. Saith the Lord concerning his unprofitable vineyard: Isa. v. 1—4. "Judge, I pray you, betwixt me and my vineyard:

what could have been done more to my vineyard that I have not done in it?" When he had planted it in a fruitful soil, and fenced it, and gathered out the stones, and planted it with the choicest vines, what should he have done more to it? He hath made you men, and endowed you with reason; he hath furnished you with all external necessaries; all creatures are at your service; he hath given you a righteous perfect law. When ye had broken it, and undone yourselves, he had pity on you, and sent his Son by a miracle of condescending mercy to die for you, and be a sacrifice for your sins; and he was in Christ reconciling the word to himself!

The Lord Jesus hath made you a deed of gift of himself, and eternal life with him, on the condition you will but accept it, and return. He hath on this reasonable condition offered you the free pardon of all your sins! he hath written this in his word, and sealed it by his Spirit, and sent it by his ministers: they have made the offer to you a hundred and a hundred times, and called you to accept it, and to turn to God. They have in his name entreated you, and reasoned the case with you, and answered all your frivolous objections. He hath long waited on you, and staid your leisure, and suffered you to abuse him to his face! He hath mercifully sustained you in the midst of your sins; he hath compassed you about with all sorts of mercies; he hath also intermixed afflictions, to remind you of your folly, and call you to your senses, and his Spirit has been often striving with your hearts, and saying there, 'Turn, sinner, turn to him that calleth thee: Whither art thou going? What art thou doing? Dost thou know what will be the end? How long wilt thou hate thy friends, and love thine enemies? When wilt thou let go all, and turn and deliver thyself to God, and give thy Redeemer the possession of thy soul? When shall it once be?' These pleadings have been used with thee, and when thou hast delayed, thou hast been urged to make haste, and

God hath called to thee, "To-day, while it is called to-day, harden not thy heart." Why not now, without any more delay? Life hath been set before you; the joys of heaven have been opened to you in the gospel; the certainty of them hath been manifested; the certainty of the everlasting torments of the damned hath been declared to you; unless you would have had a sight of heaven and hell, what could you desire more? Christ hath been, as it were, set forth crucified before your eyes, Gal. iii. 1. You have been a hundred times told that you are but lost men till you come unto him; as oft you have been told of the evil of sin, of the vanity of sin, the world, and all the pleasures and wealth it can afford; of the shortness and uncertainty of your lives, and the endless duration of the joy or torment of the life to come. All this, and more than this have you been told, and told again, even till you were weary of hearing it, and till you could make the lighter of it, because you had so often heard it, like the smith's dog, that is brought by custom to sleep under the noise of the hammers and when the sparks fly about his ears; and though all this have not converted you, yet you are alive, and might have mercy to this day, if you had but hearts to entertain it. And now let reason itself be the judge, whether it be the fault of God or yours, if after this you will be unconverted and be damned. If you die now, it is because you will die. What should be said more to you, or what course should be taken that is more likely to prevail? Are you able to say, and make it good, 'We would fain have been converted and become new creatures, but we could not; we would fain have forsaken our sins, but we could not; we would have changed our company, and our thoughts, and our discourse, but we could not.' Why could you not, if you would? What hindered you but the wickedness of your hearts? Who forced you to sin, or who held you back from duty? Had not you the same teaching, and time, and liberty to be godly, as your godly neighbours had? Why then could not you have been godly as well as they? Were the church doors shut against you, or did you not keep away yourselves, or sit and sleep, or hear as if you did not hear? Did God put in any exceptions against you in his word, when he invited sinners to return; and when he promised mercy to those that do return? Did he say, 'I will pardon all that repent except thee?' Did he shut thee out from the liberty of his holy worship? Did he forbid you to pray to him any more than others? You know he did not. God did not drive you away from him, but you forsook him, and ran away yourselves, and when he called you to him, you would not come. If God had excepted you out of the general promise and offer of mercy, or had said to you, 'Stand off, I will have nothing to do with such as you; pray not to me, for I will not hear you; if you repent never so much, and cry for mercy never so much, I will not regard you.' If God had left you nothing to trust to but desperation, then you had had a fair excuse; you might have said, 'To what end do I repent and turn, when it will do no good?' But this was not your case: you might have had Christ to be your Lord and Saviour, your head and husband, as well as others, and you would not, because you felt yourselves not sick enough for the physician: and because you could not spare your dis ease. In your hearts you said as those rebels, Luke xix. 14. "We will not have this man to reign over us." Christ would have gathered you under the wings of his salvation, and you would not. Matt. xxiii. 37. What desires of your welfare did the Lord express in his holy word? With what compassion did he stand over you, and say, "O that my people had hearkened unto me, and that they had walked in my ways!" Psalm xvii. 13. lxxvi. 13. "O that there were such a heart in this people, that they would fear me, and keep all my commandments always; that it might be well with them and with their children for ever!" Deut. v. 29. "O that they were wise, that they understood this, that they would consider their latter end!" Deut. xxxii. 29. He would have been your God, and done all for you that your souls could well desire: but you loved the world and your flesh above him, and therefore you would not hearken to him: though you complimented him, and gave him high titles; yet when it came to the closing, you would have none of him. Psalm lxxxi. 11, 12. No marvel then if he gave you up to your own hearts' lusts, and you walked in your own counsels. He condescends to reason, and pleads the case with you, and asks you, 'What is there in me, or my service, that you should be so much against me? What harm have I done thee, sinner? Have I deserved this unkind dealing at thy hand? Many mercies have I showed thee: for which of them dost thou thus despise me? Is it I, or is it Satan, that is thy enemy? Is it I, or is it thy carnal self that would undo thee? Is it a holy life, or a life of sin that thou hast cause to fly from? If thou be undone, thou procurest this to thyself, by forsaking me, the Lord that would have saved thee.' Jer. ii. 7. "Doth not thy own wickedness correct thee, and thy sin reprove thee? Thou mayst see that it is an evil and bitter thing that thou hast forsaken me." Jer. ii. 19. "What iniquity have you found in me that you have followed after vanity, and forsaken me?" Jer. ii. 5, 6. He calleth out, as it were, to the brutes, to hear the controversy he hath against you. Mic. ii. 3—5. "Hear, O ye mountains, the Lord's controversy, and ye strong foundations of the earth; for the Lord hath a controversy with his people, and he will plead with Israel. O my people, what have I done unto thee, and wherein have I wearied thee? testify against me, for I brought thee up out of Egypt, and redeemed thee." "Hear, O heavens, and give ear, O earth, for the Lord hath spoken. I have nourished and brought up children, and they have rebelled against me.

The ox knoweth his owner, and the ass his master s crib; but Israel doth not know, my people doth not consider! Ah sinful nation, a people laden with iniquity, a seed of evil doers!" &c. Is. i. 2—4. "Do you thus requite the Lord, O foolish people, and unwise? Is not he thy Father that bought thee? Hath he not made thee, and established thee?" Deut. xxxii. 6. When he saw that you forsook him, even for nothing, and turned away from your Lord and life, to hunt after the chaff and feathers of the world, he told you of your folly, and called you to a more profitable employment, Isa. lv. 1—3. "Wherefore do ye spend your money for that which is not bread, and your labour for that which satisfieth not? Hearken diligently unto me, and eat ye that which is good, and let your soul delight itself in fatness. Incline you ear, and come unto me; hear, and your soul shall live; and I will make an everlasting covenant with you, even the sure mercies of David. Seek ye the Lord while he may be found: call ye upon him while he is near. Let the wicked forsake his way, and the unrighteous man his thoughts, and let him return unto the Lord, and he will have mercy upon him; and to our God, for he will abundantly pardon," and so Isa. i. 16—18. And when you would not hear, what complaints have you put him to, charging it on you as your wilfulness and stubbornness. Jer. ii. 12, 13. "Be astonished, O heavens, at this, and be horribly afraid; for my people have committed two evils; they have forsaken me, the fountain of living waters, and hewed them out cisterns, broken cisterns, that can hold no water." Many a time hath Christ proclaimed that free invitation to you, Rev. xxii. 17. "Let him that is athirst come, and whosoever will, let him take the water of life freely." But you put him to complain, after all his offers; "They will not come to me, that they may have life." John v. 40. He hath invited you to feast with him in the kingdom of his grace, and you have had excuses from your grounds, and your cattle, and your worldly business; and when you would not come, you have said you could not; and provoked him to resolve that you should never taste of his supper, Luke xiv. 16—25. And who is it the fault of now but yourselves? and what can you say is the chief cause of your damnation but your own wills? you would be damned. The whole case is laid open by Christ himself, Prov. i. 20—33. "Wisdom crieth without, she uttereth her voice in the streets; she crieth in the chief place of the concourse,—How long, ye simple ones, will ye love simplicity, and the scorners delight in their scorning, and fools hate knowledge? Turn ye at my reproof. Behold, I will pour out my Spirit upon you, I will make known my words unto you. Because I have called, and ye refused. I have stretched out my hands and no man regarded; but ye have set at naught all my counsels, and would none of my reproofs. I also will laugh at your calamity, I will mock when your fear cometh: when your fear cometh as desolation, and your destruction cometh as a whirlwind; when distress and anguish cometh upon you, then shall they call upon me, but I will not answer; they shall seek me early, but they shall not find me; for that they hated knowledge, and did not choose the fear of the Lord. They would none of my counsels: they despised all my reproofs; therefore shall they eat of the fruit of their own way; and be filled with their own devices. For the turning away of the simple shall slay them, and the prosperity of fools shall destroy them. But whoso hearkeneth to me shall dwell safely, and shall be quiet from the fear of evil." I thought best to recite the whole text at large to you, because it doth so fully show the cause of the destruction of the wicked. It is not because God would not teach them, but because they would not learn. It is not because God would not call them, but because they would not turn at his reproof. Their wilfulness is their undoing.

USE.—From what hath been said, you may further learn these following things:

1. From hence you may see, not only what blasphemy and impiety it is to lay the blame of men's destruction upon God; but also how unfit these wicked wretches are to bring in such a charge against their Maker! They cry out upon God, and say he gives them not grace, and his threatenings are severe, and God forbid that all should be condemned that be not converted and sanctified; and they think it hard measure that a short sin should have an endless suffering; and if they be damned, they say they cannot help it, when in the mean time they are busy about their own destruction, even the destruction of their own souls, and will not be persuaded to hold their hands. They think God were cruel, if he should condemn them; and yet they are so cruel to themselves, that they will run into the fire of hell, when God hath told them it is a little before them; and neither entreaties, nor threatenings, nor any thing that can be said, will stop them. We see them almost undone; their careless worldly, fleshly lives tell us that they are in the power of the devil; we know, if they die before they are converted, all the world cannot save them; and knowing the uncertainty of their lives, we are afraid every day lest they drop into the fire: and therefore we entreat them to pity their own souls, and not to undo themselves when mercy is at hand; and they will not hear us. We entreat them to cast away their sin, and come to Christ without delay, and to have some mercy on themselves, but they will have none; and yet they think that God must be cruel if he condemn them. O wilful miserable sinners! it is not God that is cruel to you, it is you that are cruel to yourselves; you are told you must turn or burn, and yet you turn not. Your are told that if you will needs keep your sins, you shall keep the curse of God with them; and yet you will keep them. You are told that there is no way to happiness but by

holiness; and yet you will not be holy. What would you have God say more to you? What would you have him do with his mercy? He offereth it to you, and you will not have it. You are in the ditch of sin and misery, and he would give you his hand to help you out, and you refuse his help; he would cleanse you of your sins, and you had rather keep them; you love your lust, and love your gluttony and sports, and drunkenness, and will not let them go; would you have him bring you to heaven whether you will or not? Or would you have him bring you and your sins to heaven together? Why that is an impossibility; you may as well expect he should turn the sun into darkness. What! an unsanctified fleshly heart be in heaven? it cannot be. There entereth nothing that is unclean. Rev. xxi. 17. "For what communion hath light with darkness, or Christ with Belial?" 2 Cor. vi. 14, 15. "All the day long hath he stretched out his hands to a disobedient and gainsaying people." Rom. x. 21. What will you do now? Will you cry to God for mercy? Why, God calleth upon you to have mercy upon yourselves, and you will not! Ministers see the poisoned cup in the drunkard's hand, and tell him there is poison in it, and desire him to have mercy on his soul, and forbear, and he will not hear us! Drink it he must and will; he loves it, and therefore, though hell comes next, he saith he cannot help it. What should one say to such men as these? We tell the ungodly careless worldling, it is not such a life that will serve the turn, or ever bring you to heaven. If a bear were at your back, you would mend your pace; and when the curse of God is at your back, and Satan and hell are at your back, will you not stir, but ask, What needs all this ado? Is an immortal soul of no more worth? O have mercy upon yourselves! But they will have no mercy on themselves, nor once regard us. We tell them the end will be bitter. Who can dwell with the everlasting fire? And yet they will have no mercy on themselves. And yet will these shameless transgressors say, that God is more merciful than to condemn them; when it is themselves that cruelly and unmercifully run upon condemnation; and if we should go to them, and entreat them, we cannot stop them; if we should fall on our knees to them, we cannot stop them, but to hell they will go, and yet will not believe that they are going thither. If we beg of them for the sake of God that made them, and preserveth them; for the sake of Christ, that died for them; for the sake of their own souls, to pity themselves, and go no further in the way to hell, but come to Christ while his arms are open, and enter into the state of life while the door stands open, and now take mercy while mercy may be had, they will not be persuaded. If we should die for it, we cannot so much as get them now and then to consider with themselves of the matter, and turn and yet they can say, 'I hope God will be merciful. Did you never consider what he saith, Isa. xxvii. 11. "It is a people of no understanding; therefore, he that made them will not have mercy on them, and he that formed them will show them no favour.' If another man will not clothe you when you are naked, and feed you when you are hungry, you will say he is unmerciful. If he should cast you into prison, or beat and torment you, you would say he is unmerciful; and yet you will do a thousand times more against yourselves, even cast away both soul and body for ever, and never complain of your own unmercifulness! Yea, and God that waited upon you all the while with his mercy, must be taken to be unmerciful, if he punish you after all this. Unless the holy God of heaven will give these wretches leave to trample upon his Son's blood, and with the Jews, as it were, again to spit in his face, and do despite to the spirit of grace, and make a jest of sin, and a mock at holiness, and set more light by saving mercy than by the filth of their fleshly pleasures; and unless, after all this he will save them by the mercy which they cast away and would have none of, God himself must be called unmerciful by them! But he will be justified when he judgeth, and he will not stand or fall at the bar of a sinful worm.

I know there are many particular cavils that are brought by them against the Lord; but I shall not here stay to answer them particularly, having done it already in my *Treatise of Judgment*, to which I shall refer them. Had the disputing part of the world been as careful to avoid sin and destruction, as they have been busy in searching after the cause of them, and forward indirectly to impute it to God, they might have exercised their wits more profitably, and have less wronged God, and sped better themselves. When so ugly a monster as sin is within us, and so heavy a thing as punishment is on us, and so dreadful a thing as hell is before us, one would think it should be an easy question, who is in the fault, whether God or man be the principal or culpable cause? Some men are such favourable judges of themselves, that they are more prone to accuse the infinite perfection and goodness itself, than their own hearts, and imitate their first parents, that said, "The serpent tempted me; and the woman that thou gavest me gave unto me, and I did eat;" secretly implying that God was the cause. So say they, "The understanding that thou gavest me was unable to discern; the will that thou gavest me was unable to make a better choice; the objects which thou didst set before me did entice me; the temptations which thou didst permit to assault me prevailed against me." And some are so loth to think that God can make a self-determining creature, that they dare not deny him that which they take to be his prerogative, to be the determiner of the will in every sin, as the first efficient immediate physical cause; and many could be content to acquit God from so much causing of evil, if they could but reconcile it with his being the chief cause of good; as if truths would be no longer truths than we are able to see them in their perfect order and coherence: because our ravelled wits cannot see them right together, nor assign each truth its proper place, we presume to conclude that some must be cast away. This is the fruit of proud self-conceitedness, when men receive not God's truth as a child his lesson, in holy submission to the omniscience of our Teacher, but censurers, that are too wise to learn.

Object. But we cannot convert ourselves till God convert us; we can do nothing without his grace; it is not in him that willeth, nor in him that runneth, but in God that showeth mercy.

Answ. 1. God hath two degrees of mercy to show; the mercy of conversion first, and the mercy of salvation last; the latter he will give to none but those that will and run, and hath promised it to them only. The former is to make them willing that are unwilling; and though your own willingness and endeavours deserve not his grace, yet your wilful refusal deserveth that it should be denied to you. Your disability is your very unwillingness itself, which excuseth not your sin, but maketh it the greater. You could turn if you were but truly willing; and if your wills themselves are so corrupted, that nothing but effectual grace will move them, you have no more cause to seek for that grace, and yield to it, and do what you can in the use of means, and not neglect it, and set against it. Do what you are able first, and then complain of God for denying you grace, if you have cause.

Object. But you seem to intimate all this while that man hath free-will.

Answ. 1. The dispute about free-will is beyond your capacity; I shall therefore now trouble you with no more but this about it. Your will is naturally a free, that is, a self-determining faculty; but it is viciously inclined, and backward to do good; and therefore we see, by sad experience, that it hath not a virtuous moral freedom: but that it is the wickedness of it which deserveth the punishment; and I pray you, let us not befool ourselves with opinions. Let the case be your own. If you had an enemy that was so malicious as to fall upon you, and beat you, or take away the lives of your children, would you excuse him, because he said, I have not free-will; it is my nature; I cannot choose unless God give me grace? If you had a servant that robbed you, would you take such an answer from him? Might not every thief and murderer that is hanged at the assize give such an answer: I have not free-will; I cannot change my own heart; what can I do without God's grace? and shall they therefore be acquitted? If not, why then should you think to be acquitted for a course of sin against the Lord?

2. From hence also you may observe these three things together:—1. What a subtle tempter Satan is. 2. What a deceitful thing sin is. 3. What a foolish creature corrupted man is. A subtle tempter indeed, that can persuade the greatest part of the world to go into everlasting fire, when they have so many warnings and dissuasives as they have! A deceitful thing is sin indeed, that can bewitch so many thousands to part with everlasting life, for a thing so base and utterly unworthy! A foolish creature is man indeed, that will be cheated of his salvation for nothing, yea, for a known nothing; and that by an enemy, and a known enemy. You would think it impossible that any man in his wits should be persuaded for a little to cast himself into the fire, or water, or into a coal-pit, to the destruction of his life; and yet men will be enticed to cast themselves into hell. If your natural lives were in your own hands, that you should not die till you would kill yourselves, how long would most of you live? And yet when your everlasting life is so far in your own hands under God, that you cannot be undone till you undo yourselves, how few of you will forbear your own undoing? Ah, what a silly thing is man! and what a bewitching and befooling thing is sin!

3. From hence also you may learn, that it is no great wonder if wicked men be hinderers of others in the way to heaven, and would have as many unconverted as they can, and would draw them into sin, and keep them in it. Can you expect that they should have mercy on others, that have none upon themselves? and that they should hesitate much at the destruction of others, that hesitate not to destroy themselves? They do no worse by others than they do by themselves.

4. Lastly, You may hence learn that the greatest enemy to man is himself; and the greatest judgment in this life that can befall him, is to be left to himself; that the great work that grace hath to do, is to save us from ourselves; that the greatest accusations and complaints of men should be against themselves; that the greatest work that we have to do ourselves, is to resist ourselves; and the greatest enemy that we should daily pray, and watch, and strive against, is our own carnal hearts and wills; and the greatest part of your work, if you would do good to others, and help them to heaven, is to save them from themselves, even from their blind understandings and corrupted wills, and perverse affections, and violent passions, and unruly senses. I only name all these for brevity's sake, and leave them to your further consideration.

Well, sirs, now we have found out the great delinquent and murderer of souls (even men's selves, their own wills,) what remains but that you judge according to the evidence, and confess this great iniquity before the Lord, and be humbled for it, and do so no more? To these three ends distinctly, I shall add a few words more. 1. Further to convince you. 2. To humble you. And, 3. To reform you if there yet be any hope.

1. We know so much of the exceeding gracious nature of God, who is willing to do good, and delighteth to show mercy, that we have no reason to suspect him of being the culpable cause of our death,

or to call him cruel; he made all good, and he preserveth and maintaineth all; the eyes of all wait upon him, and he giveth them their meat in due season; he openeth his hand, and satisfieth the desires of all the living. Psalm cxlv. 15, 16. He is not only righteous in all his ways, and therefore will deal justly; and holy in all his works, and therefore not the author of sin; but he is also good to all, and his tender mercies are over all his works. Psalm cxlv. 17, 19.

But as for man, we know his mind is dark, his will perverse, and his affections carry him so headlong, that he is fitted by his folly and corruption to such a work as the destroying of himself. If you saw a lamb lie killed in the way, would you sooner suspect the sheep, or the dog, or the wolf, to be the author of it if they both stand by? Or if you see a house broken open and the people murdered, would you sooner suspect the prince or judge, that is wise and just, and had no need, or a known thief or murderer? I say therefore, as James i. 13—15, "Let no man say, when he is tempted, that he is tempted of God, for God cannot be tempted with evil, neither tempteth he any man to draw him to sin; but every man is tempted, when he is drawn away of his own lust, and enticed. Then when lust hath conceived, it bringeth forth sin; and sin, when it is finished, bringeth forth death." You see here that sin is the offspring of your own concupiscence, and not to be charged on God, and that death is the offspring of your own sin, and the fruit which it will yield you as soon as it is ripe. You have a treasure of evil in yourselves, as a spider hath of poison, from whence you are bringing forth hurt to yourselves, and spinning such webs as entangle your own souls. Your nature shows it is you that are the cause.

2. It is evident that you are your own destroyers, in that you are so ready to entertain any temptation almost that is offered you. Satan is scarcely more ready to move you to any evil, that you are ready to hear, and to do as he would have you. If he

would tempt your understanding to error and prejudice, you yield. If he would hinder you from good resolutions, it is soon done. If he would cool any good desires or affections, it is soon done. If he would kindle any lust, or vile affections and desires in you, it is soon done. If he will put you on to evil thoughts, or deeds, you are so free, that he needs no rod or spur. If he would keep you from holy thoughts, and words, and ways, a little doth it, you need no curb. You examine not his suggestions, nor resist them with any resolution, nor cast them out as he casts them in, nor quench the sparks which he endeavoureth to kindle; but you set in with him, and meet him half way, and embrace his motions, and tempt him to tempt you. And it is easy to catch such greedy fish that are ranging for a bait, and will take the bare hook.

3. Your destruction is evidently of yourselves, in that you resist all that would help to save you, and would do you good, or hinder you from undoing yourselves. God would help and save you by his word, and you resist it: it is too strict for you. He would sanctify you by his Spirit, and you resist and quench it. If any man reprove you for your sin, you fly in his face with evil words: and if he would draw you to a holy life, and tell you of your present danger, you give him little thanks, but either bid him look to himself, he shall not answer for you; else, at best, you put him off with heartless thanks, and will not turn when you are persuaded. If ministers would privately instruct and help you, you will not come to them; your unhumbled souls feel but little need of their help; if they would catechise you, you are too old to be catechised, though you are not too old to be ignorant and unholy. Whatever they can say to you for your good, you are so self-conceited and wise in your own eyes, even in the depth of ignorance, that you will regard nothing that agreeth not with your present conceits, but contradict your teachers, as if you were wiser than they; you resist

all that they can say to you by your ignorance, and wilfulness, and foolish cavils, and shifting evasions, and unthankful rejections, so that no good that is offered can find any welcome acceptance and entertainment with you.

4. Moreover, it is apparent that you are self-destroyers, in that you "draw the matter of your sin and destruction even from the blessed God himself." You like not the contrivances of his wisdom; you like not his justice, but take it for cruelty; you like not his holiness, but are ready to think he is such a one as yourselves, Psalm l. 21. and makes as light of sin as you; you like not his truth, but would have his threatenings, even his peremptory threatenings, prove false; and his goodness, which you seem most highly to approve, you partly resist, as it would lead you to repentance; and partly abuse, to the strengthening of your sin, as if you might more freely sin because God is merciful, and because his grace doth so much abound.

5. Yea, you fetch destruction from the blessed Redeemer, and death from the Lord of life himself! and nothing more emboldeneth you in sin, than that Christ hath died for you; as if now the danger of death were over, and you might boldly venture; as if Christ were become a servant to Satan and your sins, and must wait upon you while you are abusing him; and because he is become the Physician of souls, and is able to save to the uttermost all that come to God by him, you think he must suffer you to refuse his help, and throw away his medicines, and must save you whether you will come to God by him or not: so that a great part of your sins are occasioned by your bold presumption upon the death of Christ,—not considering that he came to redeem his people from their sins, and to sanctify them a peculiar people to himself, and to conform them in holiness to the image of their heavenly Father, and to their head. Matt. i. 21. Tit. ii. 14. 1 Pet. i. 15, 16. Col. iii. 10, 11. Phil. iii. 9, 10.

6. You also fetch your own destruction from all the providences and works of God. When you think of his eternal fore-knowledge and decrees, it is to harden you in your sin, or possess your minds with quarrelling thoughts, as if his decrees might spare you the labour of repentance and a holy life, or else were the cause of sin and death. If he afflict you, you repine; if he prosper you, you the more forget him, and are the more backward to the thoughts of the life to come. If the wicked prosper, you forget the end that will set all reckonings straight, and are ready to think it is as good to be wicked as godly; and thus you draw your death from all.

7. And the like you do from all the creatures and mercies of God to you. He giveth them to you as the tokens of his love and furniture for his service, and you turn them against him, to the pleasing of your flesh. You eat and drink to please your appetite, and not for the glory of God, and to enable you to perform his work. Your clothes you abuse to pride; your riches draw your hearts from heaven, Phil. iii. 18; your honours and applause puff you up; if you have health and strength, it makes you more secure, and forget your end. Yea, other men's mercies are abused by you to your hurt. If you see their honours and dignity, you are provoked to envy them; if you see their riches, you are ready to covet them; if you look upon beauty, you are stirred up to lust; and it is well if godliness be not an eye-sore to you.

8. The very gifts that God bestoweth on you, and the ordinances of grace which he hath instituted for his church, you turn to sin. If you have better parts than others, you grow proud and self-conceited; if you have but common gifts, you take them for special grace. You take the bare hearing of your duty for so good a work, as if it would excuse you for not obeying it. Your prayers are turned into sin, because you "regard iniquity in your

hearts," Ps. lxvi. 18. and depart not from iniquity when you call on the name of the Lord. 2 Tim. ii. 19. Your "prayers are abominable, because you turn away your ear from hearing the law," Prov. xxviii. 9, and are more ready to offer the sacrifice of fools, thinking you do God some special service, than to hear his word and obey it. Eccles.v. 1.

9. Yea, the persons that you converse with, and all their actions, you make the occasions of your sin and destruction; if they live in the fear of God, you hate them. If they live ungodly, you imitate them; if the wicked are many, you think you may the more boldly follow them; if the godly be few, you are the more emboldened to despise them. If they walk exactly, you think they are too precise; if one of them fall in a particular temptation, you stumble and turn away from holiness, because that others are imperfectly holy; as if you were warranted to break your necks, because some others have by their heedlessness strained a sinew, or put out a bone. If a hypocrite discover himself, you say, 'They are all alike,' and think yourselves as honest as the best. A professor can scarce slip into any miscarriage, but because he cuts his finger, you think you may boldly cut your throats. If ministers deal plainly with you, you say they rail. If they speak gently or coldly, you either sleep under them, or are little more affected than the seats you sit upon. If any errors creep into the church, some greedily entertain them, and others reproach the Christian doctrine for them, which is most against them. And if we would draw you from any ancient rooted error, which can but plead two, or three, or six, or seven hundred years' custom, you are as much offended with a motion for reformation as if you were to lose your life by it, and hold fast old errors, while you cry out against new ones. Scarce a difference can arise among the ministers of the gospel, but you will fetch your own death from it; and you will not hear or at least not obey, the unquestiona

ble doctrine of any of those that agree not with your conceits. One will not hear a minister, because he saith the Lord's prayer; and another will not hear him because he doth not use it. One will not hear them that are for episcopacy; and another will not near them that are against it. And thus I might show it you in many other cases, how you turn all that comes near you to your own destruction; so clear is it that the ungodly are self-destroyers, and that their perdition is of themselves.

Methinks now, upon the consideration of what is said, and the review of your own ways, you should bethink you what you have done, and be ashamed and deeply humbled to remember it. If you be not, I pray you consider these following truths:—

1. To be your own destroyers, is to sin against the deepest principle in your natures, even the principle of self-preservation. Every thing naturally desireth or inclineth to its own felicity, welfare, or perfection; and will you set yourselves to your own destruction? When you are commanded to love your neighbours as yourselves, it is supposed that you naturally love yourselves; but if you love your neighbours no better than yourselves, it seems you would have all the world to be damned.

2. How extremely do you cross your own intentions! I know you intend not your own damnation, even when you are procuring it; you think you are but doing good to yourselves, by gratifying the desires of your flesh. But, alas, it is but as a draught of cold water in a burning fever, or as the scratching of an itching wild-fire, which increaseth the disease and pain. If indeed you would have pleasure, profit, or honour, seek them where they are to be found, and do not hunt after them in the way to hell.

3. What pity is it that you should do that against yourselves which none else on earth or in hell can do! If all the world were combined against you, or all the devils in hell were combined against you, they could not destroy you without yourselves, nor make

you sin but by your own consent: and will you do that against yourselves which no one else can do? You have hateful thoughts of the devil, because he is your enemy, and endeavoureth your destruction; and will you be worse than devils to yourselves? Why thus it is with you, if you had hearts to understand it: when you run into sin, and run from godliness, and refuse to turn at the call of God, you do more against your own souls than men or devils could do besides; and if you should set yourselves and bend your wits to do yourselves the greatest mischief, you could not devise to do a greater.

4. You are false to the trust that God hath reposed in you. He hath much intrusted you with your own salvation; and will you betray your trust? He hath set you, with all diligence, to keep your hearts; and is this the keeping of them? Prov. iv. 23.

5. You do even forbid all others to pity you, when you will have no pity on yourselves. If you cry to God in the day of your calamity, for mercy, mercy—what can you expect, but that he should thrust you away, and say, 'Nay, thou wouldst not have mercy on thyself; who brought this upon thee but thy own wilfulness?' And if your brethren see you everlastingly in misery, how shall they pity you that were your own destroyers, and would not be dissuaded?

6. It will everlastingly make you your own tormentors in hell, to think that you brought yourselves wilfully to that misery. O what a piercing thought it will be for ever to think with yourselves that this was your own doing! that you were warned of this day, and warned again, but it would not do; that you wilfully sinned, and wilfully turned away from God! that you had time as well as others, but you abused it; you had teachers as well as others, but you refused their instruction; you had holy examples, but you did not imitate them; you were offered Christ, and grace, and glory, as well as others, but you had more mind of your fleshly pleasures! you had a price in your hands, but you had not a

heart to lay it out. Prov. xvii. 16. Can it fail to torment you to think of this your present folly? O that your eyes were open to see what you have done in the wilful wronging of your own souls! and that you better understood these words of God. Prov. viii. 33—36. "Hear instruction and be wise, and refuse it not. Blessed is the man that heareth me, watching daily at my gates, waiting at the posts of my doors: for whoso findeth me findeth life, and shall obtain favour of the Lord. But he that sinneth against me, wrongeth his own soul. All they that hate me love death."

And now I am come to the conclusion of this work, my heart is troubled to think how I shall leave you, lest after this the flesh should still deceive you, and the world and the devil should keep you asleep, and I should leave you as I found you, till you awake in hell. Though in care of your poor souls, I am afraid of this, as knowing the obstinacy of a carnal heart; yet I can say with the prophet Jeremiah, xvii. 16. "I have not desired the woful day, thou Lord knowest." I have not with James and John desired that "fire might come from heaven" to consume them that refused Jesus Christ. Luke ix. 54. But it is the preventing of the eternal fire that I have been all this while endeavouring: and O that it had been a needless work! That God and conscience might have been as willing to spare me this labour as some of you could have been. Dear friends, I am so loth that you should lie in everlasting fire, and be shut out of heaven, if it be possible to prevent it, that I shall once more ask you, what do you now resolve? Will you turn or die? I look upon you as a physician on his patient, in a dangerous disease, that saith to him, 'Though you are far gone, take but this medicine, and forbear but those few things that are hurtful to you, and I dare warrant your life; but if you will not do this, you are but a dead man.' What would you think of such a man, if the physician, and all the friends he hath, cannot persuade him to take one medicine to save his life, or to forbear one or two poisonous things that would kill him? This is your case. As far as you are gone in sin, do but now turn and come to Christ, and take his remedies, and your souls shall live. Cast up your deadly sins by repentance, and return not to the poisonous vomit any more, and you shall do well. But yet, if it were your bodies that we had to deal with, we might partly know what to do for you. Though you would not consent, yet you might be held or bound while the medicine were poured down your throats, and hurtful things might be kept from you. But about your souls it cannot be so; we cannot convert you against your wills. There is no carrying madmen to heaven in fetters. You may be condemned against your wills, because you sinned with your wills; but you cannot be saved against your wills. The wisdom of God has thought meet to lay men's salvation or destruction exceedingly much upon the choice of their own will, that no man shall come to heaven that chose not the way to heaven; and no man shall come to hell, but shall be forced to say, 'I have the thing I chose; my own will did bring me hither.' Now, if I could but get you to be willing, to be thoroughly, and resolvedly, and habitually willing, the work were more than half done. And alas! must we lose our friends, and must they lose their God, their happiness, their souls, for want of this? O God forbid! It is a strange thing to me that men are so inhuman and stupid in the greatest matters, who in lesser things are civil and courteous, and good neighbours. For aught I know, I have the love of all, or almost all my neighbours, so far, that if I should send to any man in the town, or parish, or country, and request a reasonable courtesy of them, they would grant it me; and yet when I come to request of them the greatest matter in the world, for themselves, and not for me, I can have nothing of many of them but a patient hearing. I know not whether people think a man in the pulpit is in good earnest or not, and means as he speaks; for I think I have few neighbours, but, if I were sitting familiarly with them, and telling them what I have seen and done, or known in the world, they themselves shall see and know in the world to come, they would be lieve me, and regard what I say; but when I tell them, from the infallible word of God, what they themselves shall see and know in the world to come, they show by their lives, that they do either not believe it or not much regard it. If I met any one of them on the way, and told them yonder is a coal-pit, or there is a quicksand, or there are thieves lying in wait for you, I could persuade them to turn by; but when I tell them that Satan lieth in wait for them, and that sin is poison to them, and that hell is not a matter to be jested with, they go on as if they did not hear me. Truly, neighbours, I am in as good earnest with you in the pulpit as I am in my familiar discourse; and if ever you will regard me, I beseech you let it be here. I think there is not a man of you all, but, if my own soul lie at your wills, you would be willing to save it, though I cannot promise that you would leave your sins for it. Tell me, thou drunkard, art thou so cruel to me, that thou wouldst not forbear a few cups of drink, if thou knewest it would save my soul from hell? Hadst thou rather that I did burn there for ever than thou shouldst live soberly as other men do? If so, may I not say, thou art an unmerciful monster, and not a man? If I came hungry or naked to one of your doors, would you not part with more than a cup of drink to relieve me? I am confident you would. If it were to save my life, I know you would, some of you, hazard your own; and yet will you not be entreated to part with your sensual pleasures for your own salvation? Wouldst thou forbear a hundred cups of drink, to save my life, if it were in thy power, and wilt thou not do it to save thy own soul? I profess to you, sirs, I am as hearty a beggar with you this day for the saving of your own souls, as I would be for my own supply, if I were forced to come begging to your doors; and therefore if you would hear me then, hear me now. If you would pity me then, be entreated now to pity yourselves. I do again beseech you, as if it were on my bended knees, that you would hearken to your Redeemer, and turn, that you may live. All you that have lived in ignorance, and carelessness, and presumption to this day; all you that have been drowned in the cares of the world, and have no mind of God, and eternal glory; all you that are enslaved to your fleshly desires of meats and drinks, sports and lusts; and all you that know not the necessity of holiness, and never were acquainted with the sanctifying work of the Holy Ghost upon your souls; that never embraced your blessed Redeemer by a lively faith, and with admiring and thankful apprehensions of his love; and that never felt a higher estimation of God and heaven, and heartier love to them than to your fleshly prosperity, and the things below,—I earnestly beseech you, not only for my sake, but for the Lord's sake, and for your soul's sake, that you go not one day longer in your former condition, but look about you, and cry to God for converting grace, that you may be made new creatures, and may escape the plagues that are a little before you. And if ever you will do any thing for me, grant me this request, to turn from your evil ways and live. Deny me any thing that ever I shall ask you for myself, if you will but grant me this; and if you deny me this, I care not for any thing else that you would grant me. Nay, as ever you will do any thing at the request of the Lord that made you and redeemed you, deny him not this; for if you deny him this, he cares for nothing that you shall grant him. As ever you would have him hear your prayers, and grant your requests, and do for you at the hour of death and day of judgment, or in any of your extremities, deny not his request now in the day of your prosperity.

O sirs, believe it, death and judgment, and heaven and hell, are other matters when you come near them, than they seem to carnal eyes afar off: then you would hear such a message as I bring you with more awakened regardful hearts.

Well, though I cannot hope so well of all, I will hope that some of you are by this time purposing to turn and live; and that you are ready to ask me, as the Jews did Peter, (Acts ii. 37.) when they were pricked in their hearts, and said, "Men and brethren, what shall we do?" How might we come to be truly converted? We are willing, if we did but know our duty. God forbid that we should choose destruction, by refusing conversion, as hitherto we have done.

If these be the thoughts and purposes of your hearts, I say of you as God did of a promising people, Deut. v. 28, 29. "They have well said all that they have spoken: O that there was such a heart in them, that they would fear me, and keep all my commandments always!" Your purposes are good: O that there were but a heart in you to perform these purposes! And in hope hereof I shall gladly give you direction what to do, and that but briefly, that you may the easier remember it for your practice.

Direction 1.—If you would be converted and saved, labour to understand the necessity and true nature of conversion: for what, and from what, and to what, and by what it is that you must turn.

Consider in what a lamentable condition you are till the hour of your conversion, that you may see it is not a state to be rested in. You are under the guilt of all the sins that ever you committed, and under the wrath of God and the curse of his law: you are bond slaves to the devil, and daily employed in his work against the Lord, yourselves, and others: you are spiritually dead and deformed, as being devoid of the holy Life, and nature, and image of the Lord. You are unfit for any holy work. and do nothing that is truly pleasing to God. You are without any promise or assurance of his protection, and live in continual danger of his justice, not knowing what hour you may be snatched away to hell, and most certain to be lost if you die in that condition; and nothing short of conversion can prevent it. Whatever civilities or amendments are short of true conversion, will never procure the saving of your souls. Keep the true sense of this natural misery, and so of the necessity of conversion on your hearts.

And then you must understand what it is to be converted; it is to have a new heart or disposition, and a new conversation.

Quest. I. For what must we turn?

Answ. For these ends following, which you may attain: 1. You shall immediately be made living members of Christ, and have an interest in him, and be renewed after the image of God, and be adorned with all his graces, and quickened with a new and heavenly life, and saved from the tyranny of Satan, and the dominion of sin, and be justified by the curse of the law, and have the pardon of all the sins of your whole lives, and be accepted of God, and made his sons, and have liberty with boldness to call him Father, and go to him by prayer in all your needs, with a promise of acceptance; you shall have the holy Ghost to dwell in you, to sanctify and guide you; you shall have part in the brotherhood, communion, and prayers of the saints; you shall be fitted for God's service, and be freed from the dominion of sin, and be useful and a blessing to the place where you live; and shall have the promise of this life and that which is to come; you shall want nothing that is truly good for you, and your necessary afflictions you will be enabled to bear; you may have some taste of communion with God in the Spirit, especially in all holy ordinances, where God prepareth a feast for your souls; you shall be heirs of heaven while you live on earth, and may foresee by faith the everlasting glory, and so may live and die in peace; and you shall never be so low but your happiness will be incomparably greater than your misery.

How precious is every one of these blessings, which I do but briefly name, and which in this life you may receive!

And then, 2. At death your souls shall go to Christ, and at the day of judgment both soul and body shall be glorified and justified, and enter into your Master's joy, where your happiness will consist in these particulars:

1. You shall be perfected yourselves; your mortal bodies shall be made immortal, and the corruptible shall put on incorruption; you shall no more be hungry, or thirsty, or weary, or sick, nor shall you need to fear either shame, or sorrow, or death, or hell; your souls shall be perfectly freed from sin, and perfectly fitted for the knowledge, and love, and praises of the Lord.

2. Your employment shall be to behold your glorified Redeemer, with all your holy fellow-citizens of heaven, and to see the glory of the most blessed God, and to love him perfectly, and be beloved by him, and to praise him everlastingly.

3. Your glory will contribute to the glory of the New Jerusalem, the city of the living God; which is more than to have a private felicity to yourselves.

4. Your glory will contribute to the glorifying of your Redeemer, who will everlastingly be magnified and pleased in that you are the travail of his soul; and this is more than the glorifying of yourselves.

5. And the eternal Majesty, the living God, will be glorified in your glory, both as he is magnified by your praises, and as he communicateth of his glory and goodness to you, and as he is pleased in you, and in the accomplishment of his glorious work, in the glory of the New Jerusalem, and of his Son.

All this the poorest beggar of you that is converted, shall certainly and endlessly enjoy.

II. You see for what you must turn: next you must understand from what you must turn; and this is, in a word, from your carnal self, which is the end of all the unconverted:—from the flesh that would be pleased before God, and would still be enticing you;—from the world, that is the bait; and from the devil, that is the angler for souls, and the deceiver. And so from all known and wilful sins.

III. Next you must know to what end you must turn; and that is, to God as your end; to Christ as the way to the Father; to holiness as the way appointed you by Christ; and to the use of all the helps and means of grace afforded you by the Lord.

IV. Lastly, You must know by what you must turn; and that is by Christ, as the only Redeemer and Intercessor; and by the Holy Ghost, as the Sanctifier; and by the word, as his instrument or means; and by faith and repentance, as the means and duties on your part to be performed. All this is of necessity.

DIRECTION II.—If you will be converted and saved, be much in serious secret consideration. Inconsiderateness undoes the world. Withdraw yourselves oft into retired secrecy, and there bethink you of the end why you were made, of the life you have lived, of the time you have lost, the sins you have committed; of the love and sufferings, and fulness of Christ; of the danger you are in; of the nearness of death and judgment; of the certainty and excellency of the joys of heaven; and of the certainty and terror of the torments of hell, and the eternity of both; and of the necessity of conversion and a holy life. Absorb your hearts in such considerations as these.

DIRECTION III.—If you will be converted and saved, attend upon the word of God, which is the ordinary means. Read the Scripture, or hear it read, and other holy writings that do apply it; constantly attend on the public preaching of the word. As God will light the world by the sun, and not by himself without it, so will he convert and save men by his ministers, who are the lights of the world. Acts xxvi. 17, 18. Matt. v. 14. When he had miraculously humbled Paul, he sent him to Ananias, Acts ix. 10; and when he had sent an angel to Cornelius, it was but to bid him send for Peter, who must tell him what to believe and do.

DIRECTION IV.—Betake yourselves to God in a course of earnest constant prayer. Confess and lament your former lives, and beg his grace to illuminate and convert you. Beseech him to pardon what is past, and to give you his Spirit, and change your hearts and lives, and lead you in his ways, and save you from temptation. Pursue this work daily, and be not weary of it.

DIRECTION V.—Presently give over your known and wilful sins. Make a stand, and go that way no farther. Be drunk no more, but avoid the very occasion of it. Cast away your lusts and sinful pleasures with detestation. Curse, and swear, and rail no more; and if you have wronged any, restore, as Zaccheus did: if you will commit again your old sins, what blessing can you expect on the means for conversion?

DIRECTION VI.—Presently, if possible, change your company, if it hath hitherto been bad; not by forsaking your necessary relations, but your unnecessary sinful companions; and join yourselves with those that fear the Lord, and inquire of them the way to heaven. Acts ix. 19, 26. Psalm xv. 4.

DIRECTION VII.—Deliver up yourselves to the Lord Jesus, as the physician of your souls, that he may pardon you by his blood, and sanctify you by his Spirit, by his word and ministers, the instruments of the Spirit. He is the way, the truth, and the life; there is no coming to the Father but by him. John xiv. 6. Nor is there any other name under heaven, by which you can be saved. Acts iv. 12. Study, therefore, his person and natures, and what he hath done for you, and what he is to you, and what he will be, and how he is fitted to the full sup ply of all your necessities.

DIRECTION VIII.—If you mean indeed to turn and live, do it speedily, without delay. If you be not willing to turn to-day, you are not willing to do it at all. Remember, you are all this while in your blood, under the guilt of many thousand sins, and under God's wrath, and you stand at the very brink of hell; there is but a step between you and death: and this is not a case for a man that is well in his wits to be quiet in. Up therefore presently, and fly as for your lives, as you would be gone out of your house if it were all on fire over your head. O, if you did but know in what continual danger you live, and what daily unspeakable loss you sustain, and what a safer and sweeter life you might live, you would not stand trifling, but presently turn. Multitudes miscarry that wilfully delay, when they are convinced that it must be done. Your lives are short and uncertain; and what a case are you in if you die before you thoroughly turn! Ye have staid too long already, and wronged God too long. Sin getteth strength while you delay. Your conversion will grow more hard and doubtful. You have much to do, and therefore put not all off to the last, lest God forsake you, and give you up to yourselves, and then you are undone for ever.

DIRECTION IX.—If you will turn and live, do it unreservedly, absolutely, and universally. Think not to capitulate with Christ, and divide your heart between him and the world; and to part with some sins, and keep the rest; and to let that go which your flesh can spare. This is but self-deluding; you must in heart and resolution forsake all that you have, or else you cannot be his disciples. Luke xiv. 26, 33. If you will not take God and heaven for your portion, and lay all below at the feet of Christ, but you must needs also have your good things here, and have an earthly portion, and God and glory are not enough for you,—it is vain to dream of salvation on these terms; for it will not be. If you seem never so religious, if yet it be but a carnal righteousness, and if the flesh's prosperity, or pleasure, or safety, be still excepted in your devotedness to God, this is as certain a way to death as open profaneness, though it be more plausible.

Direction X.—If you will turn and live, do it resolvedly, and stand not still deliberating, as if it were a doubtful case. Stand not wavering, as if you were uncertain whether God or the flesh be the better master, or whether sin or holiness be the better way, or whether heaven or hell be the better end. But away with your former lusts, and presently, habitually, fixedly resolve. Be not one day of one mind, and the next day of another; but be at a point with all the world, and resolvedly give up yourselves and all you have to God. Now, while you are reading, or hearing this, resolve; before you sleep another night, resolve; before you stir from the place, resolve; before Satan have time to take you off, resolve. You never turn indeed till you do resolve, and that with a firm unchangeable resolution.

And now I have done my part in this work, that you may turn to the call of God, and live. What will become of it I cannot tell. I have cast the seed at God's command; but it is not in my power to give the increase. I can go no further with my message; I cannot bring it to your heart, nor make it work; I cannot do your parts for you to entertain it and consider it; nor can I do God's part, by opening your heart to entertain it; nor can I show heaven or hell to your sight, nor give you new and tender hearts. If I knew what more to do for your conversion, I hope I should do it.

But O thou that art the gracious Father of spirits, thou hast sworn thou delightest not in the death of the wicked, but rather that they turn and live; deny not thy blessing to these persuasions and directions, and suffer not thine enemies to triumph in thy sight, and the great deceiver of souls to prevail against thy Son, thy Spirit, and thy Word! O pity poor unconverted sinners, that have no hearts to pity or help themselves! Command the blind to see, and the deaf to hear, and the dead to live, and let not sin and death be able to resist thee. Awaken the secure, resolve the unresolved, confirm the wavering; and let the eyes of sinners, that read these lines, be next employed in weeping over their sins, and bring them to themselves, and to thy Son, before their sins have brought them to perdition. If thou say but the word, these poor endeavours shall prosper to the winning of many a soul to their everlasting joy, and thine everlasting glory.—*Amen.*

NOW OR NEVER.

EXTRACTED FROM

A DISCOURSE OF REV. RICHARD BAXTER.

ECCLES. IX. 10.

Whatsoever thy hand findeth to do, do it with thy might; for there is no work, nor device, nor knowledge nor wisdom, in the grave, whither thou goest.

THE mortality of man being the principal subject of Solomon in this chapter, and observing that wisdom and piety exempt not men from death, he first hence infers, that God's love or hatred to one man above another, is not to be gathered by his dealings with them here, where all things in the common course of providence come alike to all. The common sin hath introduced death as a common punishment, which levels all, and ends all the contrivances, businesses, and enjoyments of this life, to good and bad; and discriminating justice is not ordinarily manifested here: an epicure or infidel would think Solomon was here pleading his unmanly impious cause: but it is not the cessation of the life, or operations, or enjoyments of the soul that he is speaking of, as if there were no life to come, or the soul of man were not immortal; but it is the cessation of all the actions, and honours, and pleasures of this life, which to good or bad shall be no more. Here they have no more reward, the memory of them will be here forgotten. "They have no more a portion for ever in any thing that is done under the sun."

From hence he further infers, that the comforts of life are but short and transitory, and therefore that what the creature can afford, must be presently taken: and as the wicked shall have no more but present pleasures, so the faithful may take their lawful comforts in the present moderate use of the creatures. For if their enjoyment be of right and use to any, it is to them; and, therefore, though they may not use them to their hurt, to the pampering of their flesh, and strengthening their lusts, and hindering spiritual duties, benefits, and salvation; yet must they "serve the Lord with joyfulness, and with gladness of heart, for the abundance of all things" which he giveth them.

Next he infers, from the brevity of man's life, the necessity of speed and diligence in his duty. And this is in the words of my text; where you have, 1. The duty commanded. 2. The reason or motive to enforce it.

The duty is in the first part, "Whatsoever thy hand findeth to do," that is, whatever work is assigned thee by God to do in this thy transitory life, "do it with thy might;" that is, 1. Speedily, without delay. 2. Diligently; and not with slothfulness, or by halves.

2. The motive is in the latter part, "For there is no work, nor device, nor knowledge, nor wisdom, in the grave, whither thou goest;" that is, it must be *now or never*. The grave, where thy work cannot be done, will quickly end thy opportunities. The sense is obviously contained in these two propositions:—

DOCTRINE 1.—"The work of this life cannot be done when this life is ended: or, There is no working in the grave, to which we are all making haste."

DOCTRINE 2.—"Therefore, while we have time, we must do our best: or do the work of this present life with vigour and diligence."

1. It is from an unquestionable and commonly acknowledged truth, that Solomon here urgeth us to diligence in duty; and therefore to prove it would be but loss of time. As there are two worlds for man to live in, and so two lives for man to live, so each of these lives has its peculiar employment. This is the life of preparation: the next is the life of rewards or punishments. We are now but in the womb of eternity, and must live hereafter in the open world. We are now but sent to school to learn the work we must do for ever: this is the time of our apprenticeship; we are learning the trade that we must live upon in heaven. We run now, that we may then receive the crown; we fight now, that we may then triumph in victory. The grave hath no work; but heaven hath work, and hell hath suffering: there is no repentance unto life hereafter; but there is repentance to torment and to desperation. There is no believing of a happiness unseen in order to the obtaining of it; or of a misery unseen in order to the escaping of it; nor believing in a Saviour in order to these ends. But there is the fruition of the happiness which was here believed; and feeling of the misery that men would not believe; and suffering from him as a righteous Judge, whom they rejected as a merciful Saviour. So that it is not all work that ceaseth at our death; but only the work of this present life.

And indeed no reason can show us the least probability of doing our work when our time is gone, that was given us to do it in. If it can be done, it must be, 1. By the recalling of our time. 2. By the return of life. 3. Or, by opportunity in another life. But there is no hope of any of these.

1. Who knoweth not that time cannot be recalled? That which once was, will be no more. Yesterday will never come again. To-day is passing.

and will not return. You may work while it is day; but when you have lost that day, it will not return for you to work in. While your candle burneth, you may make use of its light; but when it is done, it is too late to use it. No force of medicine, no orator's elegant persuasions, no worldling's wealth, no prince's power, can call back one day or hour of time. If they could, what endeavours would there be used, when extremity hath taught them to value what they now despise! What bargaining would there be at last, if time could be purchased for any thing that man can give. Then misers would bring out their wealth, and say, 'All this will I give for one day's time of repentance more.' And lords and knights would lay down their honours, and say, 'Take all, and let us be beggars, if we may have but one year of the time that we mispent.' Then kings would lay down their crowns, and say, 'Let us be equal with the lowest subjects, so we may but have the time again that we wasted in the cares and pleasures of the world.' Kingdoms would then seem a contemptible price for the recovery of time.

The time that is now idled and talked away; the time that is now feasted and complimented away, that is unnecessarily sported and slept away; that is wickedly and presumptuously sinned away; how precious will it one day seem to all! How happy a bargain would they think they had made, if at the dearest rates they could redeem it?

The profanest mariner falls a praying, when he fears his time is at an end. If importunity would then prevail, how earnestly would they pray for the recovery of time that formerly derided praying! What a liturgy would death teach the trifling time-despising gallants, the idle, busy, dreaming, active, ambitious, covetous lovers of this world, if time could be entreated to return! How passionately then would they pour out their requests! 'O that we might once see the days of hope, and means, and mercy, which once we saw, and would not see! O that we had those days to spend in penitential tears and prayers, and holy preparations for an endless life, which we spent at cards, in needless recreations, in idle talk, in humouring others, in the pleasing of our flesh, or in the inordinate cares and businesses of the world! O that our youthful vigour might return! that our years might be renewed! that the days we spent in vanity might be recalled! that ministers might again be sent to us publicly and privately, with the message of grace which we once made light of! that the sun would once more shine upon us! and that patience and mercy would once more reassume their work!'

If cries or tears, or price or pains, would bring back lost abused time, how happy were the now distracted, dreaming, dead-hearted, and impenitent world! If it would then serve their turn to say to the vigilant believers, "Give us of your oil, for our lamps are gone out;" or to cry, "Lord, Lord, open to us," when the door is shut; the foolish would be saved as well as the wise. But "this is the day of salvation! this is the accepted time." While it is called to-day, hearken, and harden not your hearts. Awake, thou that sleepest, and use the light that is afforded thee by Christ; or else the everlasting utter darkness will shortly end thy time and hope.

2. And as time can never be recalled, so life shall never be here restored: "If a man die, shall he live (here) again?" All the days of our appointed time we must therefore wait, in faith and diligence, till our change shall come. One life is appointed us on earth, to despatch the work on which our everlasting life dependeth, and we shall have but one. Lose that, and all is lost for ever: yet you may hear, and read, and learn, and pray; but when this life is ended, it shall be so no more. You shall rise from the dead indeed to judgment, and to the life that you are now preparing for; but never to such a life as this on earth: your life is as the fighting of a

battle, that must be won or lost at once. There is no coming hither again to mend what is done amiss. Oversights must be presently corrected by repentance, or else they are everlastingly past remedy. Now, if you be not truly converted, you may be; if you find that you are carnal and miserable, you may be healed; if you are unpardoned, you may be pardoned; if you are enemies, you may be reconciled to God: but when once the thread of life is cut, your opportunities are at an end. Now you may inquire of your friends and teachers what you must do to be saved; and you may receive particular instructions and exhortations, and God may bless them, to the illuminating, renewing, and saving of your souls. But when life is past, it will be so no more. O then, if departed souls might but return, and once more be tried with the means of life, what joyful tidings would it be! How welcome would the messenger be that bringeth it! Had hell but such an offer as this, and would any cries procure it from their righteous Judge, O what a change would be among them! How importunately would they cry to God, 'O send us once again to the earth! Once more let us see the face of mercy, and hear the tenders of Christ and of salvation! Once more let the ministers offer us their helps, and teach in season and out of season, in public and in private, and we will refuse their help and exhortations no more: we will hate them, and drive them away from our houses and towns no more. Once more let us have thy word, and ordinances, and try whether we will not believe them, and use them better than we did. Once more let us have the help and company of thy saints, and we will scorn them, and abuse them, and persecute them no more. O for the great invaluable mercy of such a life as once we had! O try us once more with such a life, and see whether we will not contemn the world, and close with Christ, and live as strictly, and pray as earnestly, as those that we hated and abused for so doing! O that we might once more be admitted into the holy assemblies, and have the Lord's days to spend in the business of our salvation! We would plead no more against the power and purity of the ordinances; we would no more call that day a burden, nor hate them that spent it in works of holiness, nor plead for the liberty of the flesh therein.'

He that would have Lazarus sent from the dead to warn his unbelieving brethren on earth, no doubt would have strongly purposed himself on a reformation, if he might once more have been tried? and how earnestly would he have begged for such a trial, that begged so hard for a drop of water? But, alas! such mouths must be stopped for ever with—"Remember that thou, in thy lifetime, received thy good things."

So that "it is appointed for men once to die, and after that the judgment." But there is no return to earth again: the places of your abode, employment, and delight, shall know you no more. You must see these faces of your friends, and converse in flesh with men no more. This world, those houses, that wealth and honour, as to any fruition, must be to you as if you had never known them.

You must assemble here but a little while. Yet a little longer, and we must preach, and you must hear it no more for ever. That therefore which you will do, must presently be done, or it will be too late. If ever you will repent and believe, it must be now. If ever you will be converted and sanctified, it must be now. If ever you will be pardoned and reconciled to God, it must be now. If ever you will reign, it is now that you must fight and conquer. "O that you were wise, that you understood this, and that you would consider your latter end!" And that you would let those words sink down into your hearts, which came from the heart of the Redeemer, as was witnessed by his tears: "If thou hadst known, even thou, at least in this thy day, the things which belong unto thy peace! but now they are hid from thine eyes." And that these warnings may not be the less regarded, because you have so often heard them; when often hearing increaseth your obligation, and diminisheth not the truth, or your danger.

3. And as there is no return to earth, so is there no doing this work hereafter. Heaven and hell are for other work. The harvest doth presuppose the seed-time, and the labour of the husbandman. It is now that you must sow, and hereafter that you must reap. It is now that you must work, and then that you must receive your wages.

Is this believed and considered by the sleepy world? Alas! sirs, do you live as men that must live here no more? Do you work as men that must work no more, and pray as men that must pray no more, when once the time of work is ended? What thinkest thou! will God command the sun to stand still while thou rebellest or forgettest thy work and him! Dost thou expect he should pervert the course of nature, and continue the spring and seed-time till thou hast a mind to sow? Will he renew thy age, and make thee young again, and call back the hours that thou hast prodigally wasted on thy lusts and idleness? Canst thou look for this at the hand of God, when nature and Scripture assure thee of the contrary? If not, why hast thou not yet done with thy beloved sins? Why hast thou not yet begun to live? Why sittest thou still while thy soul is unrenewed, and all thy preparation for death and judgment is yet to make? How fain would Satan find thee thus at death? How fain would he have leave to blow out thy candle, before thou hast entered into the way of life? Dost thou look to have preachers sent after thee, to bring thee the mercy which thy contempt here left behind? Wilt thou hear and be converted in the grave and hell? or wilt thou be saved without holiness? that is, in despite of God that hath resolved it shall not be. O ye sons of sleep, of death, of darkness, awake, and live, and hear the Lord, before the grave and hell have shut their mouths upon you! Hear now, lest hearing be too late! Hear now, if you will ever hear. Hear now, if you have ears to hear! And, O ye sons of light, that see what sleeping sinners see not, call to them, and ring them such a peal of lamentations, tears, and compassionate entreaties, as is suited to such a dead and doleful state; who knows but God may bless it to awake them?

II. If any of you be so far awakened as to ask me what I am calling you to do, my text tells you in general, Up and be doing; look about you, and see what you have to do, and do it with your might.

1. "Whatsoever thy hand findeth to do," that is, whatsoever is a duty imposed by the Lord, whatsoever is a means conducing to thy own or others' welfare; whatsoever necessity calleth thee to do, and opportunity alloweth thee to do.

"Thy hand findeth;" that is, thy executive powers by the conduct of thy understanding, is now to do.

"Do it with thy might." Do thy best in it.

1. Trifle not, but do it presently, without unnecessary delay.

2. Do it resolutely; remain not doubtful, unresolved, in suspense, as if it were yet a question with thee whether thou shouldst do it, or not.

3. Do it with thy most awakened affections, and serious intention of the powers of thy soul. Sleepiness and insensibility are most unsuitable to such works.

4. Do it with all necessary forecast and contrivance; not with a distracting hindering care; but with such a care as may show that you despise not your Master, and are not regardless of his work: and with such a care as is suited to the difficulties and nature of the thing, and is necessary to the due accomplishment of it.

5. Do it not slothfully, but vigorously and with diligence. "Hide not thy hand in thy bosom with the slothful," and say not, "There is a lion in the

way." The negligent and the vicious, the waster and the slothful, differ but as one brother from another. As the self-murder of the wilful ungodly, so also the desire of the slothful killeth him, because his hands refuse to labour. "The soul of the sluggard desireth and hath nothing; but the soul of the diligent shall be made fat." "Be not slothful in business, but be fervent in spirit, serving the Lord."

6. Do it with constancy, and not with destructive pauses and intermissions, or with weariness and turning back. "The righteous shall hold on his way, and he that is of clean hands shall be stronger and stronger." "Be steadfast, unmoveable, always abounding in the work of the Lord, forasmuch as you know that your labour is not in vain in the Lord." "Be not weary in well-doing: for in due season we shall reap if we faint not."

But, that misunderstanding hinder not the performance, I shall acquaint you further with the sense, by these few explicatory cautions.

1. The might and diligence here required, exclude not the necessity of deliberation and prudent conduct. Otherwise, the faster you go, the further you may go out of the way; and misguided zeal may spoil all the work, and make it but an injury to others or yourselves. A little imprudence in the season, and order, and manner of a duty, sometimes may spoil it, and hinder the success, and make it do more hurt than good. How many a sermon, or prayer, or reproof, is made the matter of derision and contempt, for some imprudent passages or deportment! God sendeth not his servants to be jesters of the world, or to play the madman as David in his fears; we must be wise and innocent, as well as resolute and valiant: though fleshly and worldly wisdom be not desirable, as being but foolishness with God; yet the wisdom which is from above, and is first pure and then peaceable, and is acquainted with the high and hidden mysteries, and is justified of her children, must be the guide of all

our holy actions. Holiness is not blind: illumination is the first part of sanctification. Believers are children of the light. Nothing requireth so much wisdom as the matters of God, and of our salvation. Folly is most unsuitable to such excellent employments, and most unbeseeming the sons of the Most High. It is a spirit of wisdom that animateth all the saints. "Howbeit we speak wisdom among them that are perfect; yet not the wisdom of this world, nor of the princes of this world, that come to nought: but we speak the wisdom of God in a mystery, even the hidden wisdom, which God ordained before the world unto our glory." It is the treasures of wisdom that dwell in Christ, and are communicated to his members. We must "walk in wisdom toward them that are without." And our works must be "shown out of a good conversation, with meekness of wisdom."

2. Though you must work with your might, yet with a diversity agreeable to the quality of your several works. Some works must be preferred before others: all cannot be done at once. That is a sin out of season, which in season is a duty. The greatest, and the most urgent work must be preferred. And some works must be done with double fervour and resolution, and some with less. Buying and selling, and possessing, and using the world, must be done with a fear of overdoing, and in a manner as if we did them not, though they also must have a necessary diligence. God's "kingdom and its righteousness must be first sought." And our labour for the meat that perisheth, must be comparatively as none: "Labour not for the meat which perisheth, but for that meat which endureth unto everlasting life, which the Son of man shall give unto you: for him hath God the Father sealed."

3. Lastly, it is not an irregular, nor a self-disturbing vexatious violence that is required of us; but a sweet well-settled resolution, and a delightful expeditious diligence, that make the wheels more easily

get over those difficulties that clog and stop a slothful soul.

And now will you lend me the assistance of your consciences, for the transcribing of this command of God upon your hearts, and taking out a copy of this order, for the regulating of your lives? *Whatsoever* is not a work so comprehensive as to include any vanity or sin; but so comprehensive as to include all our duty.

1. To begin with the lowest: the very works of your bodily callings must have diligence. "In the sweat of your brows you must eat your bread." "Six days shalt thou labour, and do all that thou hast to do." "He that will not work, let him not eat." Disorderly walkers, busybodies, that will not work with quietness, and eat their own bread, are to be avoided and shamed by the church. "For we hear that there are some which walk among you disorderly, working not at all, but are busybodies. Now them that are such we command and exhort by our Lord Jesus Christ, that with quietness they work, and eat their own bread." Lazy servants are unfaithful to men and disobedient to God, who commandeth them to "obey their masters according to the flesh, (unbelieving, ungodly masters) in all things, (that concern their service) and that not with eye-service, as men-pleasers, but in singleness of heart, and in the fear of God, do whatsoever they do as to the Lord, and not unto men; knowing that of the Lord (even for this) they shall receive the reward of the inheritance." "But he that doth wrong (by slothfulness, or unfaithfulness) shall receive for the wrong which he hath done."

Success is God's ordinary temporal reward of diligence: "The hand of the diligent shall bear rule: but the slothful shall be under tribute. The slothful man roasteth not that which he took in hunting: but the substance of a diligent man is precious." And diseases, poverty, shame, disappointment, or self-tormenting melancholy, are his usual punishments of sloth. Hard labour redeemeth time you will have the more to lay out on greater works: the slothful is still behindhand, and therefore must leave much of his work undone.

2. Are you parents or governors of families? You have work to do for God, and for your children and servants' souls. Do it with your might: deal wisely, but seriously and frequently with them about their sin, their duty, and their hopes of heaven; tell them whither they are going, and which way they must go. Make them understand that they have a higher Father and Master that must be first served, and greater work than yours. Waken them from their natural insensibility and sloth: turn not all your family duties into lifeless customary forms; whether extemporary, or by rote; speak about God, and heaven, and hell, and holiness, with that seriousness which beseems men that believe what they say, and would have those believe it to whom they speak. Talk not either drowsily, or lightly, or jestingly of such dreadful, or joyful, inexpressible things. Remember, that your families and you are going to the grave, and to the world where there is no more room for your exhortations. There is no catechising, examining, or serious instructing them in the grave, whither they and you are going.—It must be *now* or *never:* and therefore do it with your might. " The words of God must be in your hearts, and you must diligently teach them to your children, talking of them when you sit in your houses, when you walk by the way, when you lie down, and when you rise up."

3. Have you ignorant or ungodly neighbours, whose misery calls for your compassion and relief? Speak to them, and help them with prudent diligence. Lose not your opportunities: stay not till death hath stopped your mouths, or stopped their ears. Stay not till they are out of hearing, or till heaven be lost, before you have seriously called on them to remember it. Go to their houses; take all

opportunities: stoop to their infirmities: bear with unthankful frowardness; it is for men's salvation. Remember there is no place for your instructions or exhortations in the grave or hell. Your dust cannot speak, and their dust cannot hear. Up, therefore, and be doing with all your might.

4. Hath God intrusted you with the riches of the world; with many talents or with few, by which he looketh you should relieve the needy, and especially should promote those works of piety which are the greatest charity? Give prudently, but willingly and liberally, while you have to give. It is your gain: the time of laying up a treasure in heaven, and furthering your salvation by that which hindereth other men's, and occasioneth their perdition. "As you have opportunity, do good to all men, but especially to them of the household of faith." "Cast thy bread upon the waters; for thou shalt find it after many days. Give a portion to seven and to eight; for thou knowest not what evil may be upon the earth." "In the morning sow thy seed, and in the evening withhold not thy hand: for thou knowest not whether shall prosper, this or that, or whether they both shall be alike good." "Withhold not good from them to whom it is due, when it is in the power of thy hand to do it. Say not to thy neighbour, go and come again, and to-morrow I will give, when thou hast it by thee." Lay up a foundation for the time to come. Do good before thy heart be hardened, thy riches blasted and consumed, thy opportunities taken away; part with it before it part with thee. Remember it must be *now* or *never*. There is no working in the grave.

5. Hath God intrusted you with power or interest, by which you may promote his honour in the world, and relieve the oppressed, and restrain the rage of impious malice? Hath he made you governors, and put the sword of justice into your hands? Up then and be doing with your might. Defend the innocent, protect the servants of the Lord, cherish

them that do well, be a terror to the wicked, encourage the strictest obedience to the universal Governor, discountenance the breakers of his laws. Your trust is great, and so is your advantage to do good; and how great will be your account, and how dreadful, if you be unfaithful!

6. To come yet a little nearer to you, and speak of the work that is yet to be done in your own souls; are any of you yet in the state of unrenewed nature, born only of the flesh, and not of the Spirit? "Minding the things of the flesh, and not the things of the Spirit," and consequently yet in the power of Satan, taken captive by him at his will? Up and be doing, if thou lovest thy soul. If thou carest whether thou shalt be in joy or misery for ever, bewail thy sin and spiritual distress. Go to Christ, cry mightily to him for his renewing, reconciling, and pardoning grace. Plead his satisfaction, his merits, and his promises; away with thy rebellion, and thy beloved sin; deliver up thy soul entirely to Christ, to be sanctified, governed and saved by him. Make no more demur; it is not a matter to be questioned, or trifled in. Let the earth be acquainted with thy bended knees, and the air with thy complaints and cries, and men with thy confessions and inquiries after the way of life; and heaven with thy sorrows, desires, and resolutions, till thy soul be acquainted with the Spirit of Christ, and with the new, the holy and heavenly nature, and thy heart have received the transcript of God's law, the impress of the Gospel, and so the image of thy Creator and Redeemer. For there is no conversion, renovation, or repentance unto life, in the grave whither thou goest. It must be *now* or *never*. And never saved if never sanctified: "Without holiness no man shall see the Lord."

7. Hast thou any prevailing sin to mortify, that either reigneth in thee, or woundeth thee and keepeth thy soul in darkness and unacquaintedness with God? Assault it resolutely; reject it speedily; abhor

the motions of it; turn away from the persons or things that would entice thee. Hate the doors of the harlot and of the ale-house, or the gaming-house; and go not as the "ox to the slaughter, and as a bird to the fowler's snare, and as a fool to the correction of the stocks, as if thou knewest not that it is for thy life." Why wilt thou be tasting of the poisoned cup? Wilt thou be sporting with the bait? Hast thou no where to walk or play, but at the brink of ruin? Must not the flesh be crucified, with its "affections and lusts?" Must it not be tamed and mortified, or thy soul condemned? "For if ye live after the flesh, ye shall die: but if ye through the Spirit do mortify the deeds of the body, ye shall live." Run not therefore as at uncertainty; fight not as one "that beats the air." Seeing this must be done, or thou art undone, delay and dally with sin no longer. Let this be the day; resolve, and resist it with thy might: it must be *now* or *never:* when death comes it is too late.

8. Art thou in a declined, fallen state? Decayed in grace? Hast thou lost thy first desires and love? Do thy first works, and do them with thy might. Delay not, but remember from whence thou art fallen. Cry out with Job, "O that I were as in months past; as in the days when God preserved me! when his candle shined upon my head, and when, by his light, I walked through darkness. As I was in the days of my youth, when the secret of God was on my tabernacle, when the Almighty was yet with me." Return, while thou hast day, lest the night surprise thee.

9. Art thou in the darkness of uncertainty concerning thy conversion, and thy everlasting state? Dost thou not know whether thou art in a state of life or death? And what should become of thee, if this were the day or hour of thy change? If thou art careless in thy uncertainty, and mindest not so great a business, be awakened, and call thy soul to its account; search and examine thy heart and life;

read and consider, and take advice of faithful guides. Canst thou carelessly sleep, and laugh, and sport, and follow thy business, as if thy salvation were made sure, when thou knowest not where thou must dwell for ever? "Examine yourselves whether you be in the faith; prove yourselves; know ye not your own selves, that Christ is in you, except ye be reprobates?" Give all diligence to make your calling and election sure." In the grave and hell there is no making sure of heaven; you are then past inquiries and self-examination, in order to any recovery or hope. Another kind of trial will finally resolve you. It must be *now* or *never*.

10. In all the duties of thy profession of piety, justice, or charity, to God, thyself, or others, up and be doing with thy might. Art thou seeking to inflame thy soul with love to God? Plunge thyself in the ocean of his love; admire his mercies; gaze upon the representations of his transcendant goodness; "O taste and see that the Lord is gracious!" Remember that he must be loved with all thy heart, and soul, and might; canst thou pour out thy love upon a creature, and give but a few barren drops to God?

When thou art fearing, let his fear command thy soul, and conquer all the fear of man. When thou art trusting him, do it without distrust, and cast all thy care and thyself upon him: trust him as a creature should trust his God, and the members of Christ should trust their head and dear Redeemer. When thou art making mention of his great and dreadful name, O do it with reverence, and awe, and admiration: and "take not the name of God in vain!" When thou art reading his word, let the majesty of the Author, and the greatness of the matter, and the gravity of the style, possess thee with an obedient fear. Love it, and let it be sweeter to thee than the honey-comb, and more precious than thousands of gold and silver. Resolve to do what there thou findest to be the will of God.

When thou art praying in secret, or in thy family, "do it with thy might:" cry mightily to God, as a soul under sin, wants, and danger, that is stepping into an endless life, should do. Let the reverence and the fervour of thy prayers, show that it is God himself that thou art speaking to: that it is heaven itself that thou art praying for; hell itself that thou art praying to be saved from. Wilt thou be dull and senseless on such an errand to the living God? Remember what lieth upon thy failing or prevailing: and that it must be *now* or *never*.

Art thou a preacher of the gospel, and takest charge of the souls of men? "Take heed to thyself and to the whole flock, over which the Holy Ghost hath made thee an overseer, to feed the church of God, which he hath purchased with his own blood." Let not the blood of souls, and the blood that purchased them, "be required at thy hands." Thou art charged "before God, and the Lord Jesus Christ, who shall judge the quick and the dead at his appearing, and his kingdom, that thou preach his word: be instant in season, and out of season; reprove, rebuke, and exhort, with all long-suffering and doctrine." "Teach every man, and exhort every man,—even night and day with tears." "Save men with fear, pulling them out of the fire. Cry aloud: lift up thy voice like a trumpet; tell them of their transgressions." Yet thou art alive, and they alive; yet thou hast a tongue, and they have ears: the final sentence hath not yet cut off their hopes. Preach, therefore, and preach with all thy might. Exhort them, privately and personally, with all the seriousness thou canst. Quickly, or it will be too late; prudently, or Satan will overreach thee; fervently, or thy words are likely to be disregarded. Remember, when thou lookest them in the faces when thou beholdest the assemblies, that they must be converted or condemned, sanctified on earth, or tormented in hell; and that this is the day: it must be *now* or *never*.

In a word, apply this quickening precept to all the duties of the Christian course. Be religious, and just, and charitable, in good earnest, if you would be taken for such when you look for the reward. "Work out your salvation with fear and trembling." "Strive to enter in at the strait gate; for many shall seek to enter, and shall not be able." Many run, but few receive the prize: so run that you may obtain. "If the righteous scarcely be saved, where shall the ungodly and sinner appear?" Let the doting world deride your diligence, and set themselves to hinder and afflict you: it will be but a little while before experience change their minds, and make them talk differently. Follow Christ fully: be diligent, and lose no time. The Judge is coming. Let not words, nor any thing that man can do, prevail with you to sit down, or stop you in a journey of such importance. Please God, though flesh, and friends, and all the world should be displeased. Whatever come of your reputation, or estates, or liberties, or lives, be sure you look to life eternal; and cast not that, on any hazard, for a withering flower, or a pleasant dream, or a picture of commodity, or any vanity that the Deceiver can present. "For what shall it profit you, to win the world, and lose your soul?" Obey God, though all the world forbid you. No power can save you from his justice; and none of them can deprive you of his reward. Though you lose your heads, you shall save your crowns; you no way save your lives so certainly, as by such losing them. One thing is necessary: do that with speed, and care, and diligence, which must be done, or you are lost for ever. They that are now against your much and earnest praying, will shortly cry as loud themselves in vain. When it is too late, how fervently will they beg for mercy, that now deride you for valuing and seeking it in time! But "then they shall call upon God, but he will not answer; they shall seek him early, but shall not find him: for that they hated knowledge, and did not choose the fear of the Lord: they would none of his counsel, but despised all his reproof." Up, therefore, and work with all thy might. Let unbelievers trifle, that know not that the righteous God stands over them, and know not that they are *now* to work for everlasting, and know not that heaven or hell is at the end. Let them delay, and laugh, and play, and dream away their time, that are drunk with prosperity, and mad with fleshly lusts and pleasures, and have lost their reason in the cares, and delusions, and vain-glory of the world. But shall it be so with thee, whose eyes are opened, who seest the God, the heaven, the hell, which they do but hear of as unlikely things? Wilt thou live awake, as they that are asleep? Wilt thou do in the day-light, as they do in the dark? Shall freemen live as Satan's slaves? Shall the living lie as still and useless as the dead? "Work then while it is day; for the night is coming, when none can work."

But you will say, perhaps, 'Alas! what might have we? We have no sufficiency of ourselves: without Christ we can do nothing. And this we find when it comes to the trial.'

1. I answer, It is not might that is originally thine own, that I am calling thee to exercise; but that which thou hast already received from God, and that which he is ready to bestow. Use well but all the might thou hast, and thou shalt find thy labour is not in vain.

2. Art thou willing to use the might thou hast, and to have more, and use it if thou hadst it? If thou art, thou hast then the strength of Christ: thou standest not, and workest not, by thy own strength; his promise is engaged to thee, and his strength is sufficient for thee. But if thou art not willing, thou art without excuse: when thou hast heaven and hell set open in the word of God to make thee willing, God will distinguish thy wilfulness from unwilling weakness.

3. There is more power in all of you than you use, or than you are well aware of. It wanteth but awakening to bring it into act. Do you not find, in your repentings, that the change is more in your will, than in your power? And in the awakening of your will and reason into act, than in the addition of mere abilities? And that therefore you befool yourselves for your sins and your neglects, and wonder that you had no more use of your understandings? Let but a storm at sea, or violent sickness or approaching death, rouse up and awaken the powers which you have, and you will find there was much more asleep in you than you used.

I shall, therefore, next endeavour to awaken your abilities, or tell you how you should awaken them.

When your souls are drowsy, and you are forgetting your God, and your latter end, and matters of eternity have little force and favour with you, when you grow lazy and superficial, and religion seems a lifeless thing, and you do your duty as if it were in vain, or against your wills; when you can lose your time, and delay repentance; and friends, and profit, and reputation, and pleasure, can be heard against the word of God, and take you off; when you do all by halves, and languish in your Christian course, as near to death—stir up your souls with the urgency of such questions as these:—

Question 1. Can I do no more than this for God, who gave me all, who deserveth all? Who seeth me in my duties and my sins? When he puts me purposely on the trial, what can I do for his sake and service? Can I do no more? Can I love him no more, and obey, and watch, and work no more?

Question 2. Can I do no more than this for Christ? For him that did so much for me? That obeyed so perfectly; walked so meekly; despising all the baits, and honours, and riches of the world? That loved me to the death; and offereth me freely all his benefits, and would bring me to eternal glory? Are these careless, cold, and dull endeavours, my best return for all his mercy?

Question 3. Can I do no more, when my salvation is the prize? when heaven or hell depends upon it? When I know this beforehand, and may see, in the glass of the Holy Scriptures, what is prepared for the diligent and the negligent, and what work there is, and will be for ever, in heaven and hell, on these accounts? Could I not do more, if my house were on fire, or my estate, or life, or friend, in danger, than I do for my salvation?

Question 4. Can I do no more for the souls of men; when they are undone for ever if they be not speedily delivered? Is this my love and compassion to my neighbour, my servant, friend, or child?

Question 5. Can I do no more for the church of God? for the public good? for the peace and welfare of the nation, and our posterity? in suppressing sin? in praying for deliverance? or in promoting works of public benefit?

Question 6. Can I do no more, that have loitered so long? and go no faster, that have slept till the evening of my days, when diligence must be the discovery of my repentance?

Question 7. Can I do no more, that know not now but I am doing my last? that see how fast my time makes haste, and know I must be quickly gone? that know it must be *now* or *never*.

Question 8. Can I do no better, when I know beforehand what a vexatious and heart-disquieting thing it will then be, to look back on times as irrecoverably lost, and on a life of trial as cast away upon impertinences, while the work that we lived for lay undone! Shall I now, by trifling, prepare such tormenting thoughts for my awakened conscience?

Question 9. Can I do no more, when I am sure I cannot do too much, and am sure there is nothing else to be preferred?

Question 10. Can I do no more, that have so much help? that have mercies of all sorts encouraging me, and creatures attending me; that have health to enable me, or affliction to remember and excite me; that have such a master, such a work, such a reward? who is less excusable for neglect than I?

Question 11. Could I do no more, if I were sure that my salvation lay on this one duty? that, according to this prayer, it should go with me for ever? or if the soul of my child, or servant, or neighbour, must speed for ever, as my endeavours speed with them now for their conversion? For aught I know, it may be thus.

By this time you may see what difference there is between the judgment of God and of the world; and what to think of the understandings of those men, be they high or low, learned or unlearned, who hate or oppose this holy diligence. God bids us love, and seek, and serve him, with all our heart, and soul, and might: and these men call them Zealots and Puritans that endeavour it; though, alas! they fall exceedingly short, when they have done their best. It is one of the most wonderful, monstrous deformities that ever befell the nature of man, that men, learned men—that men who in other things are wise, should seriously think that the utmost diligence to obey the Lord, and save our souls, is needless; and that ever they should take it for a crime, and make it a matter of reproach: that the serious, diligent obeying of God's laws, should be the matter of the common disdain and hatred of the world. It is not in vain that the Holy Ghost saith, "Marvel not, my brethren, if the world hate you;" implying, that we are apt to marvel at it; as I confess I have oft and greatly done. Methinks, it is so wonderful a plague and stain in nature, that it doth very much to confirm me of the truth of Scripture; of the doctrine of man's fall and original sin, and the necessity of a Reconciler, and of renewing grace.

Look upwards, sirs, and think whether heaven be worth our labour. Look downwards, and think whether earth be more worthy of it. Lay up your treasures where you must dwell for ever. If that be here, then scrape, and flatter, and get all that you can: but if it be not here, but in another life, then hearken to your Lord, and lay up for yourselves a treasure in heaven, and there let your very hearts be set. And, upon the peril of everlasting misery, hearken not to any man that will tempt you from a diligent holy life. It is a serious business; deal seriously in it, and be not laughed or mocked out of heaven.

All the commands, and promises, and threatenings of God, the most powerful preaching that, as it were, sets open heaven and hell, do not prevail with fleshly men, to leave the most sordid and unmanly sin: and shall the words or frowns of creeping dust prevail with thee against the work for which thou livest in the world, when thou hast still at hand unanswerable arguments from God, from thyself, from heaven and hell, to put thee on? Were it but for thy life, or the life of thy children, friend, yea, or enemy, or for the quenching of a fire in thy house, or in the town, wouldst thou not stir and do thy best? And wilt thou be idle when eternal life lies on it? Let Satan roar against thee by his instruments. Let sinners talk awhile of they know not what, till God hath made them change their note. These are not matters for a man to observe, that is engaged for an endless life. O what are these to the things that thou art called to prosecute? Hold on then, Christians, in the work that you have begun. Do it prudently, and do it universally. Take it together, works of piety, justice, and charity: but do it now without delay, and do it seriously with your might. I know not what cloud of darkness hath seized on those men's minds that speak against this, or what deadly damp hath seized on their hearts, that hath so benumbed and unmanned them.

For my own part, though I have long lived in a sense of the preciousness of time, and have not been wholly idle in the world; yet, when I have the deepest thoughts of the great everlasting consequence of my work, and of the uncertainty and shortness of my time, I am even amazed to think that my heart can be so slow and senseless, as to do no more in such a case. The Lord knows, and my conscience knows, that my slothfulness is so much my shame and admiration, that I am astonished to think that my resolutions are no stronger, my affections no livelier, and my labour and diligence no greater, when God is the commander, and his love the encourager, and his wrath the spur, and heaven or hell must be the issue. O, what lives should all of us live, that have things of such unspeakable consequence on our hands, if our hearts were not almost dead within us! Let who will speak against such a life, it shall be my daily grief and moan, that I am so dull, and do so little. I know that our works do not profit the Almighty, nor bear any proportion with his reward; nor can they stand in his sight, but as accepted in the Lord our righteousness, and perfumed by the odour of his merits. But I know they are necessary, and they are sweet. Without the holy employment of our faculties, this life will be but a burden or a dream, and the next an inexpressible misery. O therefore, that I had more of the love of God, that my soul could get but nearer to him, and move more swiftly upward by faith and love! O that I had more of holy life, and active diligence, though I had with it the scorns of all about me, and though they made me, as they once did better men, "as the filth of the world, and the off-scouring of all things!" O that I had more of this derided diligence, and holy converse with the Lord, though "my name was cast out as an evil doer," and I were spit at and buffeted by those that do now but secretly reproach! Might I more closely follow Christ in holiness, why should I grudge to bear his cross, and to be used as he was used? Knowing, that "if we suffer with him, we shall also reign with him; and the sufferings of this present time are not worthy to be compared with the glory which shall be revealed in us."

Alas, sirs! it is nothing but intoxicating prosperity, and sensual delights, and worldly diversions that make you think well of ungodly slothfulness, and make you think contemptuously of a heavenly life. There is not the boldest infidel in the world, nor the bitterest enemy to holiness, but shortly would wish they had rather been saints, with all the scorn and cruelty that malice can inflict on such, than to have braved it out in pride and gallantry, with the neglect of everlasting things.

Methinks I even see how you will passionately rage against yourselves, and tear your hearts with self-revenge, (if grace prevent it not by a safe repentance,) when you think too late how you lived on earth, and what golden times of grace you lost, and vilified all that would not lose them as foolishly as you. If repentance unto life made St. Paul call himself foolish, disobedient, deceived, and exceeding mad, (Tit. iii. 3. Acts xxvi. 11.) you may imagine how tormenting repentance will make you call yourselves too late.

O sirs! you cannot now conceive, what different thoughts will then possess you of a holy and unholy life. How mad you will think them that had but one life's time of preparation for eternal life, and desperately neglected it! And how sensible you will then be of the wisdom of believers, that knew their time, and used it while they had it! "Now wisdom is justified of all her children;" but then how sensibly will it be justified of all its enemies! O, with what remorse will undone souls look back on a life of mercy and opportunities, thus basely undervalued, and slept away in dreaming idleness, and fooled away for things of nought!

The language of that rich man, Luke xvi. may help you in your predictions. O how will you wonder at yourselves, that ever you could be so blind and senseless, as to be no more affected with the warnings of the Lord, and with the forethoughts of everlasting joy and misery! To have but one small part of time to do all that ever must be done by you for eternity, and say all that ever you must say, for your own or others' souls, and that this was spent in worse than nothing! To have but one uncertain life, in which you must run the race that wins or loses heaven for ever; and that you should be tempted with a thing of nought, to lose that one irrecoverable opportunity, and to sit still or run another way, when you should have been making haste with all your might! O sirs, the thoughts of this will be other kind of thoughts another day than now you feel them; you cannot now think how the thoughts of this will then affect you! That you had a time in which you might have prayed, with promise of acceptance, and had no hearts to take that time! That Christ was offered to you as well as he was offered to them that entertained him; that you are called on, and warned as well they, but obstinately despised and neglected all! That life and death were set before you, and the everlasting joys were offered to your choice, against the charms of sinful pleasures, and you might have freely had them if you would, and were told that holiness was the only way, and that it must be *now* or *never*, and yet that you chose your own destruction! These thoughts will be part of hell to the ungodly. They will wonder that reason could be so unreasonable; and that they, who had the common wit of man in other matters, should be so far beside themselves in that which is the only thing that is commendable to be wise for; that such reasonings should prevail with them against the clearest light, and nothing should be preferred before all things, and arguments fetched from chaff should conquer those that were fetched from heaven! O what heart-rending thoughts will these be, when eternity shall afford them leisure for an impartial review!

Come away speedily from the snares of sinners, and the company of deceived hardened men, and cast away the works of darkness. Heaven is before you! Death is at hand! The eternal God hath sent to call you! Mercy doth yet stretch forth its arms! You have stayed too long, and abused patience too much already: stay no longer! O now please God, and comfort us, and save yourselves, by resolving that "this shall be the day:" and faithfully performing this your resolution, "up and be doing:" believe, repent, desire, obey, and do all this with all your might; love him that you must love for ever, and love him with all your soul and might; seek that which is truly worth seeking, and will pay for all your cost and pains, and seek it first with all your might, remembering still it must be *now* or *never*.

And now I should conclude, I am loath to end for fear lest I have not yet prevailed with you What are you now resolved to do, from this day forward? It is work that we have been speaking of, and necessary work of endless consequence, which must be done, and quickly done, and thoroughly done. Are you not convinced that it is so? that ploughing and sowing are not more necessary to your harvest, than the work of holiness in this day of grace is necessary to your salvation? You are blind, if you see not this; you are dead, if you feel it not: what then will you do? O hear the God of heaven, if you will not hear us, who calleth to you Return and live! O hear him that shed his blood for souls, and tendereth you now salvation by his blood! O hear without any more delay, before all is gone, and you are gone, and he that now deceiveth you, torment you! Yet hold on a little longer in a carnal, earthly, unsanctified state, and it is too late to hope, or pray, or strive for your salvation. Yet a little longer, and mercy will have done with you for ever; and Christ will never invite you more, nor ever offer to cleanse you by his blood; nor sanctify you by his Spirit. Yet a little longer, and you shall never hear a sermon more, and never more be troubled with those preachers that were in good earnest with you, and longed once for your conversion and salvation. O sleepy, dead-hearted sinners, what should I do to show you how near you stand to eternity, and what is now doing in the world that you are going to, and how these things are thought on there! What should I do to make you know how time is valued, how sin and holiness are esteemed in the world where you must live for ever! What should I do to make you know those things to-day, which I will not thank you to know when you are gone hence! O that the Lord would open your eyes in time! O that I could but make you know these things as believers should know them! I say not as those that see them, nor yet as dreamers, that do not regard them, but as those that believe that they must shortly see them, what a joyful hour's work should I esteem this! how happy would it be to you and me! If every word were accompanied with tears; if this sermon cost me as many censures or slanders as ever sermon did, I should not think it too dear, if I could but help you to such a sight of the things we speak of, that you might truly understand them as they are: that you had but a true awakened apprehension of the shortness of your day, of the nearness of eternity, and of the endless consequence of your present work, and what holy labour and sinful loitering will be thought of in the world to come for ever. But when we see you sin, and trifle, and no more regard your endless life, and see also what haste your time is making, and yet cannot make you understand these things; when we know ourselves as sure as we speak to you, that you will shortly be astonished at the review of your present sloth and folly, and when we know that these matters are not thought of in another world, as they are among sleepy sinners here, and yet know not how to make you know it, whom it doth so exceedingly much concern, this amazeth us, and almost breaks our hearts. Yea, when we tell you of things that are past doubt, and can be no further matter of controversy, than men have sold their understandings, and betrayed their reason to their sordid lusts, and yet we cannot get reasonable men to know that which they cannot choose but know, to know that seriously and practically which always hath a witness in their breasts, and which none but the profligate dare deny; this, even this, is worse than a prison to us. It is you that are our persecutors; it is you that are the daily sorrow of our hearts; it is you that disappoint us of our hopes, and make us lose so much of the labour of our lives.

Sinners, whatever the devil and raging passion may say against a holy life, God and your own consciences shall be our witnesses, that we desired nothing unreasonable, or unnecessary at your hands.

The question that I am putting to you, is not whether you will be for this form of church-government, or for that: but it is, whether you will hearken in time to God and conscience, and be as busy to provide for heaven, as ever you have been to provide for earth? It is godliness, serious and practical godliness, that thou art called to. It is nothing but what all Christians in the world are agreed in. That I may not leave thee in any darkness which I can deliver thee from, I will tell thee distinctly though succinctly, what it is that thou art thus importuned to; and tell me, then, whether it be that which any Christian can make doubt of.

1. That which I entreat of thee, is but to live as one that verily believeth there is a God; and that this God is the Creator, the Lord and Ruler of the world: and that it is incomparably more our business to understand and obey his laws, and as faithful subjects to be conformed to them, than to observe

or be conformed to the laws of man: and to live as men that do believe that this God is Almighty, and that the greatest of men are less than crawling worms to him; and that he is infinitely wise, and the wisdom of man is foolishness to him; and that he is infinitely good and amiable; that his love is the only felicity of man; and that none are happy but those that do enjoy it; and none that do enjoy it can be miserable; and that riches, and honour, and fleshly delights are brutish vanities in comparison of the eternal love of God. Live but as men that heartily believe all this, and I have that I come for: and is any of this a matter of controversy or doubt? Not among Christians I am sure: not among wise men. It is no doubt to those in heaven, nor to those in hell, nor to those that have not lost their understandings upon earth. Live then according to these truths.

2. Live as men that verily believe that mankind is fallen into sin and misery; and that all men are corrupted, and under the condemnation of the law of God, till they are delivered, pardoned, reconciled to God, and made new creatures, by a renewing, restoring, sanctifying change. Live but as men that believe that this cure must be wrought, and this great restoring change must be made upon ourselves, if it be not done already. Live as men that have so great a work to look after; and is this a matter of any doubt or controversy? Sure it is not to a Christian: and methinks it should not be to any man else that knoweth himself, any more than to a man in a dropsy, whether he be diseased, when he feels the thirst and sees the swelling. Did you but know what cures and changes are necessarily to be made upon your diseased miserable souls, if you care what becomes of them, you would soon see cause to look about you.

3. Live but as men that verily believe that the Son of God hath suffered for your sins, and brought you the tidings of pardon and salvation, which you may have, if you will give up yourselves to him

who is the physician of souls, to be healed by him. Live as men that believe that the infinite love of God, revealed to lost mankind in the Redeemer, doth bind us to love him with all our hearts, and serve him with all our restored faculties, and to work as those that have the greatest thankfulness to show, as well as the greatest mercies to receive, and misery to escape: and as those that believe, that if sinners that, without Christ, had not hope, shall now love their sins and refuse to leave them, and to repent and be converted, and unthankfully reject the mercy of salvation so dearly bought, and freely offered them, their damnation will be doubled as their sin is doubled.

Live but as men that have such redemption to admire, such mercy to entertain, and such a salvation to attain, and that are sure they can never escape if they continue to "neglect so great salvation." And is there any controversy among Christians in any of this? There is not, certainly.

4. Live but as men that believe that the Holy Ghost is given by Jesus Christ to convert, to quicken, and to sanctify all that he will save; that "except you be born again of the Spirit, you shall not enter into the kingdom of heaven;" and that "if any man have not the Spirit of Christ, the same is none of his," and that without this, no mending of your lives, by any common principles, will serve the turn for your salvation, or make you acceptable to God. Live as men that believe that this Spirit is given by the hearing of the word of God, and must be prayed for, and obeyed, and not resisted, quenched, and grieved. And is there any controversy among Christians in any of this?

5. Live but as men that believe that sin is the greatest evil, the thing which the holy God abhorreth; and then you will never make a mock of it, as Solomon saith the foolish do; nor say, What harm is in it?

6. Live but as men that believe no sin is pardoned without repentance; and that repentance is the

loathing and forsaking of sin: and that if it be true, it will not suffer you to live in any sin, nor to desire to keep the least infirmity, nor to be loath to know your unknown sins.

7. Live as those that believe that you are to be members of the Holy Catholic Church, and therein to hold the communion of saints. And then you will know that it is not as a member of any sect or party, but as a holy member of this holy church, that you must be saved: and that it is the name of a Christian, which is more honourable than the name of any division, or subdivision among Christians.

8. Live as those that believe that there is a life everlasting, where the sanctified shall live in endless joy, and the unsanctified in endless punishment and wo: live but as men that verily believe a heaven and a hell, and a day of judgment, in which all the actions of this life must be revised, and all men judged to their endless state. Believe these things heartily, and then think a holy diligence needless if you can. Then be of the mind of the deriders and enemies of godliness if you can. If one sight of heaven or hell would serve without any more ado, instead of other arguments, to confute all the cavils of the distracted world, and to justify the most diligent saints in the judgment of those that now abhor them, why should not a sound belief of the same thing in its measure do the same?

9. Live but as those that believe this life is given us as the only time to make preparation for eternal life: and that all that ever shall be done for your salvation, must be now, just now, before your time is ended: live as those that know, and need not faith to tell them, that this time is short, and almost at an end already, and stayeth for no man, but, as a post, doth haste away. It will not stay while you are taken up at stage plays, in compliments, in idle visits, or any impertinent, needless things: it will not tarry while you spend yet the other year, or month, or day, in your worldliness, or ambition, or in your lusts and sensual delights, and put off your

repentance to another time. O sirs, for the Lord's sake, do but live as men that must shortly be buried in the grave, and their souls appear before the Lord, and as men that have but this little time to do all for their everlasting life, that ever must be done. O live as men that are sure to die, and are not sure to live till to-morrow: and let not the noise of pleasure or worldly business, or the chat or scorns of miserable fools, bear down your reason, and make you live as if you knew not what you know; or as if there was any doubt about these things. Who is the man and what is his name, that dares contradict them, and can make it good? O do not sin against your knowledge: do not stand still and see your glass running, and time making such haste, and yet make no more haste yourselves, than if you were not concerned in it: do not, O do not slumber, when time and judgment never slumber; nor sit still when you have so much to do, and know all that is now left undone must be undone for ever! Alas, sirs, how many questions of exceeding weight have you yet to be resolved in! whether you are truly sanctified? whether your sins be pardoned? whether you shall be saved when you die? whether you are ready to leave this world and enter upon another? I tell you, the answering of these and many more such questions, is a matter of no small difficulty or concern. And all these must be done in this little and uncertain time. It must be *now* or *never*. Live but as men that believe and consider these certain unquestionable things.

10. Lastly, Will you but live as men that believe that the world and the flesh are the deadly enemies of your salvation? and that believe, that "if any man love the world, (so far) the love of the Father is not in him?" and as men that believe that, "if ye live after the flesh ye shall die; but if by the Spirit ye mortify the deeds of the body, ye shall live;" and that those who are in Christ Jesus, and are freed from condemnation, are such as "walk not after the flesh, but after the Spirit?" And that

we must "make no provision for the flesh to satisfy the will or lusts thereof;" and must not "walk in gluttony and drunkenness, in chambering and wantonness, in strife and envying," but must "have our hearts where our treasure is," and our conversation in heaven; and being risen with Christ, must seek the things that are above, and set our affections on them, and not on the things that are on earth.

Sirs, will you say that any of this is our singular opinion, or matter of controversy and doubt? Are not all Christians agreed in it? Do you not, your own selves profess that you believe it? Live then but as those that do believe it, and condemn not yourselves in the things that you confess.

I have done my part to open to you the necessity of *serious diligence*, and to call up the sluggish souls of sinners to mind the work of their salvation, and to do it *speedily*, and with all their *might*. I must now leave the success to God and you. What use you will make of it, and what you will be and do for the time to come, is a matter that more concerneth yourselves than me.

Sirs, the matter is now laid before you. What will you now do? Have I convinced you now, that God and your salvation are to be sought with all your might? If I have not, it is not for want of evidence in what is said, but for want of willingness in yourselves to know the truth.

It is wonderful, to think that learned men, and gentlemen, and men that pretend to reason and ingenuity, can quietly betray their souls, and do the evil that they have no more to say for, and neglect that duty that they have no more to say against, when they know they must do it *now* or *never*. That while they confess that there is a God, and a life to come, a heaven and a hell, and that this life is purposely given us for preparation for eternity while they confess that God is most wise, and holy and good, and just, and that sin is the greatest evil, and that the word of God is true, they can yet make shift to quiet themselves in an unholy, sensual, careless life; and that while they honour the apostles and martyrs, and saints that are dead and gone, they hate their successors and imitators, and the lives that they lived.

Alas! all this comes from the want of a sound belief of the things which they never saw; and the distance of those things, and the power of passion, and sensual objects and inclinations, that hurry them away after present vanities, and conquer reason, and rob them of their humanity; and from the noise of the company of sensual sinners, that harden and deafen one another, and by the just judgment of God forsaking those that would not know him, and leaving them to the blindness and hardness of their hearts. But is there no remedy? O Thou, the Fountain of mercy and relief, vouchsafe these miserable sinners a remedy! O Thou, the Saviour of lost mankind, have mercy upon these sinners in the depth of their security, presumption, and misery! O Thou, the Illuminator and Sanctifier of souls, apply the remedy so dearly purchased!

Poor sleepy sinners, hear us! Though we speak not to you as men would do that had seen heaven and hell; and were themselves in a perfectly awakened frame, yet hear us while we speak to you the words of truth, with some seriousness, and compassionate desire for your salvation. O Look up to your God! Look out unto eternity: Look inwardly upon your souls: Look wisely upon your short and hasty time: and then bethink you how the little remnant of your time should be employed; and what it is that most concerneth you to despatch and secure before you die. Now you have sermons, and books, and warnings: it will not be so long. Preachers must have done; God threateneth them, and death threateneth them, and men threaten them, and it is you, it is you that are most severely threatened, and that are called on by God's warnings. "If any man have an ear to hear, let him hear." Now you have abundance of private helps, you have abundance of understanding gracious companions; you have the Lord's day to spend in holy exercises, for the edification and solace of your souls; you have choice of sound and serious books: O what invaluable mercies are all these! O know your time, and use these with industry, and improve this harvest for your souls! For it will not be thus always: it must be *now* or *never*. You have yet time and leave to pray and cry to God in hope: yet if you have hearts and tongues, he hath a hearing ear; the Spirit of grace is ready to assist you. It will not be thus always: the time is coming when the loudest cries will do no good. O pray, pray, pray, poor needy miserable sinners; for it must be *now* or *never*.

You have yet health and strength, and bodies fit to serve your souls: it will not be so always: languishing, and pains, and death are coming. O use your health and strength for God; for it must be *now* or *never*.

Yet there are some stirrings of conviction in your consciences: you find that all is not well with you; and you have some thoughts or purposes to repent and be new creatures. There is some hope in this, that yet God hath not quite forsaken you. O trifle not, and stifle not the convictions of your consciences, but hearken to the witness of God within you. It must be *now* or *never*.

Would you not be loath to be left to the despair ing case of many poor distressed souls, that cry out, 'O it is now too late! I fear my day of grace is past; God will not hear me now if I should call upon him: he hath forsaken me, and given me over to myself. It is too late to repent, too late to pray, too late to think of a new life; all is too late.' This case is sad; but yet many of these are in a safer and better case than they imagine, and are but frightened by the Tempter: and it is not too late, while they cry out, 'It is too late;' but if you are left to cry in hell, 'It is too late;' alas, how long and how doleful a cry and lamentation will it be!

O consider, poor sinner, that God knoweth the

time and season of thy mercies. He giveth the spring and harvest in their season; and all his mercies in their season, and wilt thou not know thy time and season, or love, and duty, and thanks to him?

Consider that God, who hath commanded thee thy work, hath also appointed thee thy time. And this is his appointed time. To-day, therefore, hearken to his voice, and see that thou harden not thy heart. He that bids thee "repent and work out thy salvation with fear and trembling," doth also bid thee do it now. Obey him in the time, if thou wilt be indeed obedient; he best understandeth the fittest time. One would think to men that have lost so much already, and loitered so long, and are so lamentably behind hand, and stand so near the bar of God, and their everlasting state, there should be no need to say any more to persuade them to be up and doing. I shall add but this: 'You are never like to have a better time.' Take this, or the work will grow more difficult, more doubtful, if through the just judgment of God, it become not desperate. If all this will not serve, but still you will loiter till time be gone, what can your poor friends do but lament your misery! The Lord knows, if we knew what words, what pains, what cost would tend to your awakening, and conversion, and salvation, we should be glad to submit to it: and we hope we should not think our labours, or liberties, or our lives too dear to promote so blessed and so necessary a work. But if when all this is done that we can do, you will leave us nothing but our tears and moans for self-destroyers, the sin is yours, and the suffering shall be yours. If I can do no more, I shall leave this upon record, that we took our time to tell you, that *serious diligence* is necessary to your salvation; and that God is the "Rewarder of them that diligently seek him," and that this was your day your only day. It must be *now* or *never*.

FIFTY REASONS

WHY A SINNER OUGHT TO TURN TO GOD WITHOUT DELAY.

[With some abridgement.]

HEBREWS III. 7, 8.

To-day, if ye will hear his voice, harden not your hearts.

1. CONSIDER to whom it is that you are commanded to turn; and then tell me whether there can be any reason for delay. It is not to an empty deceitful creature, but to the faithful all-sufficient God; to Him that is the cause of all things; the strength of the creation; the joy of angels; the felicity of the saints; the sun and shield of all the righteous; the refuge of the distressed; and the glory of the whole world. Of such power, that his word can take down the sun from the firmament, and turn the earth and all things into nothing; for he doth more in giving them their being and continuance: of such wisdom, that he was never guilty of mistake; and therefore will not mislead you, nor draw you to any thing that is not for the best: of such goodness, as that evil cannot stand in his sight, and nothing but your evil could make him displeased with you; and it is from nothing but evil, that he

calleth you to turn. It is not to a malicious enemy, that would do you mischief, but to a gracious God that is love itself; not to an implacable justice, but to a reconciled Father; not to revenging indignation, but to the embrace of those arms, and the mercy of that compassionate Lord, that is enough to melt the hardest heart, when you find yourself, as the poor returning prodigal, in his bosom, when you deserved to have been under his feet. And will the great and blessed God invite thee to his favour, and wilt thou delay and demur upon the return? The greatest of the angels of heaven are glad of his favour, and value no happiness but the light of his countenance. Heaven and earth are supported by him, and nothing can stand without him. How glad would those very devils be of his favour, that tempt thee to neglect his favour! And wilt thou delay to turn to such a God? Why, man, thou art every minute at his mercy. And yet dost thou delay? There are all things imaginable in him to draw thee. There is nothing that is good for thee, but it is perfectly in him, where thou mayst have it certain and perpetual. There is nothing in him to give the least discouragement: let all the devils in hell, and all the enemies of God on earth, say the worst they can against his majesty, and they are not able to find the smallest blemish in his absolute holiness, and wisdom, and goodness. And yet wilt thou delay to return?

2. Consider also, to what it is that thou must turn. Not to uncleanness, but to holiness; not to the sensual life of a beast, but to the noble rational life of a man, and the more noble heavenly life of a Christian; not to an unprofitable worldly toil, but to the most gainful employment that ever the sons of men were acquainted with; not to the deceitful drudgery of sin, but to that godliness which is profitable to all things, "having the promise of the life that now is, and of that which is to come."

Sirs, do you know what a life of holiness is? You do not know it, if you turn away from it. I am sure, if you knew it you would never fly from it. No, nor endure to live without it. Why, a life of holiness is nothing but living unto God; to be conversant with him, as the wicked are with the world; and to be devoted to his service, as sensualists are to the flesh. It is to live in the love of God, and of our Redeemer; and in the foretaste of his everlasting glory, and of his love; and in the sweet forethoughts of that blessed life that shall never end; and in the honest self-denying course that leadeth to that blessedness. A godly life is nothing else but a sowing the seed of heaven on earth; and a learning, in the school of Christ, the songs of praise which we must use before the throne of God; and by suffering,—a learning how to triumph and reign with Christ.

Can you delay to come into your Father's family; into the vineyard of the Lord; into the kingdom of God on earth; to be "fellow-citizens of the saints, and of the household of God;" to have the pardon of all your sins, and the sealed promise of everlasting glory? Why, sirs, when you are called on to turn, you are called to the porch of heaven, into the beginning of salvation; and will you delay to accept everlasting life?

3. Consider also, From what you are called to turn; and then judge whether there be any reason of delay. It is from the devil, your enemy; from the love of a deceitful world; from the seductions of corrupted brutish flesh; it is from sin the greatest evil. What is there in sin that you should delay to part with it? Is there any good in it? Or what hath it ever done for you that you should love it? Did it ever do you good? Or did it ever do any man good? It is the deadly enemy of Christ and you, that caused his death, and will cause yours, and is working for your condemnation, if converting and pardoning grace prevent it not. And are you

loath to leave it? It is the cause of all the miseries of the world, of all the sorrows that ever did befall you, and the cause of the damnation of them that perish; and do you delay to part with it?

4. Your delaying shows that you love not God, and that you prefer your sin before him, and that you would never part with it if you could have your will. For if you loved God, you would long to be restored to his favour, and to be near him, and employed in his service and his family. Love is quick and diligent, and will not draw back. And it is a sign also that you are in love with sin: for else, why should you be so loath to leave it? He that would not leave his sin and turn to God, till the next week, or the next month, or year, would never turn if he might have his desire. For that which makes you desirous to stay a day or a week longer, doth indeed make you loath to turn at all. And therefore it is but hypocrisy to say, that you are willing to turn hereafter, if you are not willing to do it now without delay.

5. Consider, what a case you are in, while you thus delay? Do you think you stand in a safe condition? If you knew where you are, you would sit as upon thorns as long as you are unconverted; you would be as a man that stood up to the knees in the sea, and saw the tide coming towards him, who certainly would think that there is no standing still in such a place. You have all your sin unpardoned; you are under the curse of the law; the wrath of God is upon you, and the fulness of it hangs over your heads; judgment is coming to pass upon you the dreadful doom; the Lord is at hand; death is at the door, and waits but for the word from the mouth of God, that it may arrest you, and bring you to everlasting misery: and is this a state for a man to continue in?

6. Moreover, Your delaying giveth great advantage to the Tempter. If you would presently turn and forsake your sins, and enter into a faithful cove-

nant with God, the devil would be almost out of hope, and the very heart of his temptations would be broken. He would see that now it is too late; there is no getting you out of the arms of Christ. But as long as you delay, you keep him in heart and hope; he hath time to strengthen his prison and fetters, and to renew his snares; and if one temptation serve not, he hath time to try another and another; as if you would stand as a mark for Satan to shoot at, as long as he pleases. What likelihood is there that ever so foolish a sinner should be recovered and saved from his sin?

7. Moreover, Your delaying is a vile abuse of Christ and the Holy Ghost, and may so far provoke him, as to leave you to yourself, and then you are past help. If you delight so to trample on your crucified Lord, and will so long put him to it by refusing his grace and grieving his Spirit, what can you expect but that he should turn away in wrath, and utterly forsake you.

8. Consider also, I beseech you, if you ever mean to turn, what it is that you stay for. Do you think to bring down Christ and heaven to your own terms, and to be saved hereafter with less ado? Sure, you cannot be so foolish: for God will be still the same; and Christ the same; and his promise hath still the same condition, which he will never change; and godliness will be the same, and as much against your carnal interest hereafter as it is now. When you have looked about you ever so long, you will never find a fairer or nearer way; but this same way you must go or perish. If you cannot leave sin now, how shall you leave it then? It will still be as sweet to your flesh as now: or if one grow stale by the decay of nature, another that is worse will spring up in its stead, and though the acts abate, they will all live still at the root; for sin was never mortified by age. So that if ever you will turn, you may best turn now.

9. Yea, more than that, the longer you stay, the harder it will be. If it be hard to-day, it is like to be harder to-morrow. For as the Spirit of Christ is like to forsake you for your wilful delays, so custom will strengthen sin: and custom in sinning will harden your hearts, and make you "past feeling, to work all uncleanness with greediness." Cannot you crush this serpent when it is but weak; and can you encounter it in its serpentine strength? Cannot you pluck up a tender plant; and can you pluck up an oak or cedar? O sinners! what do you mean, to make your recovery so difficult by delay? You are never like to be fairer for heaven, and to find conversion an easier work, than now you may do. Will you stay till the work be ten times harder, and yet do you think it so hard already?

10. Consider also, that sin gets daily victories by your delay. We lay out batteries against it, and preach, and exhort, and pray against it, and it gets a kind of victory over all, as long as we prevail not with you to turn. It conquereth our persuasions and advice; it conquereth all the stirrings of your consciences; it conquereth all your heartless purposes and deceitful promises. And these frequent conquests strengthen your sin, and weaken your resistance, and leave the matter almost hopeless. Before a physician hath used remedies, he hath more hope of a cure, than when he hath tried all means, and finds that the best medicines do no good, but the man is still as bad or worse. So when all means have been tried with you, and yet you are unconverted, the case draws towards desperation itself: the very means are disabled more than before; that is, your hearts are harder to be wrought upon by them. When you have long been under sermons and reading, and among good examples, and yet you are unconverted, these ordinances lose much of their force with you. Custom will make you slight them, and be dead-hearted under them. And it is these very same means and truths, that you have

frustrated, that must do the work, or it will never be done.

11. Moreover, age itself hath many inconveni ences, and youth hath many great advantages: and therefore it is folly to delay. In age the understanding and memory grow dull, and people grow incapable, and almost unchangeable. We see, by our every day's experience, that men think they should not change when they are old; that opinion or practice, in which they have been brought up, they think they should not then forsake. To learn when they are old, and to turn when they are old—you see how much they are against it. Besides, how unfit is age to be at that pains that youth can undergo? How unfit to begin the holy warfare against the flesh, the world, and the devil? God's way is to list his soldiers as soon as may be, when in youth; but the devil will persuade them that it is yet too soon; and when he can no longer persuade them that it is yet too soon, he will then persuade that it is too late. O what a happy thing it is to come to God betimes, and with the first! What ad vantage hath youth! They have the vigour of wit and of body; they are not rooted and hardened in sin, nor filled with prejudice and obstinacy against godliness, as others are.

12. You have such times of advantage and encouragement as few ages of the world have ever seen, and few nations on earth enjoy at this day. What plain and plentiful teaching have you! What abundance of good examples, and the society of the godly! Private and public helps are common. Seldom has the church seen such days on earth. And yet is not the way to heaven fair enough for you? Yet are you not ready to turn to God? Will you delay till harvest time be over, and the winter of persecution come again? Have you sun, and wind, and tide to serve you, and will you stay to set out in storms and darkness?

13. Moreover, Your delay doth cast your con·

version and salvation into hazard, yea, into many and grievous hazards. And is your everlasting happiness a matter to be wilfully hazarded, by causeless and unreasonable delays? If you delay to-day, you are utterly uncertain of living till to-morrow. If you put by this one motion, you know not whether ever you may have another. You know not whether ever the Spirit of God will put another thought of turning into your hearts; or at least, whether he will incline your hearts to turn.

14. Moreover, the delay of conversion continueth your sin, and so you will daily increase their number, and increase your guilt, and make your souls abundantly miserable. Are you not deep enough in debt to God already, and have you not sins enough to answer for upon your souls? Would you fain have one year's sins more, or one day's sins more, to be charged upon you? O, if you did but know what sin is, it would amaze you to think what a mountain lieth already upon your consciences! One sin unpardoned will sink the sinner into hell; and you have many a thousand upon your souls already, and would you yet have more? Methinks you should rather look about you, and bethink you how you may get a pardon for all that is past.

15. And as sin increaseth daily by delay, so consequently the wrath of God increaseth, and you will run further into his displeasure, and possibly you may cut down the bough that you stand upon, and hasten destruction to yourselves. When you live daily upon God, and are kept out of hell, by a miracle of his mercy, methinks you should not desire yet longer to provoke him, lest he withdraw his mercy, and let you fall into misery.

16. And do but consider, What will become of you if ye be found in these delays? You are then lost, body and soul, for ever. Now if you had but hearts to know what is good for you, the worst of you might be converted and saved; for God doth freely offer you his grace. But if you die in your

delays, in the twinkling of an eye you will find yourselves utterly undone for ever.

17. Consider, That your very time, which you lose by these delays, is an inconceivable loss. When time is gone, what would you then give for one of those years, or days, or hours, which you now foolishly trifle away? O wretched sinners, are there so many thousand souls in hell that would give a world, if they had it, for one of your days; and yet can you afford to throw them away in worldliness, and sensuality, and loitering delays? I tell you, time is better worth than all the wealth and honours of the world. The day is coming when you will value time: when it is gone you will know what a blessing you made light of.

18. Consider also, that God hath given you no time to spare. He hath not lent you one day or hour, more than is needful for the work that you have to do; therefore you have no reason to lose any by your delays. Do you imagine that God would give a man an hour's time for nothing? much less to abuse him and serve his enemy. No, let me tell you, that if you make your best of every hour, if you should never lose a moment of your lives, you would find all little enough for the work you have to do. I know not how others think of time, but for my part I am forced daily to say, How swift, how short is time! And how great is our work! And when we have done our best, how slowly it goeth on! O precious time! What hearts have they, what lives do those men lead, that think time long! That have time to spare, and to pass in idleness!

19. To convince you more, Consider, I beseech you, the exceeding greatness of the work you have to do; and tell me then, whether it be time for you to delay. Especially you, that are yet unconverted, and strangers to the heavenly nature of the saints,—you have far more to do than other men. You have a multitude of head-strong passions to subdue, and

abundance of deadly sins to kill, and rooted vices to root up: you have a false opinion of God, and his ways, to be plucked up; and the customs of many years' standing to be broken: you have blind minds that must be enlightened with heavenly knowledge, and abundance of spiritual truths that are above the reach of flesh and blood, that you must needs learn and understand: you have much to know, that is hard to be known: you have a dead soul to be made alive, and a hard heart to be melted; and a seared conscience to be softened, and made tender; and the guilt of many thousand sins to be pardoned: you have a new heart to get, and a new end to aim at, and seek after, and a new life to live; abundance of enemies you have to fight with, and overcome; abundance of temptations to resist and conquer; many graces to get, and preserve and exercise, and increase; and abundance of holy work to do for the service of God, and the good of yourselves and others. O what a deal of work doth every one of these words contain! And yet what abundance more might I name! And have you all this to do, and yet will you delay? And they are not indifferent matters that are before you: it is no less than the saving of your souls, and obtaining the blessed glory of the saints. Necessity is upon you. These are things that must be done, or else wo to you that ever you were born! And yet have you another day to lose? Why, sirs, if you had a hundred miles to go in a day or two, upon pain of death, would you delay? O think of the work that you have to do, and then judge whether it be not time to stir?

20. And methinks it should exceedingly terrify you to consider, What multitudes perish by such delays; and how few that wilfully delay, are ever converted and saved! Many a soul, that once had purposes hereafter to repent, is now in the misery where there is no repentance that will do them any good. For my part, though I have known some very few converted when they were old; yet I must

needs say, both that they were very few indeed, and I had reason to believe, that they were such as had sinned before in ignorance, and did not wilfully put off repentance, when they were convinced that they must turn. Though I doubt not but God may convert even these if he please, yet I cannot say that I have ever known many, if any such, to be converted. Sure I am that God's usual time is in childhood, or youth, before they have long abused grace, and wilfully delayed to turn when they were convinced. Some considerable time, I confess, may have elapsed before their first convictions and purposes be brought to any great ripeness of performance: but O how dangerous it is to delay!

21. Consider also, Either conversion is good or bad for you; either it is needful or unnecessary. If it be bad, and a needless thing, then let it alone altogether. But if you are convinced that it is good and necessary, is it not better now than to stay any longer? Is it not the sooner the better? Are you afraid of being safe or happy too soon? If you are sick, you care not how soon you are well; if you have a bone out, you care not how soon it is set; if you fall into the water, you care not how soon you get out; if your house be on fire, you care not how soon it be quenched; if you are put in fear by any doubts or ill tidings, you care not how soon your fears be over. And yet are you afraid of being too soon out of the power of the devil, and the danger of hell; and of being too soon the sons of God, and the holy, justified heirs of heaven?

22. Consider also, Either you can turn now, or not. If you can and yet will not, you are utterly without excuse. If you cannot to-day, how much less will you be able hereafter, when strength is less, and difficulties greater, and burdens more? Is it not time, therefore, to apply to Christ for strength; and should not the very sense of your inability dissuade you from delay?

23. Consider how long you have stayed already,

and put God's patience to it by your folly. Have not the devil, the world, and the flesh, had many years time of your life already? Have you not long enough been swallowing the poison of sin; and long enough been abusing the Lord that made you; and the blood of the Son of God that was shed for you; and the Spirit of grace, that hath moved and persuaded you? Are you not yet gone far enough from God? And have you not yet done enough to the destroying of yourselves, and casting away everlasting life? O wretched sinners! it is rather time for you to fall down on your faces before the Lord, and with tears and groans to lament it day and night, that ever you have gone so far in sin, and delayed so long to turn to him as you have done. Sure, if after so many years' rebellion, you are yet so far from lamenting it, that you had rather have more of it, and had rather hold on a little longer no wonder if God forsake you, and let you alone.

24. Have you any hopes of God's acceptance and your salvation, or not? If you have such hopes,—that, when you turn, God will pardon all your sins, and give you everlasting life,—is it, think you, an ingenuous thing to desire to offend him yet a little longer, from whom you expect such exceeding mercy and glory? Have you the faces to speak out what is in your hearts and practice; and to go to God with such words as these? 'Lord, I know I cannot have the pardon of one sin without the blood of Christ, and the riches of thy mercy. Nor can I be saved from hell without it: but yet I hope for all this from thy grace. I beseech thee let me live a little longer in my sins; a little longer let me trample on the blood of Christ, and despise thy commandments, and abuse thy mercies; and then pardon me all that ever I did, and take me into glory.'—Could you for shame put such a request to God as this? If you could, you are past shame: if not, then do not practise and desire that which you cannot, for shame, speak out and request.

25. Moreover, It is an exceeding advantage to you to come to God betimes; and an exceeding loss, that you will suffer by delay, if you were sure to be converted at the last. If you speedily come in, you may have time to learn, and get more understanding in the matters of God, than otherwise can be expected. For knowledge will not be had but by time and study. You may also have time to get strength of grace, when beginners can expect no more than infant strength. You may grow to be men of parts and abilities, to be useful in the church, and profitable to those about you, when others cannot go or stand, unless they lean on the stronger for support. If you come in betimes, you may do God service; which, in the evening of the day, you will neither have strength nor time to do. You may have time to get assurance of salvation, and to be ready with comfort, when death shall call; when a weakling is like to be perplexed with doubts and fears, and death is like to be terrible, because of their unreadiness.

26. And did you ever consider, who and how many stay for you while you delay? Do you know who it is that you make to wait your leisure? God himself stands over you with the offers of his mercy, as if he thought it long till your return, saying, "O that there were such a heart in them!" and "when will it once be!" "How long, ye simple ones, will ye love simplicity, and scorners delight in scorning, and fools hate knowledge? Turn ye at my reproof." And do you think it wise, or safe, for you to make the God of heaven wait on you, while you are serving his enemy? Can you offer God a baser indignity, than to expect he should support your lives, and feed you, and preserve you, and patiently forbear while you abuse him to his face, and drudge for the flesh, the world, and the devil? Should a worm thus use the Lord that made him, marvel not, if he withdraw his supporting mercy, and let such wretches drop into hell!

And it is not God only, but his servants, and creatures, and ordinances, that are all waiting on you. The angels stay for the joy that is due to them upon your conversion. Ministers are studying, and preaching, and praying for you; godly neighbours are praying, and longing for your change. The springs and rivers are flowing for you; the winds blow for you; the sun shines for you; the clouds rain for you; the earth bears fruit for you; the beasts must labour, and suffer, and die for you: all things are doing, and would you stand still, or else do worse? What haste makes the sun about the world, to return in its time to give you light! What haste make other creatures in your service! And yet must you delay? Must God stay, and Christ and the Spirit stay? Must angels stay, must ministers stay, must the godly stay, and the ordinances stay, and all the creatures stay your leisure, while you are abusing God, and your souls, and others, and while you delay, as if it were too soon to turn?

27. Consider, That when you were lost, the Son of God did not delay the work of redemption. He presently undertook it, and turned by the stroke of condemning justice. In the fulness of time he came and performed what he undertook; he failed not one day of his appointed time. And will you now delay to accept the benefit and to turn to him? Must he make such haste to save you at so dear a rate, and now will you delay to be saved?

28. Moreover, God doth not delay to do you good. You have the day and night in their proper seasons; the sun doth not fail to rise upon you at the appointed time; you have the spring and harvest in their proper seasons; the former and the latter rain in season. When you are in want, you have seasonable supplies; and when you are in danger, you have seasonable deliverances. And is it meet or equal that you should refuse to bring forth sea-

sonable fruit, but still be putting off God with your delays?

29. Moreover, When you are in trouble and necessity, you are then in haste for deliverance and relief. Then you think every day a week, till your danger or suffering be past. If you be under the pain of a disease, or in danger of death, or under poverty, or oppression, or disgrace, you would have God relieve you without delay; and yet you will not turn to him without delay. Then you are ready to cry out, 'How long, Lord, how long till deliverance come?' But you will not hear God, when he crieth to you, in your sins—How long will it be ere you turn from your transgressions? When shall it once be? When you are to receive any outward deliverance, you care not how soon; but when you are to turn to God, and receive his grace and title to glory, then you care not how late, as if you had no mind of it. Can you, for shame, beg of God to hasten your deliverance, when you remember your delays, and still continue to trifle with him and draw back?

30. Your present prosperity, and worldly delights, are passing away without delay; and should you delay to make sure of better in their stead? Time is going; and health is going; youth is going; yea, life is going; your riches are taking wing; your fleshly pleasures do perish in the very using. Shortly you must part with house and lands, with goods and friends; and all your mirth and earthly business will be done. All this you know, and yet will you delay to lay up a durable treasure, which you may trust upon, and to provide you a better tenement before you be turned out of this? What will you do for a habitation, for pleasures and contents, when all that you have now is spent and gone, and earth will afford you nothing but a grave? If you could but keep that you have, I should not much wonder, that knowing so little of God and another world, you look not much after it; but when you perceive death

knocking at your doors, and seeing all your worldly comforts are packing up and hasting away, methinks you should presently turn, and make sure of heaven, without any more delay.

31. Consider also, Whether it be equal that you should delay your conversion, when you can seasonably despatch your worldly business; and when your flesh would be provided for, you can hearken to it without delay. You have wit enough to sow your seed in season, and will not delay it till the time of harvest. You will reap your corn when it is ripe, and gather your fruit when it is ripe, without delay. You observe the seasons in the course of your labours, day by day, and year by year. You will not lie in bed, when you should be at your work, nor delay all night to go to your rest; nor suffer your servants to delay your business. If you be sick, you will seek help without delay, lest your disease should grow to be incurable. And yet will you delay your conversion, and the making sure of heaven? Why, sirs, shall these trifles be done without delay, and shall your salvation be put off? Can you have time for every thing, except that one thing which all the rest are merely to promote, and in comparison of which they are all but dreams? Can you have time to work, to plough, and sow, and reap, and cannot you have time to prepare for eternal life? Why, sirs, if you cannot find time yet to search your hearts, to turn to God, and prepare for death, give over eating and drinking, and sleeping, and say, you cannot have time for these. You may as wisely say so for these smaller matters, as for the greater.

31. Moreover, if men offer you conveniences and commodities for your bodies, you will not stand delaying, and need so many persuasions to accept them. If your landlord would for nothing renew your lease; if any man would give you houses or lands, would you delay so long before you would accept them? A beggar at your door will not only

thankfully take your alms, without your entreaty and importunity, but will beg for it, and be importunate with you to give it. And yet will you delay to accept the blessed offers of grace, which are so much greater?

33. Yet consider, that it is God that is the giver, and you that are the miserable beggars and receivers. And therefore it is fitter you should wait on God, and call on him for his grace, when he seemeth to delay, and not that he should wait on you. He can live without your receiving, but you cannot live with out his giving. The beggar must be glad of an alms at any time; and the condemned person of a pardon at any time; but the giver may well expect that his gifts be received without delay, or else he may let them go without.

34. And methinks you should not deal worse with God, when he comes to you as a physician to save your own souls, than you would do with a neighbour, or a friend, when it is not for your own good, but for theirs. If your neighbour lay a dying, you would go and visit him without delay. If he fell down in a swoon, you would catch him up without delay. If he fell into the fire or water, you would pluck him out without delay. Yea, you would do thus much to a very beast. And yet will you delay, when it is not another, but yourselves that are sinking and drowning, and within a step of death and desperation?

35. If yet you perceive not how unreasonably you deal with God and your souls, I beseech you, consider, whether you do not deal worse with him than you do with the devil himself. If Satan or his servants persuade you to sin, you delay not so long but you are presently at it. You are ready to follow every tippling companion or gamester that puts up the finger. You are as willing to go, as they are to invite you. The very sight of the cup does presently prevail with the drunkard; and the sight of a harlot prevaileth with the fornicator; and sin

can be presently entertained without delay. But when God comes, when Christ calleth, when the Spirit moveth, when the minister persuadeth, when conscience is convinced, we can have nothing but wishes, and purposes, and promises, with delays.

Nay, more than this: so eager are they on their sin, that we are not able to entreat them to delay it. When the passionate man is but provoked, we cannot persuade him to delay his railing language, so long as to consider first of the issue. We cannot entreat the drunkard to put off his drunkenness but for one twelve months, while he trieth another course. All the ministers in the country cannot persuade the worldling to forbear his worldliness, and the proud persons their pride, and the ungodly person his ungodliness, for the space of one month, or week, or day. And yet when God hath a command and a request to them, to turn to him and be saved, here they can delay, without our entreaty.

36. Consider also, that it is not possible for you to turn too soon: nor will you ever have cause to repent of your speediness. Delay may undo you; but speedy turning can do you no harm. Should there be any delay, where it is not possible to be too hasty? Do you think that there is ever a saint in heaven, yea, or on earth, that is sorry he continued not longer unconverted? No: you shall never hear of such a repentance from the mouth of any that is indeed converted.

37. But I must tell you on the contrary, that if ever you be so happy as to be converted, you will repent it, and a hundred times repent it, that you delayed so long before you yielded. O, how it will grieve you, when your hearts are melted with the love of God, and are overcome with the infinite kindness of his pardoning, saving grace, that ever you had the hearts to abuse such a God, and deal so unkindly with him, and stand out so long against that compassion that was seeking your salvation! O, how it will grieve your hearts, to consider that

you have spent so much of your lives in sin, for the devil, and the flesh, and the deceitful world! O, you will think with yourselves, 'Was not God more worthy of my youthful days? Had I not better have spent them in his service, and in the work of my salvation? Alas, that I should waste such precious days, and now be so far behind-hand as I am! Now I want that faith, that hope, that love, that peace, that assurance, that joy in the Holy Ghost, which I might have had, if I had spent those years for God, which I spent in the service of the world and the flesh.'

38. And I pray you, consider whether it belongs of right to God or you, to determine of the day and hour of your coming in. It is he that must give you the pardon of your sins; and doth it not belong to him to appoint the time of your receiving it? You cannot have Christ and life without him: it is he that must give you the kingdom of heaven: and is he not worthy, then, to appoint the time of your conversion, that you may be made partakers of it? But if he say, To-day, dare you say, I will stay till to-morrow?

39. Nay, consider, whether God or you be likelier to know the meetest time. Dare you say that you know better when to turn than God doth? I suppose you dare not; and if you dare not say so, for shame, let not your practice say so. God saith, "To-day, while it is called to-day, hear my voice, and harden not your hearts." And dare you say, It is better to stay one month longer, or one day longer? God saith, "Behold, this is the accepted time! Behold, this is the day of salvation!" And will you say, It is time enough to-morrow? Do you know better than God? If your physician do but tell you in a pleurisy or a fever, You must let blood this day—before to-morrow; you have so much reason as to submit to his understanding, and think that he knows better than you

and cannot you allow as much to the God of wisdom?

40. Consider also, that the speediness of your conversion, when God first calls you, doth make you the more welcome, and is a thing exceedingly pleasing to God. Our proverb is, A speedy gift is a double gift. If you ask any thing of a friend, and he give it you presently and cheerfully at the first asking, you will think you have it with a good-will; but if he stand long delaying first, and demurring upon it, you will think that you have it with an ill-will, and that you owe him the smaller thanks. If a very beggar at your door must stay long for an alms, he will think he is the less beholden to you. How much more may God be displeased, when he must stay so long for his own, and that for your benefit! God loveth a cheerful giver, and consequently, a cheerful obeyer of his call; and if it be hearty and cheerful, it is the likelier to be speedy, without such delays.

41. And I would desire you but to do with God as you would be done by. Would you take it well of your children, if they should tear all their clothes, and cast their meat to the dogs, and tread it in the dirt, and when you entreat them, they will not regard you? Would you stand month after month entreating and waiting on them, as God doth on you? If your servant will spend the whole day and year in drinking and playing, when he should do your work, will you wait on him all the year with entreaties, and pay him at last, as if he had served you? And can you expect that God should deal so with you?

42. And consider, I entreat you, that your delay is a denial, and so may God interpret it, for the time of your turning is part of the command. He that saith, Turn, saith, Now, even to-day, without delay. He giveth you no longer day. If time be lengthened, and the offer made again and again,

that is more than he promised you, or you could have promised yourselves. His command is, Now return and live. And if you refuse the time, the present time, you refuse the offer, and forfeit the benefit. And if you knew but what it is to give God a denial in such a case as this, and what a case you were in, if he should turn away in wrath and never come near you more; you would then be afraid of jesting with his hot displeasure, or trifling with the Lord.

43. And, methinks, you should remember, that God does not stay thus on all, as he doth on you. Thousands are under despair, and past all remedy, while patience is waiting yet upon you. Can you forget that others are in hell at this very hour, for as small sins as those that you are yet entangled and linger in? Good Lord, what a thing is a senseless heart! That at the same time when millions are in misery, for delaying or refusing to be converted, their successors should fearlessly venture in their steps!

44. And I must tell you, that God will not always thus wait on you, and attend you by his patience, as hitherto he hath done. Patience hath his appointed time. And if you out-stay that time, you are miserable. I can assure you, sirs, the glass is turned upon you, and when it is run out, you shall never have an hour of patience more. Then God will no more entreat you to be converted. He will not always stand over you with salvation, and say, O that this sinner would repent and live! O that he would take the mercies that I have provided for him! Do not expect that God should do this always with you; for it will not be.

45. Your delays weary the servants of Christ that are employed for your recovery. Ministers will grow weary of preaching to you, and persuading you. When we come to men that were never warned before, we come in hopes that they will hear and obey; and this hope puts life and

earnestness into our persuasions: but when we have persuaded men but a few times in vain, and leave them as we found them, our spirits begin to droop and flag; much more, when we have preached and persuaded you many years, and still you are the same, and are but where you were,—this dulls a minister's spirit, and makes him preach heavily and coldly, when he is almost out of heart and hope.

Truly, sirs, I must tell you, for my own part, that if it had not been for those that gave me better encouragement by their obedience, I should never have held out with you a quarter of this time. If all had profited as little as some, and all remained in an unconverted state as some; if the humble, penitent, obedient ones among you, had not been my comfort and encouragement under Christ, I had been gone from you many years ago; I could never have held out till now: either my corruption would have made me run away with Jonah, or my judgment would have commanded me to shake off the dust off my feet as a witness against you, and depart.

But to what end do I speak all this to you? To what end? Why, to let you see how you abuse both God and man, by your delays and disobedience. You cannot possibly do us, that are your teachers, a greater injury or mischief in the world. It is not in your power to wrong us more. Are our studies and our labours worth nothing? Are our watchings and waitings worth nothing? Are our prayers, and tears, and groans to be despised? God will not despise them, if you do; believe it, he will set them all on your account, and you will one day have a heavy reckoning of them, and pay full dear for them. Is it equal dealing with us, that when we are watching for your souls, as men that know we must give an account, you should rob us of our comfort, and make us do it with sighs and sorrow? Yea, that you should undo all that we are doing, and make us lose our labour and our hopes? And yet do you not think to pay for this? Many years we have been persuading you but to turn and live, and yet you are unturned; you have been convinced long, and thinking on it; and wishing long, and talking of it; and promising long, and yet it is undone, and here is nothing but delays. We see, while you delay, death takes away one this week, and another the next week, and you are passing into the other world apace; and yet those that are left behind will take no warning, but still delay: we see that Satan delays not while you delay: he is day and night at work against you: if he seem to make a truce with you, it is that he may be doing secretly, while you suspect him not: we see that sin delayeth not while you delay; it is working like poison or infection in your bodies, and seizing upon your vital powers; it is every day blinding you more and more, it is hardening your hearts more and more, and searing your consciences, to bring you past all feeling and hope. And must we stand by and see this miserable work with our people's souls, and all be frustrated and rejected by themselves that we do for their deliverance? I pray you deal but fairly with us, and tell us whether ever you will turn or not. If you will not, but are resolved for sin and hell, say so, that we may know the worst; speak out your minds, that we may know what to trust to. But if still you say, you will turn—when will you do it? You will do it, and you hope you shall: but when? How long would you have us wait yet? Nay, I must tell you, that you even weary God himself. It is his own expression, (Mal. ii. 17. Isa. xliii. 24.) "Thou hast wearied me with thine iniquities." (Isa. i. 14.) And I must say to you as the Prophet, (Isa. vii. 13.) "Is it a small thing for you to weary men, but you will weary my God also?" Consider what it is that you do.

46. Consider also, that you are at a constant and unspeakable loss every day and hour that you delay

your conversion. O! little do you know what you deprive yourselves of every day. If a slave in the galleys or prison might live at court, as a favourite of the prince, in honour, and delight, and ease, would he delay either years or hours? Or would he not rather think within himself, Is it not better to be at ease and in honour, than to be here? As the prodigal said, "How many hired servants of my father have bread enough and to spare, and I perish with hunger!" All this while I might be in plenty and delight.—All the while that you live in sin, you might be in favour of God, in the high and heavenly employments of the saints; you might have the comforts of daily communion with Christ and with the saints; you might be laying up for another world, and might look death in the face with faith and confidence, as one that cannot be conquered by it; you might live as the heirs of heaven on earth. All this, and more than this, you lose by your delays; all the mercies of God are lost upon you; your food and raiment, your health and wealth, which you set so much by, all is lost, and worse than lost, for they turn to your greater hurt; all our pains with you, and all the ordinances of God which you possess, and all your time is lost, and worse. And do you think it, indeed, a wise man's part to live any longer at such a loss as this, and that wilfully and for nothing? If you knew your loss, you would not think so.

47. Nay more, you are all this while doing that which must be undone again, or you will be undone for ever. You are running from God, but you must come back again, or perish when all is done. You are learning a hundred carnal lessons and false conceits, that must be all unlearned again; you are shutting up your eyes in wilful ignorance, which must be opened again: you must learn the doctrine of Christ, the great Teacher of the Church, if you stay never so long, or else you would be cut off from his people. Acts iii. 22. and vii. 37.

When you have been long accustoming yourselves to sin, you must unlearn and break all these customs again. You are hardening your hearts daily, and they must again be softened. And I must tell you, that though a little time and labour may serve to do mischief, yet it is not quickly undone again. You may sooner set your house on fire than quench it. You may sooner cut and wound your bodies, than heal them again; and sooner catch a cold or a disease than cure it; you may quickly do that which must be longer undoing. Besides, the cure is accompanied with pain; you must take many a bitter draught, in groans or tears of godly sorrow, for these delays; the wounds, that you are now giving your souls, must smart, and smart again, before they are searched and healed to the bottom. And what man of wisdom would make himself such work and sorrow? Who would travel on an hour longer, that knows he is out of his way, and must come back again? Would you not think him a madman that would say, I will go on a little further, and then I will turn back.

48. And methinks if it were but this, it would terrify you from your delays, that it is likely to make your conversion more grievous, if you should have so great mercy from God, after all, to be converted. God must send either some grievous affliction to fire and frighten you out of your sins, or else some terrible horrors of conscience, that should make you groan, and groan again, in the feelings of your folly. The pangs and throes of conscience, in the work of conversion, are far more grievous in some than in others. Some are even on the rack, and almost brought beside their wits, and the next step to desperation, with horror of soul and the sense of the wrath of God; so that they lie in doubts and complaints many a year together, and think that they are even forsaken of God. And to delay your conversion is the way to draw on either this or worse.

49. Consider also, that delays are contrary to the very nature of the work, and the nature of your souls themselves. If indeed you ever mean to turn, it is a work of haste, and violence, and diligence, that you must needs set upon. You must "strive tc enter in, for the gate is strait, the way is narrow that leads to life, and few there be that find it." "Many shall seek to enter, and shall not be able." "When once the master of the house is risen up, and hath shut to the door, and ye begin to stand without, and knock at the door, saying, Lord, Lord, open to us, he shall answer, I know you not whence you are, depart from me, all ye workers of iniquity." It is a race that you are to run, and heaven is the prize. "And you know that they which run in a race run all, but one receiveth the prize; and therefore you must so run, as that you may win and obtain."

And what is more contrary to this than delay? You are soldiers in fight, and your salvation lieth in the victory; and will you trifle in such a case, when death or life is even at hand? You are travellers to another world, and will you stay till the day is almost past, before you will begin your journey? Christianity is a work of that infinite consequence, and requireth such speedy and vigorous despatch, that delay is more unreasonable in this than in any thing in all the world.

50. If all this will not serve to make you turn, let me tell you, that while you are delaying, your judgment doth not delay; and that when it comes, these delays will multiply your misery, and the remembrance of them will be your everlasting torment. Whatever you are thinking of, or whatever you are doing, your dreadful doom is drawing on apace, and misery will overtake you, before you are aware. When you are in the alehouse, little thinking of ruin, even then is your damnation coming in haste; when you are drowned in the pleasures or cares of the world, your judgment is still hastening. You may delay, but it will not delay. It is the saying of

the Holy Ghost, "Whose judgment now of a long time lingereth not, and their damnation slumbereth not." You may slumber, and that so carelessly, that we cannot awake you, but your damnation slumbereth not, nor hath done of a long time, while you thought it slumbered; and when it comes, it will awaken you. As a man that is in a coach on the road, or in a boat on the water, whatever he is speaking, or thinking, or doing, he is still going on, and hastening to his journey's end, or going down the stream; so whatever you think, or speak, or do, whether you believe it, or mock at it, whether you sleep or wake, whether you remember it or forget it, you are hastening to destruction, and you are every day a day nearer to it than before. "Behold the Judge standeth before the door." The Holy Ghost hath told you, "the Lord is at hand." "The day is at hand; the time is at hand; the end of all things is at hand." Rom. xiii. 12. Rev. xxii. 10. 1 Pet. iv. 7. "Behold, saith the Lord, I come quickly, and my reward is with me, to give to every man according as his work shall be." And do you, as it were, see the Judge approaching, and yet will you delay?

And withal consider, that when it comes, it will be most sore to such as you; and then what thoughts do you think you shall have of these delays? You are unable to conceive how it will torment your consciences, when you see that all your hopes are gone, to think to what you have brought yourselves by your trifling. To feel yourselves in remediless misery, and remember how long the remedy was offered you, and you delayed to use it till it was too late. To see that you are for ever shut out of heaven, and remember that you might have had it as well as others, but you lost it by delay. O then it will come with horror into your mind, How often was I persuaded, and told of this? How often had I inward motions to return? How often did I purpose to be holy and to give up my heart and life to God? I was even ready to have yielded, but I still delayed, and now it is too late.

And now, having laid you down no less than fifty moving considerations, if it be possible to save you from these delays, I conclude with this request to you, whoever you be that read these lines, that you would but consider of all these reasons, and then entertain them as they deserve. There is not one of them that you are able to gainsay, much less all of them. If after the reading of all these, you can yet believe that you have reasons to delay, your understandings are forsaken of God; but if you are forced to confess that you should not delay, what will you do then? Will you obey God and your own consciences, or will you not? Will you turn this hour without delay? Take heed of denying it, lest you have never such a motion more. You know not but God, who calls you to it, may be resolved that t should be now or never. I do beseech you, yea, as his messenger, I charge you in his name, that you delay not an hour longer, but presently be resolved, and make an unchangeable covenant with God; and, as ever you would have favour in that day of your distress, delay not now to accept his favour in the day of your visitation.

O what a blessed family were that, who upon the reading of this, would presently say, We have done exceeding foolishly in delaying so great a matter so long; let us agree together to give up ourselves to God without any more delay. This shall be the day; we will stay no longer. The flesh, and the world, and the devil, have had too much already. It is a wonder of patience that hath borne with us so long; we will abuse the patience of God no longer, but begin to be absolutely his this day. If this may be the effect of these exhortations, you shall have the everlasting blessing; but if still you delay, I hope I am free from the guilt of your blood.

EXTRACTS

FROM

BAXTER'S DYING THOUGHTS.

The reader has witnessed in the preceding pages the fervent zeal and deep anxiety of the pious author in urging on the impenitent the necessity of immediately turning to God and repairing to the Saviour in order to escape eternal death. In the following selections are exhibited some of the peaceful and happy reflections which the author indulged, in relation to his own prospects in the near view of death.

The sanctifying operations of the Spirit of God are the earnest of heaven, and the sure prognostic of our immortal happiness. It is "a change of grand importance" to man, to be renewed in his mind, his will, and life. It repairs his depraved faculties. It causes man to live as man, who was degenerated to a life too much like the brutes. Men are "slaves to sin, till Christ makes them free." "Where the spirit of the Lord is, there is liberty." If "the love of God shed abroad on our hearts," be not our excellence, health, and beauty, what is? "That which is born of the flesh is flesh, and that which is born of the Spirit is spirit." Without Christ, and his Spirit, we can do nothing. Our dead notions and reason, though we see the truth, have not power to overcome temptations, nor raise up man's soul to its original, and end, nor possess us with the love and joyful hopes of future blessedness. It were better for us to have no souls, than have our souls void of the Spirit of God. *Heaven is the design and end* of this important cnange. What is our knowledge and faith, but to know and believe that heaven consists in the glory and love of God there manifested, and that it was purchased by Christ, and given by his covenant? What is our hope, but "the hope of glory," which we through the Spirit wait for? What is our love, but a desire of communion with the blessed God, begun here, and perfected hereafter? What Christ teaches and commands, he works in us by his Spirit. He sends not his Spirit to make men craftier than others for this world, but "wiser to salvation," and more holy and heavenly. "The children of this world are in their generation wiser than the children of light." Heavenly mindedness is the special work of the Spirit. In producing this change, *the Spirit overcomes all opposition from the world, the flesh, and the devil.* Christ first overcame the world, and teaches and causes us to overcome it, even its flatteries and its frowns. "Our faith is our victory." Christ *promised his Spirit to all true believers*, to be in them as his advocate, agent, seal, and mark; and indeed, the Spirit here, and heaven hereafter, are the chief of all his promises. *That this Spirit is given to all true believers, is evident by the effects of it.* They have ends, affections, and lives, different from the rest of mankind. They live upon the hopes of a better life, and their heavenly interest overrules all the opposite interests of this world: in order to which they live under the conduct of divine authority; and to obey and please God is the great business of their lives. The men of the world discern this difference, and therefore hate and oppose them, because they find themselves condemned by their heavenly temper and conversation Believers are conscious of this difference; for they desire to be better, and to trust and love God more, and to have more of the heavenly life and comforts; and when their infirmities make them doubt of their own sin cerity they would not change their governor, rule, or hopes, for all the world; and it is never so well and pleasant with them, as when they can trust and love God most; and in their worst and weakest condition they would fain be perfect. Indeed, whatever real goodness is found among men, it is given by the same Spirit of Christ: but it is notorious, that in heavenly mindedness and virtue, no part of the world is comparable to serious Christians. This Spirit, Christ also expressly promised, as *the means and pledge, the first fruits and earnest of the heavenly glory;* and, therefore, it is a certain proof that we shall have such a glory. He that gives us a spiritual change, which in its nature and tendency is heavenly; he that sets our hopes and hearts on heaven, and turns the endeavours of our lives towards future blessedness, and promised this preparatory grace as the earnest of that felicity, may well be trusted to perform his word in our complete eternal glory.

"And now, O my soul! why shouldst thou draw back, as if the matter was doubtful? Is not thy foundation firm? Is not the way of life, through the valley of death, made safe by him that conquered death? Art thou not yet delivered from the bondage of thy fears? Hast thou not long ago found in thee the motions and effectual operations of this Spirit? and is he not still residing and working in thee, as the agent and witness of Christ? If not, whence are thy aspirations after God, thy desires to be nearer to his glory, to know him and love him more? Whence came all the pleasure thou hast had in his sacred truth, and ways, and service? Who subdued for thee thy folly, pride, and vain desires? Who made it thy choice to sit at the feet of Jesus, and hear his word, as the better part, and count the honors and preferments of the world but dross? Who breathed in thee all those requests thou hast sent up to God? Remember what thou wast in the hour of temptation, how small a matter has drawn thee to sin. Forget not the days of thy youthful vanity. Overlook not the case of thy sin ful neighbours, who, in the midst of light, still live in darkness, and hear not the loudest calls of God. is it no work of Christ's Spirit that has made thee to differ? Thou hast nothing to boast of, and much to be humbled, and also to be thankful for. Thy holy desires are, alas! too weak; but they are holy. Thy love has been too cold; but it is the most holy God whom thou hast loved. Thy hopes have been too low; but thou hast hoped in God, and for his heavenly glory. Thy prayers have been too dull and interrupted; but thou hast prayed for holiness and heaven. Thy labours have been too slothful; but thou hast laboured for God and Christ, and the good of mankind. Though thy motion was too weak and slow, it has been godward, and therefore it is from God. O bless the Lord, not only for giving thee his word, and sealing it with uncontrolled, miracles, but also for frequently and remarkably fulfilling his promises, in the answer of thy prayers, and in great deliverance of thyself and of many others; and that he has by regeneration been preparing thee for the light of glory! And wilt thou yet doubt and fear, against all this evidence, experience and foretaste?"

Why should it seem a difficult question, *How my soul may willingly leave this world, and go to Christ in peace?* The same grace which regenerated me, must bring me to my desired end. "*Believe* and *trust* thy Father, thy Saviour, and thy Comforter. *Hope* for the joyful entertainments of the promised blessedness. And long by *love* for nearer divine union and communion. Thus, O my soul, mayst thou depart in peace."

How clearly does *reason* command me to trust him, absolutely and implicitly to trust him, and to distrust myself! He is essential, infinite perfection, wisdom, power, and love. There is nothing to be trusted in any creature, but God working in it, or by it. I am altogether his own, by right, by devotion, and by consent. He is the giver of all good to every creature, as freely as the sun gives its light, and shall we not trust the sun to shine? He is my Father, and has taken me into his family, and shall I not trust my heavenly Father? He has given me his Son, as the greatest pledge of his love, and "shall he not with him also freely give me all things?" His Son purposely came to reveal his Father's unspeakable love, and shall I not trust him who has proclaimed his love by such a messenger from heaven? He has given me the spirit of his Son, even the spirit of adoption, the witness, pledge, and earnest of heaven, the seal of God upon me, "holiness to the Lord," and shall I not believe his love, and trust him? He has made me a member of his Son, and will he not take care of me, and is not Christ to be trusted with his members? I am his interest and the interest of his Son, freely beloved, and dearly bought, and may I not trust him with his treasure? He has made me the care of *angels*, who "rejoiced at my repentance," and shall they lose their joy, or ministration? He is in covenant with me, and has "given me many great and precious promises," and can he be unfaithful? My Saviour is the forerunner, who has entered into the holiest, and is there interceding for me, having first conquered death to assure us of a future life, and ascended into heaven, to show us whither we must ascend, and having "said to his brethren, I ascend to my Father and your Father, to my God and your God;" and shall I not follow him through death, and trust such a guide and captain of my salvation? He is there to "prepare a place for me, and will receive me unto himself," and may I not confidently expect it? He told a malefactor on the cross, "to-day shalt thou be with me in paradise," to show believing sinners what they may expect. His apostles and other saints have served him on earth with all these expectations. "The spirits of just men made perfect," are now possessing what I hope for, and I am a "follower of hem, who, through faith and patience, inherit the promised" felicity; and may I not trust him to save me, who has already saved millions?

What abundant *experience* have I had of God's fidelity and love, and after all shall I not trust him? His undeserved mercy gave me being, chose my parents, gave them affectionate desires for my real good, taught them to instruct me early in his word, and educate me in his fear, made my habitation and companions suitable, endowed me with a teachable disposition, put excellent books into my hands, and placed me under wise and faithful schoolmasters and ministers. His mercy fixed me in the best of lands, and in the best age that land had seen. His mercy early destroyed in me all great expectations from the world, taught me to bear the yoke from my youth, caused me rather to groan under my infirmities, than struggle with powerful lusts, and chastened me betimes, but did not give me over unto death. Ever since I was at the age of *nineteen*, great mercy has trained me up in the school of affliction, to keep my sluggish soul awake in the constant expectations of my change, to kill my proud and worldly thoughts, and to direct all my studies to things the most necessary. How has a life of constant but gentle chastisement urged me to "make my calling and election sure," and to prepare my accounts, as one that must quickly give them up to God? The face of death, and nearness of eternity, convinced me what books to read, what studies to prosecute, what companions to choose, drove me early into the vineyard of the Lord, and taught me to *preach as a dying man to dying men.* It was divine love and mercy which made sacred truth so pleasant to me, that my life, under all my infirmities, has been almost a constant recreation. How far beyond my expectations has a merciful God encouraged me in his sacred work, choosing every place of my ministry and abode to this day, without my own seeking, and never sending me to labour in vain! How many are gone to heaven and how many are in the way, through a divine blessing on the word which in weakness I delivered! Many good Christians are glad of now and then an hour to meditate on God's word, and refresh themselves in his holy worship, but God has allowed and called me to make it the constant business of my life. In my library, I have profitably and pleasantly dwelt among the shining lights, with which the learned, wise, and holy men of all ages, have illuminated the world. How many comfortable hours have I had in the society of living saints, and in the love of faithful friends! How many joyful days in solemn worshipping assemblies, where the Spirit of Christ has been manifestly present, both with ministers and people!

"To thee, O Lord, as to a faithul Creator, I commit my soul. I know that thou art 'the faithful God, which keepeth covenant and mercy with them that love thee, and keep thy commandments. Thou art faithful, who hast called me to the fellowship of thy Son Jesus Christ our Lord.' Thy faithfulness has saved me from temptation, and kept me from prevailing evil, and will 'preserve my whole spirit, and soul, and body, unto the coming of Christ.' It is 'in faithfulness thou hast afflicted me;' and shall I not trust thee to save me? 'It is thy faithful saying, that thy elect shall obtain the salvation which is in Christ Jesus, with eternal glory; for if we be dead with him, we shall also live with him; if we suffer, we shall also reign with him.' To thee, O my Saviour, I commit my soul; it is thine by redemption, thine by covenant; it is sealed by thy Spirit, and thou hast promised not to lose it. Thou wast 'made like unto thy brethren, that thou mightest be a merciful and faithful high priest in things pertaining to God, to make reconciliation for our sins. By thy blood we have boldness to enter into the holiest, by a new and living way consecrated for us.' Cause me to 'draw near with a true heart, in full assurance of faith.' Thy name is faithful and true. True and faithful are all thy promises. Thou hast promised 'rest to weary souls that come to thee.' I am weary of suffering, sin, and flesh; weary of my darkness, dulness, and distance. Whither should I look for rest, but to my heavenly Father? I am but a 'bruised reed,' but thou 'wilt not break' me. I am but 'smoking flax,' but thou 'wilt not quench' what thy grace hath kindled. Thou, in whose name the nations trust, 'wilt bring forth judgment unto victory. The Lord redeemeth the souls of his servants, and none of them that trust in him shall be desolate. I will wait on thy name, for it is good; I trust in the mercy of God for ever and ever. The Lord is good, a strong hold in the day of trouble, and he knoweth them that trust in him. Sinful fear brings a snare, but whoso putteth his trust in the Lord shall be safe. Blessed is the man that maketh the Lord his trust. Thou art my hope, O Lord God, thou art my trust from my youth. By thee have I been holden up from the womb, my praise shall be continually of thee. Mine eyes are unto thee, O God, the Lord! in thee is my trust, leave not my soul destitute. I had fainted, unless I had believed to see the goodness of the Lord in the land of the living,' even where they that live shall die no more." The sun may cease to shine on man, and the earth to bear us; but God will never cease to be faithful to his promises. Blessed be the Lord, who hath commanded me so safe and quieting a duty, as to trust in him, and cast all my cares upon him, who has promised to care for me!

I will hope for the salvation of God. Hope is the ease, yea the life of our hearts, which would otherwise break, and even die, within us. Despair is no small part of hell. God cherishes hope, as he is the lover of souls. Satan, our enemy, cherishes despair, when his more usual way of presumption fails. Hope anticipates salvation, as fear does evil. It is the hypocrite's hope that perishes; and all who hope for durable happiness on earth must be deceived

But "happy is he that hath the God of Jacob for his help, whose hope is in the Lord his God, which made heaven and earth, which keepeth truth for ever. Wo to me, if in this life only I had hope. But the righteous hath hope in his death. And hope maketh not ashamed. Blessed is the man that trusteth in the Lord, and whose hope the Lord is. Lay hold, then, O my soul, upon the hope set before thee; it is thy sure and steadfast anchor, without which thou wilt be as a shipwrecked vessel. Thy foundation is sure, even God himself. Our faith and hope are both in God. Christ, who dwells in our hearts by faith, is in us the hope of glory. By this hope, better than the law of Moses could bring, we draw nigh unto God. We hope for that we see not, and with patience wait for it. We are saved by hope." It is an encouraging grace, it excites our diligence, and helps to full assurance unto the end. It is a desiring grace, and is earnest to obtain the glory hoped for. It is a comforting grace, for "the God of hope fills us with all joy and peace in believing, that we may abound in hope through the power of the Holy Ghost."

God needs not flatter such worms as we are, nor promise us what he never means to perform. He has laid the rudiments of our hope in a nature capable of desiring, seeking, and thinking of another life. He has called me by grace to actual desires and endeavours, and has vouchsafed some foretastes. I look for no heaven, but the perfection of divine life, light, and love in endless glory, with Christ and his saints; and this he has already begun in me. And shall I not boldly hope, when I have capacity, the promise, and the earnest and foretaste? Is it not God himself that caused me to hope? Was not nature, promise, and grace from him? And can a soul miscarry and be deceived, that departs hence in a hope of God's own producing and encouraging? "Lord, I have lived in hope, I have prayed, laboured, suffered, and waited in hope, and by thy grace I will die in hope; and is not this according to thy word and will? And wilt thou cast away a soul that hopes in thee, by thine own command and operation?" Had wealth, and honour, and continuance on earth, or the favour of man, been my reward and hope, my hope and I had died together. Were this our best, how vain were man. But the Lord liveth, and my Redeemer is glorified, and intercedes for me; and the same Spirit is in heaven who is in my heart, as the same sun is in the firmament and in my habitation. The promise is sure to all Christ's seed; for millions are now in heaven, who once lived and died in hope; they were sinners once, as now I am; they had no other Saviour, Sanctifier, or promise, than I now have. "Confessing that they were strangers and pilgrims on the earth, they desired a better country, that is, a heavenly, where they now are. And shall I not follow them in hope, who have sped so well? Then, O my soul, hope unto the end. Hope in the Lord, from henceforth and for ever. I will hope continually, and will yet praise him more and more. My mouth shall show forth his righteousness and salvation. The Lord is at my right hand, I shall not be moved. Therefore my heart is glad, and my glory rejoiceth, my flesh also shall rest in hope. God hath showed me the path of life; in his presence is fulness of joy, at his right hand there are pleasures for evermore."

Lord, let me come to thee in the confidence of thy love. I long to be nearer, in the clearer sight, the fuller sense, and more joyful exercise of love for ever! Father, into thy hand I commend my spirit! Lord Jesus, receive my spirit! *Amen.*

www.ingramcontent.com/pod-product-compliance
Lightning Source LLC
LaVergne TN
LVHW050521100826
845148LV00002B/408

* 9 7 8 1 4 2 5 5 2 0 6 1 8 *